The Tragedy of Nazi Germany

Peter Phillips

 London: Routledge & Kegan Paul

First published 1969
by Routledge & Kegan Paul Ltd
Broadway House, 68–74 Carter Lane, E.C.4
Printed in Great Britain by
Butler & Tanner Ltd, Frome and London
© *Peter Phillips 1969*
No part of this book may be reproduced
in any form without permission from
the publisher, except for the quotation
of brief passages in criticism
SBN 7100 6496 9

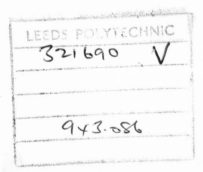

Dedication

This book is dedicated to those
who suffered and died under Nazi tyranny.
May they not have suffered and died
entirely in vain.

'The late Munich comedian, Karl Vallentin—one of the greatest of the rare race of metaphysical clowns—once enacted the following scene: the curtain goes up and reveals darkness; and in this darkness is a solitary circle of light thrown by a street lamp. Vallentin, with his long-drawn and deeply worried face, walks round and round the circle of light, desperately looking for something. "What have you lost?" a policeman asks who has entered the scene. "The key to my house." Upon which the policeman joins him in his search. They find nothing; and after a while he enquires: "Are you sure you lost it here?" "No," says Vallentin, and pointing to a dark corner of the stage: "Over there." "Then why on earth are you looking for it here?" "There is no light over there," says Vallentin.

History, may be, is the circle of light. But the key we are looking for is likely to be in a place unillumined by the street lamps.'

Erich Heller: 'Oswald Spengler'
in *The Disinherited Mind*

Contents

	Preface	xi
1	Are the Germans Human?	1
2	Power	30
3	Absolute Power	76
4	Absolute Corruption	161
5	There but for the Grace of God . . .	206
	Bibliographical Note	234

Preface

THIS BOOK IS NOT a history of Nazi Germany; it is an essay on
aspects of it, intended for an audience considerably wider than
an academic one. This is one reason why it is free of footnote
references.

I want to record my deep gratitude for immeasurable, constant
encouragement to write this book to, first and foremost, my wife,
Peggy; to my daughter, Pippa, and to my son, Patrick; and to my
friends, Ann Blainey, Geoffrey Blainey, Gwen Rice and Michael
Bradley.

In studying Nazi Germany, I have been greatly encouraged and
stimulated by undergraduate students whom I have taught, and
from whom I have learnt much, while I have been a member of
the Department of History of the University of Adelaide.

A number of Germans and Frenchmen helped provide me with
material and checked sources for me when my circumstances
prevented my doing so myself. Since most of them want to remain
unnamed, it would be invidious to name any. But each one will
know that I am grateful to him or her.

Finally, it makes me very happy to be able to mention my large
debt to certain historians and political scientists, who taught me
when I was an undergraduate student, or whose work has stimu-
lated me, even when—indeed, especially when—I have disagreed
with them. Particularly, I want to thank Karl Bracher, Alan
Bullock, J. C. Fest, Christopher Hill, Walter Hubatsch, William
Kornhauser, John Legge, Golo Mann, Erich Matthias, Friedrich
Meinecke, Rudolf Morsey, Ernst Nolte, Douglas Pike, Gerhard
Ritter, R. W. Southern, Fritz Stern, Hugh Stretton, H. R.
Trevor-Roper and Thilo Vogelsang.

PETER PHILLIPS

December 1968

I   Are the Germans Human?

THIS BOOK IS ABOUT EVIL. The evil to be explained can be characterized by such words as Hitler, Nazism, totalitarian despotism, the SS, Auschwitz, Belsen, and the *Einsatzkommando* extermination squads in the East; it is characterized by the slaughter of five or six million Jews, and perhaps as many Slavs, slaughtered in appallingly inhumane ways.

Since parts of the explanation suggested in this book are very controversial, a personal note must be introduced at the start. It is needed because some of the material in Chapter 4, on concentration camps and the extermination policy, comes from personal experience. It is also needed because many parts of what follows suggest that I am sympathetic to Germany—and even to Nazis. I am. But it is not the sympathy of approbation. I abhor many things Germans did, and I abominate beyond words the atrocities of the Nazi régime. It is the sympathy of understanding that these are real people, human beings caught in human situations. This kind of sympathy—so essential to the historians and, indeed, to any civilized person—was nurtured by intimate post-war contacts with Germans, some of whom were Nazis, by the acquaintance with evil and its human springs that the study of history—and life itself —can bring. All these helped teach me that hatred is sterile.

I did not come to this sympathy easily or quickly. In Germany I had been lucky enough (the choice of word is more than charitable to myself) to stay alive after having spent some time in POW camps and well over the average expectation of life in concentration camps, to which I had been sent after escaping from a POW camp and becoming involved with French resistance workers. When I came home in 1945 I hated the Germans. Anyone, even a friend, who bought a Volkswagen or any other German product went down in my estimation, so unbalanced was I. I would not listen to German being spoken. The result of this was that, since I had only picked up the language in Germany, my knowledge of it became so rusty that I had to relearn it to study Nazi Germany. I found it difficult, sometimes impossible, to hear the middle movement of the Pathétique Sonata, perhaps the most listenable of all music, partly because its ineffable beauty brought thoughts of life and death, and so, inevitably, of concentration camp, but partly also because Beethoven was German. Most concentration camp inmates hated the Germans—there was nothing odd in that. Only a very few exceptional inmates like the Dutch Jew, Elie Cohen, could within a very short time have sloughed off any hate they might have felt so that he could say in *Human Behaviour in the Concentration Camp* that, given similar circumstances, any people would have behaved as the Germans did.

Although I hated the Germans, I did not want to wreak revenge when released. In this I was no different from most other inmates. Perhaps our fear of the SS was still so overpowering we thought them invulnerable to anything we could do; perhaps we felt no adequate revenge was possible; perhaps we realized how much evil we ourselves had committed on fellow inmates in our desperate and ruthless efforts at self-preservation.

Like most other inmates, I did not want to talk to anyone about my experiences. We felt that no one who had not been an inmate could begin to understand what concentration camp life was like. On release, I told nothing to the British investigating officer probably for this reason; in any case, he did not want to probe and there were thousands more to pass across his desk. Like other inmates, I did not speak of my experiences to those near and dear to me, partly for the reason already given, partly because I knew it would bring pain to them that such things could have happened to someone they cared for. I am still considerably inhibited in this way. I still find it difficult to tell even my wife and children any more than snippets of what happened.

I tried to forget. But I could not. If I succeeded in daytime, I failed in nightmares, reliving time and again in sleep what I did not want to remember. Yet, these nightmares served one useful purpose. Some of them remind me of my own inhumanity to other inmates as well as the inhumanity of concentration camp officials to me. I held no official position in the camps, I was merely an ordinary inmate, but to stay alive one had to do inhumanely self-centred things. One instance. I stood and watched while the man who was then my best friend was beaten and kicked to death in front of me and several other inmates. I did not move an inch or utter a sound of protest for fear of the inevitable death that would come to me if I did. I may even have been glad that it was he who was being brutally killed, and not I. Other inmates have confessed to such a feeling in similar circumstances, and I am no braver—if that is the word—than they. I have probably repressed that terrible memory. Another example. I never volunteered to be killed in place of someone else; the camp officials cared only for numbers, not individuals, for extermination. Like many others, I feel guilty that I survived, and by so doing, ensured someone else's death. Such guilt thoughts helped me hate the Germans more.

Failure to forget made me, after many years, decide to face up to the whole horrifying subject of concentration camps, Nazism, Hitler and the rest. If I could understand, perhaps I could exorcize the horror of the memories. I undertook an intensive study of Nazi Germany. Remembering my own inhumanity to others made me wonder—perhaps paradoxically—whether even the worst SS man was still human. So, after many years of hatred, I came to the kind of sympathy that (in the words of Charles Darwin) 'feels for the most debased'. History cannot be properly studied without it. Nazi evil certainly cannot be understood and explained without it. No evil can.

The Nazi evil is one of the worst in history—some say the worst. Despotic denial of freedom, and the atrocious inhumanity that always in some measure goes with it, are no modern discoveries. Names like Caligula, Nero, Ivan the Terrible prove that Hitler had his predecessors, even if, compared with him, they were mere tyros. Certainly, except for Stalin's liquidations, at no time and in no other place has the extent of the inhumanity been so great if measured in terms of numbers annihilated. The savage holocausts of Attila, Genghis Khan, Tamburlane were, statistically, child's play compared with Hitler's. However bloodcrazed they might have been, earlier despots intent on butchery and carnage lacked the technical and administrative resources available to the modern death-dealing tyrant. A totalitarian Cain in the twentieth century can be a slayer of millions. This is a macabre tribute to the development of modern technology and administration.

3

No doubt the horror in photographs of the atrocities of Auschwitz, Belsen, Dachau and other extermination centres is no greater than that in Goya's *The Disasters of War*, depictions of atrocities in Napoleon's War in Spain; or in Callot's *Grandes Misères de la Guerre*, etchings of cruelties perpetrated in the Thirty Years War. In fact, the horror may be less since the camera is not so adept at communicating emotion as the great artist.

The terrible treatment meted out by the Syracusans to the Athenians defeated in the Sicilian expedition so vividly described in Book Seven of Thucydides' *The Peloponnesian War*; the monstrous cruelty of the anti-Albigensian crusaders who totally wiped out those they deemed heretics; the ruthless killing by whites of Red Indians in America, Bushmen and Hottentots and Bantu in Southern Africa, Aborigines in Australia, and uncounted Indians after the 1857 Mutiny, are sad witness that the Nazis did not invent inhuman atrocities.

But where the earlier despotisms and atrocities do little more than leave a nasty taste in the mouth, Nazi tyranny and crimes against humanity shock profoundly because they seem to most people unnatural in the twentieth century—at least in the Western world. Despite the erosions of faith, hope and charity caused by Auschwitz, Stalinist purges and Hiroshima, in the West today belief in inevitable progress and the fundamental goodness of man persists strongly from the nineteenth century, so aptly called the century of hope. Shakespeare, for once, was wrong when he remarked that it is the poor that are hopeful; rather, it is in the affluent breast that hope springs eternal.

It is also much easier to be kind and merciful when the house is centrally heated and has running-water, a W.C. and a bath; when the chairs are dunlopilloed, a car is in the garage, clothes are plentiful, three good meals a day are regular, the children at school, and a 40-hour week, an adequate pay-packet and an annual paid holiday assured, and, for everyday, at least six hours leisure and eight hours sleep are possible. In the English-speaking world since the nineteenth century the pattern of life has been steadily approaching this acme of materialism, at least for the upper and middle classes. For them, violence has, by and large, been confined to wars abroad, the sensational newspapers, TV Westerns, and James Bond sex-and-sadism spasms. They—and most historians —with their eyes glued on the topside of society, have overlooked or been ignorant of the commonplace violence, cruelty and in-humanity that have been so much a part of working-class domestic life. Not surprisingly, working-class people leave few records for historians. Only very rarely has a novelist—an Arthur Morison or a Louis-Ferdinand Céline—used the working class as material for its own sake. Less often, but still only occasionally has a Gerhart Hauptmann, Emile Zola or D. H. Lawrence exploited for ulterior purposes the drama of a strike or the begriming brought by indus-trialism. The official portraitist of society does not venture down slum streets.

Nor does he heed the pessimistic warnings of the direction being taken by Western Civilization uttered by all the greatest Western imaginative writers in the twentieth century: Eliot, Gide, Joyce, Kafka, D. H. Lawrence, Mann, Pound, Proust, Yeats. The official picture is one of steady, swift material progress over the last 100 years, engineered by fantastic leaps forward in science and technology, inspired by spreading education, and organized by ever newer methods of mass production and distribution conceived in executive suites and huge office blocks. The twentieth-century English-speaking world may be a pecuniary paradise for psycho-logists, but there can be no doubt that it is an age of material comfort. And comfort soothes the savage breast.

Adding to this sense of comfort has been the growth of a steady, stable, evolutionary democracy. Two of its main pillars have been restraint of conflict and respect for the humanity of the other man. Those who call themselves democrats have not infrequently fallen short of their ideals, but, by and large, they have not fallen so far short that their way of life deserves the invective of the acidulous American writer, H. L. Mencken, who called democracy the wor-ship of jackals by jackasses. Winston Churchill was never more right when he judged that democracy, for all its many and manifest faults, is the least imperfect form of government yet invented.

Unlike John Wesley who looked on all the world as his parish, Englishmen—and, for that matter, English-speaking peoples generally—look upon their parish as all the world. This attitude has affected their view of history, particularly political history. They see the natural, proper course of political development after the English or American model as 'freedom broadening down from precedent to precedent' and culminating in parliamentary demo-cracy. Unblushingly ignoring the fact that most of the world is,

B

5

and always has been, ruled non-democratically, they see any foreign kinds of development as deviations from the norm, unnatural. This is the Podsnap interpretation of history, and there are still numerous twentieth-century Podsnaps who think the natives begin at Boulogne.

This comfortable, stably ruled condition of English-speaking man is one reason why many of them have preferred to close their eyes, or merely blink at, Nazi totalitarianism and atrocities. Optimists—and they are the majority—close their eyes out of cosiness, *joie de vivre*, and a credulousness that it won't—can't—happen here. Pessimists do so out of pain, fear of overpopulation and the spread of the bomb, and the barbiturate that all one can do is eat, drink, and be as merry as possible, for tomorrow we all die nuclearized. So, whether pessimists or optimists, they shudder away in revulsion from, or masochistically enjoy, the obscenity of the ashes to ashes of Auschwitz. Some, perhaps rationalizing a little, possibly from charity, advocate we should forgive and forget. After all, Hitler, Himmler, and the exterminated Jews and Slavs have been dead these 20 and more years. Let the dead bury their dead.

Understandable as all this is, there are cogent reasons for not forgetting and forgiving. In the first place, those who suffered German inhumanity neither want to, nor indeed can forget. Although time is reputed to dull the worst memories, and although the sufferings can be thrust to the back of the mind in daylight, they recur constantly in sleep in nightmares—and always will until the last sufferer is dead. It is something one has to learn to live with. Victims and their sufferings do not deserve to be forgotten, if only in the same way as Armistice Days—and the Crucifixion—do not deserve to be forgotten.

It ill becomes those who did not suffer at the hands of the Nazis, to advocate forgiving and forgetting. After all, it is by no means sure that any crime against humanity should be forgiven, except in the sense that a transgressor—even a Hitler or Himmler or Eichmann—should not cease to be regarded as still human. He should not be regarded as irremediably marred, as beyond the pale. We should do all we can to love the sinner again; but, equally, we should still continue to hate the sin. And this certainly needs remembering.

If we do not continue to hate the sin, if we do forget these crimes

6

against humanity, then we overlook the evidence on which we base our proper condemnation of the motives which caused them, and our condemnation will lack effectiveness. It may be that neither Germany nor any other country will sink to such abysmal depths of inhumanity as under Hitler. And if they do not, it may be partly because these crimes and their motives have been remembered and understood. Understanding cannot be won without as full a remembering as possible. No one, surely, could reasonably suggest that the Nazis have been the last criminals against humanity, or that we understand more than a fraction of the reasons why such crimes continue to be committed. Since 1945, although not in such terrible volume, cruel atrocities have been committed—still are being committed—in sacred ideological names. Shibboleths still single out those for slaughter, and, since 1945, modern Gileadites have massacred Ephraimites in Korea, French Algeria, Kenya, Portuguese Angola, in Russian Siberian slave camps, Chinese purges, Indonesia's annihilation of Communists, and on both sides of the 17th parallel in Vietnam.

When Christina Rossetti wrote 'Better by far that you should forget and smile, than that you should remember and be sad', she was partly right. Yet, however much we want, we cannot banish sadness completely from our lives, and it is not even desirable that we should so want. Sadness is an important part of what makes us human. 'History, though it may make a man wise, cannot fail to make him sad.' When Bishop Stubbs said that, he did not intend a weak withdrawal from the fight, or resignation to the crimes, follies and misfortunes of mankind that Gibbon thought constituted history. He intended a vigorous sadness which understands man's infinite capacity for good and bad, weakness and strength, loving the best and doing the worst. We keep alive the sad stories of the past—the evil that men do—to help ourselves and others know how to live better, by enlarging our understanding of man's humanity and inhumanity, that is, our humanity and our inhumanity, actual and potential. To do this we must court sadness, since, without this catharsis, no healthy moral life is possible, no lessening of man's inhumanity to man is feasible. Cure cannot come without understanding. To understand we must be willing to bear sadness. This certainly does not mean sentimentality or self-righteousness, seeing ourselves always as those wronged. We have to see ourselves not merely as potential victims, but also as

7

potential executioners. Even with Nazis, we have to say 'There but for the grace of God, go I.' We need to be all those who were in the garden of Gethsemane (Peter and Judas included), Pilate in his house, and the centurion in his barracks.

That is—or should be—why we mourn past tragedies on anniversaries: a Good Friday, an Armistice Day. The words 'lest we forget' have become so trite, so stifled by lip-service, in our world which has witnessed the death of millions by violence. But clearly we owe it to those who died and to ourselves to have remembrance days. We owe it far from least to those millions who died because of their race between 1933 and 1945. This was their Calvary, and ours, too. All Calvaries are shared by those who died there, and those alive.

We remember not only in tribute to the past, a worthy enough aim on its own, but also for the future. Hitlerism and Nazism were not confined to Hitler and the Nazis. They were only the worst instances. The flaws which they enlarged to the extreme are human flaws, shared in some measure by all of us. The Nazis were the worst perpetrators of the kind of crimes they committed. But they were only the worst. Even Nazis are, in significant ways, 'as other men'.

For all these reasons, it is essential not to forgive and forget. If Dionysius is right, that history is philosophy teaching by example, we must remember in order to understand what is, undoubtedly, *human* inhumanity, and what are its myriad, complex causes. The historian himself may not wish to pronounce moral judgments on this inhumanity. He may prefer to leave that to the philosopher skilled in ethics or the clergyman practised in theology. But obviously the historian by his training and his aims should be best fitted to establish the facts about past inhumanity and its multiple causes. After all, inhumanity, if only because it is so human, is very much part of the proper study of mankind.

2

The monstrous enormity of Nazi crimes stuns the mind, especially one swathed in English-speaking stability and moderation. One murder—ten—may be able to be grasped, though not accepted, by the mind. But when the number is millions, and the millions are men, women and children, and they are slaughtered in gas-chambers and mass graves, it is hard beyond measure to compre-

8

hend the fact as real or human. So, the reaction of the historian to the enormity gravitates to the sheer stupor of mere narration. Or if comprehension is attempted, the explanations are only likely to be profound and aware of the complicity of human behaviour if comparatively small aspects of Nazism are studied. Explanations of the whole tyranny and holocaust lean to the superficial.

All this has coloured the literature, historical and otherwise, on Nazi Germany. The two most common explanations are, first, that it was the product of the country's history and German national character; and, second, that it was a conspiracy of Hitler and his Nazi thugs with men at the top level, whether generals, industrialists, non-democratic politicians or a Presidential camarilla, each being blamed according to the bias of the particular historian. Both explanations are open to serious objections.

German history is rich enough to supply evidence for any thesis about the German people, especially if the material is selected with care and awkward counter-evidence quietly disregarded. In fact, the history of most, if not all, countries, is amply enough endowed for the same purpose. It may be that a few theses about the German people would be harder than others to 'prove', one obvious example being the absence of the kind of revolutionary tradition that distinguishes French history. A skilful advocate, however, could make something of German history between 1517 and 1648, 1813 and 1815, 1848, and 1914 and 1919. Tracing a continuous line of German behaviour to Hitler and Nazism from the 'barbarian' German tribes who sacked the Roman Empire, or from the medieval Teutonic Knights who carved out domains in the East with the sword, merely displays abysmal ignorance of the great diversity, multifariousness, and protean character of German history. It also ignores the fact that it is very difficult, if not impossible, to regard Germany as one country during most of its past. It has had few clear geographical boundaries, especially eastwards. For most of its history it has been divided up into many, at times hundreds of, separate states. The division between north and south Germany has existed from the earliest Roman times and was aggravated first by the Reformation, which left the north Protestant and the south Catholic, and then by the Industrial Revolution which concentrated in the north, and left the south primarily agricultural.

Local feuds still cut deeper in Germany than elsewhere in

9

Europe, probably because unification happened only so recently. Yorkshiremen and Lancastrians are rivals at more than cricket, and a Breton and a Norman can say and do very hard things to each other. But there always seems to be some—probably national —unguent to ease the worst friction. Though in different degree, the same is true of present-day dissensions between Yankee and Southerner. In Germany, the rivalries seem more acrid, especially between Prussia and other states. This is not really surprising since, in effect, Prussia conquered most of them, and lorded it too often like a conqueror. To listen to a Bavarian call a Prussian in dialect a *Saupreiss* (a Prussian swine) is to hear a note not used by a Yorkshireman, Lancastrian, Breton, Norman, Yankee or Southerner.

Actually, parts of Germany have developed in very different ways. Dialects vary, so that, certainly in the past, Germans from one district might be unable to understand Germans from another. Even among the aristocracy, until late in the nineteenth century, the south-western states sought culture in France rather than in the north. Germany has never had a cultural capital, as England has had in London, and France in Paris. Instead of visiting Berlin, the Rhinelander preferred Paris, the Bavarian Vienna, the Silesian Prague. Until the nineteenth century, cultured Germans spoke French in their own circles, and German only to their servants, and it was a German monarch, Charles V, who said that German was fit for speaking only to horses. Metternich referred to Italy as no more than a geographical expression, but he would have been almost as right had he said it of Germany. It is very difficult to know precisely when such an aphorism would have ceased to apply —even after 1870.

For the sake of argument, however, assume Germany to be like England or France. Do her political thinkers all fit (as is often claimed) into a family tree of despotic thought with only the very occasional, odd, libertarian black sheep?

The game of tracing the intellectual genealogy of despotic thought from Luther to Hitler is an easy one; but it is child's play. In any parlour game it is simple to win if the rules are suitably made or interpreted by the player and he plays all the hands, or if the contest is against dead men who cannot answer back. According to the game played on Nazism by writers like Rohan O'Butler, McGovern, Shirer and Viereck, one accepted rule is that intellectuals generally, and political philosophers in particular, exercise a major influence on state and society. How much influence they do exercise is, however, very debatable. Other historians argue that they merely reflect trends in a society and are, as it were, Dukes of Plaza Toro who lead their regiments from behind. Nevertheless, as mere reflections, they reveal something to the historian about a society—though hardly in the distorted images presented by Shirer and the like.

Another rule is to take any anti-democratic or illiberal utterance as proving a liking for despotism. Many who were not despotic in cast of mind, or wholly so, are classed as despotic; the rules are free and easy in this game. Luther, for instance, propagated strong Pauline thoughts on the bounden submission of subject to ruler, but can also justifiably be regarded as a religious liberator. In any case, it seems to be always forgotten that Luther laid down that any action ordered by the ruler imperilling the immortal soul must be resisted by the subject. Shirer includes Kant in his rogues' gallery, on the grounds of the philosopher's insistence on the supremacy of duty over feeling. This surely shows—to put it charitably—complete misunderstanding of Kant's contribution to the furthering and enlarging of the concept of freedom. Hegel is cast by all the players as a knave because he 'glorified' the Prussian state. Yet, those who have understood him (or read him at all) realize that in his own day he was regarded as a liberal; not a liberal of the British kind, it is true, but one concerned with the maintenance and extension of a kind of freedom which (despite Sir Isaiah Berlin's eloquent arguing) has been valid philosophically and politically to many continental Europeans. Nietzsche is reputed to have been an outstanding Nazi ancestor, the evangelist of the Superman and 'the blond beast', but perhaps the only thing Nietzsche and the Nazis had in common was rejection of rationality. If that is to be a test of proto-Nazism, then many strange bed-fellows will lie under that blanket-term: to name only three, Dostoevsky, Bergson, Kierkegaard, none of them German. Recent scholarship over the last decade has shown that the editing of Nietzsche's writing, by his sister and her husband, completely perverted Nietzsche's meaning by highly biased selection, vital omissions and downright forgery. In fact, it is now conclusively proved that Nietzsche stood diametrically opposed to every Nazi tenet. In any event, whether these four examples or others are used as trump cards, none of them, however despotic-ally-minded, can sensibly be seen as totalitarians or Nazis. Every one of them would have rejected Nazi ideas.

The players also insist on the game having only one suit; they ignore all those Germans opposing tyranny by word and by deed. They ignore the Liebnitzs and Lassalles and those who in 1848 went to the barricades and the rostrum at Frankfort. They over-look that there *has been* a liberal tradition in Germany. It has not been a tradition nearly so glorious, potent and effective as that in English-speaking countries or France, but this is no reason for consigning it to the rubbish-bin of history. The Rohan O'Butlers, McGoverns, Shirers and Vierecks overlook, too, that, despite the failure of 1848 and the worst that Bismarck could do, there was a strong, popular, anti-autocratic movement in Germany. In the last Reichstag before 1914 the liberty-loving parties—the Social Democrats, Centre and Progressives—were in a majority, muster-ing 243 of the 397 seats, and the number would have been higher if the constituency boundaries had not been heavily weighted against the Social Democrats. There is a long roll-call of Germans who have held the preservation of life and liberty, and the pursuit of happiness to be rights inherent and inalienable.

It is easy to forget that rubbers can be comfortably won on non-German tables. It is no trouble to trace a French genealogical tree of tyranny from Bodin (if no earlier ancestor is required) to Pétain —some would want to say to De Gaulle. Spain, Portugal, Italy, Poland, Russia present no difficulties. The cards seem to lie the other way with England; but even it offers no grand or little slam: Hobbes, Filmer, Bolingbroke, George III's supporters, Carlyle prevent it. And just as de Tocqueville, notwithstanding his liberalism, can be convicted of being anti-democratic, so too can remarks of that arch-liberal, John Stuart Mill, be taken to show that he anticipated several severe critics of twentieth-century democracy. 'It is better to be a human being dissatisfied than a pig satisfied; better to be Socrates dissatisfied than a fool satis-fied' is a saying of Mill's not easily digestible by an egalitarian.

The argument from national character is cousin to that from the genealogical tree of tyranny. 'National character' is often in-voked as a magical Open Sesame to unlock the mysteries of his-torical problems. The English are law-abiding by nature, hence their long social stability and staid politics; and this, despite the

12

fact that the English 200 years ago were notorious as the most riotous and lawless of all Europeans. The French are naturally excitable and licentious, hence their political instability and the *Folies Bergères*; and this, despite the stand-pat conservatism and a Puritanism, as bigoted as any in Victorian England, of the French peasants composing about half the population. The Poles are by nature proud and liberty-loving, hence the turbulence of their past; and this, despite the fact that they have accepted despotic rule throughout almost all their history.

In the West in the twentieth century the Germans have been the unloved nation *par excellence*. The Russians have not been hated nearly as much, although Russia was a worse autocracy under the Tsars than Germany under the Kaisers, although Communist Russia produced a totalitarian tyranny as bad as the German, and although Stalin killed as many as atrociously as Hitler. The reasons probably are that Russia was on the Allied side in both world wars, the Communist atrocities have not been publicized nearly as much as the Nazis', and Western intellectuals have for long been very warm to the left, as if the intellectual climate has been affected by a leftwards Gulf-Stream. The English were perhaps *the* hated race in the nineteenth century; but their industrial and imperial successes had to be admired as well as envied, and they had the advantage that they were hated in a century of comparative peace. The Germans, on the other hand, have failed in two world wars, as well as living in a totalitarian society and killing in extermination camps.

But if an anthology of criticisms of Germans were to be compiled, most of the best entries would be from Germans themselves. The invective of a Shirer or an A. J. P. Taylor is crude or pale beside that of Nietzsche against his fellow-countrymen, and the censure of foreigners is rarely as profound as Goethe's or Heine's or a host of other Germans'. Germany has produced its severest critics.

3

The litany of hate against Germans includes many 'crimes'. The most popular are militarism, arrogance, subservience, crudity and cruelty. Militarism is the capital crime; the rest are subsidiary, not hanging matters.

Are Germans militaristic? Yes. But, a very modified yes. In

13

A History of Militarism, Alfred Vagts has shown how easily and how often militariness and militarism are confused. Militarism means a domination of the military man over the civilian, an undue emphasis on military needs, policies, spirit, values and ideals. Gerhard Ritter, in one of the profoundest studies of the subject, *Staatskunst und Kriegshandwerk: Das Problem des 'Militarismus' in Deutschland* (Statecraft and the Military Profession: the Problem of 'Militarism' in Germany) has cogently demonstrated that before the twentieth century, Germany was not militarist, unless the word be taken to mean that mere military thinking and behaviour play too great a part in a society, in which case it cannot be denied that in the generation before 1914—but not earlier—there was a German militarism. But the first and last military German to dominate civilian life was Ludendorff from 1916 to 1918, and the worst German militarist excesses were those of a civilian, Adolf Hitler, largely against his generals' opposition.

Militariness means a readiness to defend one's country's interests by force of arms, the acceptance of the military profession as honourable and necessary. Only a complete pacifist could validly condemn militariness. Others, aware that wars are facts of life, however unpleasant, would agree that every nation has to cultivate some militariness; and happy are the countries like Sweden and Switzerland, the United States and Britain where its cultivation has been less necessary than in lands not so fortunately placed geographically, diplomatically and historically. The history of every country has its drum-and-fife, pike-and-musket chapters. Even England from Cromwell to Wellington was as busy at war as any, although the fact of its bellicosity is conveniently misted over by its wars being mostly naval; England paid foreigners to do its fighting by land. Mars has not been merely a German god.

In the anti-German mind, 'Prussian discipline', and the jackboot and the goosestep are notorious badges of German militarism. Each badge is, however, the result of ignorance or misconception. Prussian discipline cannot possibly be shown to have ever been the most ferocious in Europe. A French officer, not a Prussian, gave his name to the word 'martinet'. The eighteenth century is reputed to have been the heyday of Prussian discipline. Then, discipline in all European armies was very harsh. It needed to be, given the conditions of war. Muzzle-loading, smooth-bored

14

(that is, non-rifled) muskets were extremely inaccurate, and were lethal only when fired in volleys at close range. Being loaded by the muzzle, they could not be used effectively lying down, and so fighting was almost always in a standing position. Therefore, soldiers had to be drilled to march towards the enemy in as straight lines as possible for the volley to do maximum damage. This was very hard to accomplish over rough ground or even on heather or turf. They also had to be drilled to hold their fire until they were right on top of the enemy—until, as the phrase went, 'the whites of their eyes could be seen', a very short distance. An important part of infantry tactics was to induce the enemy to fire his volley first, since then it would be delivered further off and be less deadly. One's own lines could then advance closer, since it took considerable time for the enemy to reload, and a much more shattering volley could be fired because at a shorter distance away. From this it can easily be realized that the strictest, and therefore very harsh, discipline was essential.

In the twentieth century German army discipline has been strict and stern. But has it been any stricter and sterner than in, say, the Communist Russian army or the democratic American army, except in second-rate novels like Hans Helmut Kirst's? No one who knows anything of the German army in either of the world wars would deny the good relationships between officers and men. This relationship has undoubtedly been one important reason for the fine fighting qualities of German units.

Due to the low esteem in which military history has for some time been held, military matters before modern times are almost universally regarded with ignorant contempt or blank incomprehension. For instance, epaulettes: these, made of metal, were a vestigial remains of armour to absorb sword blows, as were the shiny metal helmets and their crests. So were the metal cords garlanding a soldier's chest. The highly coloured and variegated uniforms also performed a necessary technological function. Before the invention in the mid-nineteenth century of smokeless powder, a battlefield was soon obscured with a mist of smoke, and a general could only recognize his own regiments by their colours, which of course needed to be brightly distinguishable. Only the ignorant, khaki-obsessed, democratic, anti-war twentieth century could regard such uniforms as the whim of aristocratic popinjays careless of the lives of their men. Even aristocrats were not fools enough to hold their own lives and those of their men so lightly for a sartorial flourish.

The word jackboot sounds sinister, but as military footwear it is extremely efficient. Soldiers need their calves guarded against cold, mud, brambles and barbed wire. The jackboot did this better than the British puttee in World War One or gaiter in World War Two. German preference for the jackboot rather than puttee or gaiter may be due to the need to fight in the east where roads are rarely sealed or metalled and the country is rougher than in the west. The jackboot is, finally, no more serviceable than the British, French, American or Russian army boot for stamping on faces, breaking ribs, or kicking in the groin—although it was used much more for these purposes in World War Two in concentration camps.

The goosestep also had its utility. It inculcated discipline. It also kept the soldier warm through its vigour. It is no mere coincidence that a similar step, combined with arms swinging across the chest, is part of Russian drill. Both Prussia and Russia have cold climates. If Englishmen think the goosestep ridiculously militaristic, they might reflect that the Guards trooping the Colour in slow time could be considered equally ridiculous and militaristic. They can, however, take consolation in the fact that the Guards' bearskins were designed to absorb sword-blows and to inspire awe and fear by giving added height to the guardsman. In the British army of the 1960s, the exaggerated footstampings of left, right and about turns, the extraordinary vigour of salutes seem (to put it charitably) a trifle unnecessary and no less ultra-formal than Prussian heel-clicking.

The seventeenth and eighteenth centuries are often thought of as periods of rampant Prussian militarism. Yet, it was much more militariness. There is no evidence that Prussians liked the vocation of war any more than Frenchmen, Russians or Austrians. Prussia needed a larger army proportionate to her population because of her special circumstances just as England needed a large navy because of her special circumstances. The Prussian domains were separated and scattered over North Germany, and therefore took more soldiers to defend than more compact countries like her enemies, Austria, France, Sweden or Poland. Also, France constantly meddled in Germany, stirring up rivalries leading to war, in order to keep Germany divided, weak, and no threat to herself.

16

Her purpose was helped by Austria's traditional effort to dominate Germany, including Prussia. If Prussia was to survive, it was imperative that she be a strong, military power.

In the eighteenth century, Prussian rulers devised schemes to urge noblemen into the Army. A Junker captain could take his own serfs, or those of his relatives, into the service for a few months each year, and then give them leave to work the land. This meant economy for the ruler's treasury—Prussia with its many acres of sandy wastes was not a rich country. Frederick the Great insisted that noblemen must always be officers and never engage in bourgeois activities. So, as Commander-in-Chief, he had the whip hand over them: they could never resign or retire to another profession. In this way he lessened the opposition and independence of the Junker class which had been, and continued to be, a formidable threat to the rulers. In any event, in those days, the Prussian nobility could surely not be called more belligerent than the French, Austrian, Polish, Russian, Swedish—only more efficient. It is a little known fact that, up to 1914, of the 213 years of its existence, Prussia was at peace for 168 years. England, France and others would be hard put to it to produce as favourable figures.

Frederick the Great is often characterized as the outstanding militarist. Yet only half his reign of 46 years was taken up with war considerations, and of those 23 years only in a few did he actually wage war. The remaining half of his reign was given over to peace, except for a minor fracas at the end of his reign. Frederick is dwarfed by Louis XIV, Charles XII of Sweden and Peter the Great as a war-maker. Despite popular belief, he did not like war and fought only for limited objectives. Notoriety has come to him because of his cynical tearing away of the seven veils of the diplomatic, dynastic dance which other monarchs, like Louis XIV, used to conceal the nakedness of their international ambitions.

Bismarck is another German regarded as a militarist. He, too, did not like war. Of his 28 years of power, in only six did he wage wars, and all those wars were short, the Austro-Prussian war in 1866 being one of the shortest wars between major powers in history. From 1870 to 1890, Bismarck concentrated on keeping the peace, with considerable success.

It was not the Germans, but the French, in the Revolutionary and Napoleonic Wars, who introduced the idea and practice of militarizing the nation. The peacemakers at the Vienna Congress regarded France rightly as a militarist menace. True, the German rulers militarized their people in World War One; but then so did every other major participant.

It is now agreed by historians that Germany was not solely or pre-eminently responsible for World War One. Germans welcomed it with cheering, almost hysterical crowds in Berlin. But there were similarly enthusiastic crowds in London, Paris, Vienna and St Petersburg. The start of World War Two was almost wholly a German responsibility, though it would be more correct to call it Hitler's war. The German people, mindful of the shocking sacrifices in 1914–18, greeted its coming with a glumness and pessimism that angered Hitler, just as he had been downcast when they had been overjoyed at the preservation of peace in 1938. In 1940 their enthusiasm for the war leapt with the defeat of France, but it is only human to be glad when winning.

In World War Two, the Germans were militarized and militarist to an extent never known before. This was the product of a totalitarian régime and a mass industrialized war, in which propaganda whipped up passions, and hate generated more hate. The human nature of the Germans, of course, played its part. So would the human nature of any people subject to the extreme pressures exerted by Führer, Gestapo, Goebbels, total war. Like the Ammonites, Germans—not all of them—came to worship Moloch. Not because of a hereditary militaristic characteristic, but because they were warped by the totalitarian régime, lost in a moral void, at the mercy of forces beyond their control. In short, not because they were naturally militaristic, but because they were human.

Are Germans arrogant? Yes, some are, at times, excessively so. But not notably more than other peoples. Some of their behaviour in two world wars is sufficient proof of the excessive arrogance of a number of them in the twentieth century. In the generation before 1914, also, German arrogance was disagreeably exhibited by many, led by the Kaiser, the Pan Germans, and noisy, nationalist professors like the historian Treitschke, who domineered in his crowded lecture halls in the University of Berlin from 1874 to 1896, in a number of books, in frequent contributions to the leading conservative periodical *Die Prussische Jahrbücher* and in his impassioned orations as a Reichstag deputy.

There is no need to resort to German genes to explain this

arrogance. Wars naturally bring out arrogance, especially in victory. The successes of the wars of unification were heady. Then, Germany achieved unparalleled industrial triumphs. Her cultural achievements in music, philosophy, literature, science and scholarship generally, were unequalled anywhere. All this may have produced delusions of grandeur. The psychologist might call it paranoia. On the other hand, he might conclude that, despite all their prowess, Germans still felt a sense of inferiority as latecomers on the international scene, *parvenus* in international society. To compensate for this sense of inferiority (the psychologist might argue), Germans developed a superiority complex, as many individuals do. But this is one of the cases psychologists toss the coin 'Heads I win, tails you lose.' Nevertheless, each explanation is from circumstances acting on human beings, not from national character.

The Junker, monocled, square-headed, never out of a tight-fitting uniform, is the stock figure of German arrogance. No doubt, they existed. But they were caricatures of reality. Most Junkers were reserved and at times haughty, but not much more so than the pre-1939 upper-class Englishman. Interconnections between aristocracy and middle class broke down some of the upper-class Englishman's haughtiness, though very little of his reserve. Until World War One, the absence of as many similar interconnections kept the Junkers a caste, rather than a class. In this they did not vary from the French aristo, the Spanish Don, or the Italian Conte. Survival of caste is not due to national character.

Like most gentlemen the world over, most Prussian Junkers valued uprightness, honour, truth, reliability, honesty. He had a strong sense of duty to state and society in general, and in particular to his soldiers if he were an officer, and his tenants if he were a landowner. He was exceptional among European aristocrats in making almost a fetish of thrift. Theodor Fontane, an acute and not uncritical observer of the Prussian Junker, presents in his writings in the latter part of the nineteenth century, a much less unfavourable portrait of the Junker and his Prussia than the habitual one in the mind of foreigners and German Socialists.

Junkers are usually held to be completely reactionary and loyal to the Hohenzollern autocrats. In fact, as Felix Carsten has shown in an important article in the journal *History* (October 1948), the Junker was more often than not in conflict with his ruler, in the way French and English nobility were with their kings before the one tamed the other in the seventeenth century. In the first half of the nineteenth century many Prussian landowners, including Junkers, were liberals, ashamed of the incompetence and harshness of the royal bureaucracy. In 1848 they joined the capitalist middle class demanding constitutional government as the only means to allow a new, modern and just order of society to develop. When war came in 1870, Junker officers—as many French tales reveal—behaved in victory and occupation with honour, restraint and decency.

Although not a few Junkers were attracted to Nazism in its early days of power, Junker names were pre-eminent in the conspiracies against Hitler culminating in the unsuccessful assassination attempt on 20 July 1944. No love was lost on either side: Junker's or Hitler's. The Führer's *Table Talk* contains numerous spiteful and contemptuous remarks about them, and he wreaked such vengeance on them and their families after 20 July 1944 that it can be truly said that it was not alone the post-war Communist confiscation of Junker property in the East that destroyed once and for all that caste with all its many faults and virtues.

They did have their faults, which do not lack publicity. Without doubt, too, the caste system of which *Junkertum* was the cornerstone was an anachronism by 1900, or perhaps earlier. But it is a double mistake to exaggerate the arrogance of Junkers, and to imagine it peculiar to Germany. It is also all too easy to forget that in these democratic days, gentlemen have a bad press and 'aristocracy' is a dirty word in the vocabularies of historians forgetful of their tendency to bias.

'*Deutschland, Deutschland über alles, über alles in der Welt*' is to the foreigner another symbol of German arrogance. Almost always he translates it to mean that Germans desire world dominance. In fact, to Germans it means that the Fatherland should be placed above all selfish and worldly considerations; the mistake derives from the ambiguity of the English words, 'above all', and the presence of '*in der Welt*', 'in the world'. Foreigners are wrong in supposing it to have always been the German national anthem. Although composed in 1841, it was not adopted as the national anthem until 1922, and then by a Social Democrat President of the Weimar Republic, Friedrich Ebert. Until 1918, the national anthem was '*Heil Dir im Siegerkranz*' ('Hail to Thee in the Victor's Wreath'), originally written by a Schleswig pastor for

Danes to sing on their King's birthday. It went to the same tune as 'God Save the Queen'. This national anthem may have been bombastic, but, surely, no more so than the British. Nor is *La Marseillaise* coy in giving vent to extremism and bloodthirsty aggressiveness. National anthems of all countries are not remarkable for expressing a hope that the meek shall inherit the earth.

Before 1914, many believed that Germany was bent on a *Weltpolitik*, when she started a naval race with England. What was forgotten then—and still is by most historians—is that Germany's sea lanes to the outside world have to pass through the English channel or go north of Scotland. Without a navy, German overseas commerce was completely at the mercy of the English in the event of war. It is also interesting to recall that, despite Germany's naval building, in 1912 the defence expenditure per head in England was the equivalent of 32 marks, in France 27 marks, and in Germany only 21 marks.

National arrogance on the world stage in the generations before 1914 was not peculiarly German. English gunboat diplomacy was neither mild nor polite. In Imperial posts, many Englishmen's behaviour—and, much more so, that of their memsahibs—was justly considered arrogant, and worse, by subject races. The popular imperialist ideas of Joseph Chamberlain, and many Englishmen's belief that the English nation was the final and finest work of evolutionary history, might well be regarded as the acme of arrogance—except perhaps by Englishmen. Of course, it is not put in this way in English history books. There the conjugation runs: 'The English are proud, the French vainglorious, the Germans arrogant.'

Are Germans subservient? The foreigner must find this hard to answer affirmatively if he has already convicted them of arrogance. Nevertheless, many have succeeded, if only by arguing that a German when on top is arrogant, and, when beaten, subservient. To adapt Oliver Goldsmith: 'There is no use arguing with an anti-German; for when his pistol misses fire, he knocks you down with the butt-end of it.'

Germans are indicted for worshipping titles. It is true they make something of a fetish of titles. But Austrians make an even greater one, for all their supposed lightheartedness, love of pleasure, and *Schlamperei*, or carelessness. Their worship of titles does not convict them of subservience, as it does the German. Germans are sometimes even accused of being too obedient to the law, as though this was a flaw in character. Stalin expressed to Churchill and Roosevelt his view that German subservience was shown by over-obedience to the law. But Stalin is surely not a reliable witness on the subject of either law or a people's subservience. Whether German law-abidingness is a fact is debatable: between 1920 and 1930, the rate of crimes against property in Germany was, each year, two to four times as great as in England, whether the year was one of depression or inflation (as between 1920 and 1923 and 1929–30) or of comparative prosperity (as between 1924 and 1928). It also appears that traffic offences in West Germany since 1945 are several times more numerous than in England or the U.S.A. However, Germans are probably less likely to question orders than Englishmen or Americans. But less likely than Frenchmen or Russians? There are no statistics, even for World War Two when '*Befehl ist Befehl*' (orders is orders) became a common German defence to war crimes charges and a subject for mocking among the Allies, as though each Allied airman carefully considered before he obeyed *his* orders—even to bomb Hamburg or Dresden.

Subservience in Germany, it is said, has long been inculcated in homes by autocratic fathers and in schools by autocratic teachers. The myth of the tyrannical German father has been properly punctured by Robert H. Lowie's *Towards Understanding Germany*. It is true that father was autocratic in Germany. But was he not also in Victorian England? Schoolteachers in Germany did train the lower orders in subservience to their betters. But did they not also in English elementary schools? In the German *Gymnasium*, the equivalent of the English secondary or grammar school, independence of mind was as often encouraged as anywhere else, which partly accounts, no doubt, for the high quality of German scholarship.

Are the Germans crude? Yes, generally: all peoples are. Only the élite of a nation has the opportunity to avoid crudity, through being nurtured in affluence, comfort, education, good manners, taste and sensibility. Even so, many with this chance fail to make good use of it. That the generality of all populations is crude is betrayed by the common level of manners, habits of eating and drinking, loving, methods of communication, speech itself, popular entertainments on TV and cinema screens, best-sellers, newspapers, the architecture and furnishings of homes. For most of the population crudity is part of the human lot, simply because their circumstances allow nothing else. It is easy to find examples of crudity in any people, as the crudities are, by their very nature, all too striking. 'Men's evil manners live in brass; their virtues we write in water.'

The Germans are accused of crudity in eating and drinking. Nowadays, they are certainly overweight. But so are the Americans, for whom obesity has become almost a national problem. If the average American silhouette is less fat than the German, this is perhaps because there are more slimming establishments in America. Germans have not always been famous for fat, and their present girth may be due to appetites remembering the lean days after 1943 and the post-1945 starvation years when tens of thousands died for lack of food and many more suffered malnutrition.

They are often thought to be the greatest beer-drinkers in the world. But the Belgians and Australians easily outdrink them. German beer-cellars are much more noisy than the quiet, almost staid, English public house. But, though crude, the beer-cellar noise is usually cheerful and sociable, with much back-slapping, singing of songs, and laughter. There are few alcoholic fights, particularly compared to Australia.

German methods of torture are instanced as examples of their crudity. The Gestapo are judged unsubtle compared with the Russian secret police. Some people would say that the Russian secret police have shown that very different methods are possible, for instance in the Great Purges of 1936 to 1938, but then they wanted unmarked victims who would 'confess their crimes' at show trials. At other times, their methods were as crude as Nazi ones. The Nazis neither wanted show trials nor brainwashing. Even after the failure of the 20 July 1944 plot, the Nazi courts were uninterested in the kind of 'confessions' Stalin wanted. Nazi torture to extract information from, say, resistance workers was crude but extremely effective, as all too many dead and alive can witness. It is a sad, but true fact that crudity in torture *is* efficient.

The German language is often called crude and ugly. Its gutteralness can grate, and the frequency of mouthfilling nouns compounded of words added to each other can be disconcertingly abrupt and jargonish to a foreigner. Nevertheless, in the hands of a Luther, Goethe, Heine, Bismarck, Rilke, German has strength

23

and beauty. English can sound very ugly, despite Shakespeare, Shelley and Yeats. Even the softer French and Italian languages depend on a cherishing care to bring out their beauty. There are few uglier noises than an ill-educated inhabitant of Marseilles or Genoa in full spate.

It needs a Judge Jeffreys to convict the Germans of total crudity when they have produced such a Croesan cultural wealth. In music, they are unequalled; by normal standards two of the three greatest composers in the world—Bach and Beethoven—were German; and there are a host of other great German musicians. German philosophy is immensely impressive, if misguided in the view of English empirical philosophers, and not even the most blinkered Oxford analytical philosopher could be contemptuous of Kant. German literature is as rich as any, and includes one of the few writers fit to stand beside Shakespeare: Goethe. The other arts and scholarships in general abound in German names and achievements. One reason for this is the seriousness with which even the bus-driver and bank-clerk take culture. Many more German cities —and towns—have for long supported orchestras and theatres than their English counterparts—or those of other nations.

Often this seriousness is charged against the German. He has, it is claimed, no sense of humour. Clive Bell in his book *Civilisation* contends that a sense of humour is a mark of a civilized, uncrude people. A civilized person must be able to laugh at even the most serious things, perhaps because, as Horace Walpole remarked, life is a comedy to those who think, a tragedy to those who feel. It is true that there is no great German humorous writer—no Dickens, Moliére, Cervantes, Gogol, Pirandello—but few countries have internationally recognized humorous writers. But there are many lesser German humorists and irony, exemplified in some of the Romantics and, above all, in Thomas Mann, is a peculiarly well-developed German literary trait. Most Germans do have a sense of humour as anyone can testify who has heard the agile, biting, wry wit of the Berliner, the quick merry humour of the Rhinelander, and the slow, gentle but pomposity-pricking joking of the Suabian.

Is the German cruel? Yes, at times, incontinently, atrociously cruel. How could that be denied by anyone aware of SS tortures, concentration camps, German brutality on the Russian front, and the Thirty Years War? Yet, in that war, foreigners perpetrated as

24

many cruelties as Germans, and on the Russian front in World War Two the Communists were not far, if at all, behind the Germans in cruelty. Cruelty in the twentieth century, however, seems immensely worse than that of earlier times because we regard ourselves as so much more advanced, civilized, humane. And in many ways we are. Nevertheless, the twentieth century has shown that these qualities can be little more than a veneer easily cracked under pressure. Perhaps the fault lies with the nineteenth century, breeding illusions of progress, and faith in man's goodness or perfectibility.

Every people has added to the sum of human cruelty. Blake rightly said: 'Cruelty has a human heart.' The history of every land has its cruel pages, although national historians may omit their own. Even those peoples with temperate political, social and military climates have atrocities to their discredit. Americans have their treatment of Red Indians and countless torturings and lynchings of negroes. The British have Hogarth to record eighteenth-century domestic cruelties. And in war the British soldier has many times been wrought up to cruelty as foul as any. In 1812, Wellington's troops in Spain stormed Badajoz with great difficulty, heroism and loss of life. Despite all Wellington could do, the troops raged through the town for three days, slaughtering, looting and raping, completely out of control—and their victims were not the defeated French, but Spanish civilians, Britain's allies. It was this sort of barbarity that made Wellington call his troops 'the scum of the earth'. He was wrong. Soldiers of all nations behaved similarly. Then, loot was a soldier's perquisite. Until the days of gold rushes and industrialism, it was one of the very few ways a man could rise above his station. Loot could buy a farm, inn or small business for a soldier with nothing previously in his purse. When a town resisted and fell, women were fair game for rapists. It had been so in the distant days when Tacitus recorded that German women, seeing their tribesmen beaten, bared their breasts to show that they knew their inevitable fate was mass rape by the Romans. There must be few continentals whose family tree does not include at least one bastard conceived in rape.

Rape is a subject eschewed by historians. The scholarly discipline of history grew up in the nineteenth century, and the prevailing middle-class reticence about sex naturally bowdlerized rape from the history books. In any case, it was hardly a matter for schoolchildren to read about. Another reason for historians' silence about rape and other common cruelties is that they have very largely confined their attentions to top people, who, obviously, need not resort to rape. The obsession with top people is not merely the result of snobbery or of a liking for the vicarious rubbing of shoulders with the great. It is, simply because top people leave records, whilst the common people do not, except very unusually. Even today political scientists are mostly interested in Presidents, Prime Ministers, Cabinets, party leaders, trade unions, pressure groups. The few attempts they have made to study common behaviour are to do with 'urgent' questions: elections, attitudes to capital punishment, racism. So far, they have penetrated little below the top crust. Sociologists have investigated much more of the underside of society, but, except in a few countries, theirs is a subject still struggling for recognition. In any event, it is of too recent origin to reveal much about common behaviour in the past.

For all these reasons, it is impossible to estimate how cruel, crude, subservient, arrogant and militarist a people is. But surely we do know enough to be certain that even if Germans show these defects in greater measure than other peoples—something extremely hard to establish—it is only in greater measure. Germans are not unique in having these flaws. Nor can it even be shown that they are distinctively German national characteristics. The flaws belong to the human race.

The casting of such stones at Germans is at best silly, naïve and irresponsible. At worst, it savours of pharasaic self-righteousness. It helps those holding such an attitude to find without any trouble a convenient receptacle for their moral indignation. It helps them feel decent, progressive, humanitarian like those in the 1920s, '30s and '40s who anathematized the British Empire whilst overlooking that they themselves still continued to enjoy the products of sweated labour in Hong Kong factories, Indian mills, Kenyan farms and West Indian sugar plantations.

These anti-Germans are our moderns for whom effortless superiority has given way to effortless virtue. They are on the side of the angels without having to go through the fires that angels have to endure before they are awarded their wings, harps and haloes. They are our Pharisees. The Pharisee is not only holier than us; he is also wrong. His over-simplification of the problem

26

of Nazi Germany is one that judges some 60 million Germans as
either fools or knaves, or both. But some 60 million Germans cannot all be fools or knaves. And to dismiss them so is to miss the
importance of more terrible and tragic things than folly or knavery
—it is to miss the most real and human and powerful of the driving
passions and reasons for a totalitarian despotism and the atrocities
it commits.

4

The neglect of such passions and reasons at any level other than
that of the top people is the Achilles heel of the second most
common explanation of Nazi Germany: that it was all the doing of
Hitler and his Nazi thugs who were assisted into power, or helped
in the awful use of that power, by a conspiracy of the Reichswehr,
industrialists, anti-democratic politicians, a Presidential camarilla
—all, some, or one being singled out for guilt depending on the
historian's preference.

Certainly, Nazism was assisted by some members of these
groups, actively or passively. Certainly, some profited from the
régime. Certainly, some acted from bad intentions; but others did
so with good intentions, perhaps forgetting what part of the
cosmos is paved with them. Certainly, Nazi thugs played an important part. Certainly Hitler was a vital factor, and his almost
incredible extraordinariness makes it all too easy to slip into the
belief that it was all, or mostly, his doing, as it is all too easy to
believe the same of Stalin and the Communist régime between
1924 and 1953.

Adolf Hitler was born in Austria at Braunau on Inn on 20 April
1889, the son of an obscure Austrian customs official who had
risen from peasant origins into the lower middle class. Hitler was
devoted to his mother who died, a widow, in his youth. He was
mediocre at school and unsuccessful in his ambition to become an
artist, largely through lack of ability. As a young man he roamed
Vienna and Munich, at times scratching a bare living and sleeping
in doss-houses. Although born in Austria, he served in the German army in World War One, but was undistinguished except for
reaching the rank of corporal, and winning both 1st and 2nd class
Iron Crosses. After the war he became a minor politician in
Bavaria. It was not until 1923 that he became a figure fit for an
occasional newspaper headline. And yet within ten years he be-

came Chancellor of Germany. Within another six, he launched a war that was one of the most terrible in history. Before it was lost, he presided over an almighty totalitarian régime. Twelve years after becoming Chancellor, at half past three on the afternoon of Monday, 30 April 1945, ten days after his 57th birthday and less than 48 hours after his only marriage, he ended his own life in the bunkers of the ruined Reich Chancellery, within gunshot of Russian tanks advancing in the capital of the Third Reich which, in his proud boast, was to last a thousand years, and was now crashing in ruins in the final Götterdämmerung days of the weird nightmarish tragedy that was Nazi Germany. Over 50 million dead from the war preceded him to the grave, at least six million of them victims of his inhuman execution squads in gas chambers and mass shootings.

No one can call such a man in any way ordinary. Indeed, he seems almost not to be human. He seems to have been a ruler before whom not only the ruled (even those at the top) but events themselves wilted. Therefore, it is not at all to be wondered at that he alone is blamed for all that happened between 30 January 1933 and VE-Day on 8 May 1945, not only by Germans eager for a scapegoat, but also by others more responsible.

'The history of the world is but the biography of great men.' Since Carlyle wrote that 100 years ago, historians have advanced far. But most still hold the view that the history of the world is but the story of the top men. The little men leave all too scanty evidence. So, Shirer's *The Rise and Fall of the Third Reich* devotes about 900 of his 1,000 or more pages to domestic and international politics at the top until 1939 and war until 1945. A similar emphasis is evident in Alan Bullock's *Hitler: A Study in Tyranny*, although he has more excuse than Shirer, since his book purports to be a biography, despite its subtitle, and is of incomparably finer quality than Shirer's book. Yet, Hitler, and still less Nazi tyranny, cannot be understood without comprehending the little and middle-rank man. This is the mass age. Hitler, above all, was a man of the masses. The Nazi régime was very much a mass régime.

The men, women and children below the top ranks were the foundations of the dictator and his totalitarian structure. They, most of all, provided its tremendous strength. Not because they —or even most of them—supported it actively, but because they were human beings caught in the grip of human emotions, desires, fears, predicaments, dilemmas. Many motives led to active support: idealism, love of Germany, hero-worship, a sense of adventure, hatred, ambition, power-lust, greed. A mixture of reasons ensured passive support or lack of opposition: fear of the Gestapo and concentration camp, political and social apathy, and a wary decision, like Candide's, that one could do little else than to cultivate one's own garden. Even in the concentration camp the inmate's craving for food for a starving stomach, or fear of his own extermination, assisted considerably the SS to carry out its horrible business.

Many, technically free, were caught on the horns of dilemmas that forbade opposition. The soldier who could not betray or desert Germany in time of war. The judge who did not resign because he feared his place would be filled by a fanatical Nazi who would impose harsher punishments and many more death sentences. The priest who stifled his conscience's sense of outrage at Nazi measures because he knew speaking out would bring exile from his parish and the loss to his flock of any spiritual ministrations. All these and more had given hostages to fortune as had the ordinary man with wife and children dependent on him. They were compelled to reflect, like Francis Bacon, that such hostages are 'impediments to great enterprises' of virtue as well as mischief.

A totalitarian tyranny like Nazi Germany is so strong because it rests on the Führer *and* the unemployed man back in work; on Göring *and* the ordinary German proud of the Fatherland's recovery of international prestige; on Himmler *and* the insignificant citizen fearful of Dachau; on the Field-Marshal *and* the private, driven by patriotism, discipline, or a sheep-like character; on Goebbels *and* the newspaper reader or radio listener who never heard the other side of the story—and did not much care; on Krupps *and* the small trader hating the competition of the department store; on Baldur von Shirach *and* the boy proud of his Hitler Youth uniform; on *Mein Kampf and* the small Nazi official making money on the side by use of his party position. *Ein Volk, Ein Reich, Ein Führer*. Historians of Nazi Germany have paid too much attention to the last two. They have emphasized *Volk* in its racist sense, and not enough in its other sense, the common people.

2 Power

ROMANTICS IN THE NINETEENTH CENTURY, and the twentieth as well, have bewailed the loss of innocence brought by modern changes. In the Robin Hood world of long ago, the sun shines forever, it is eternal summer, the merry men are never without food or drink, and the good and innocent always triumph. Under the greenwood tree, life is as you like it. Reality was very different. Before modern times, even well-fed aristocrats could *expect* to live no more than 30 or 40 years. Old tombstones tell how many children died in infancy, and the death of half or more of children born to a family made bereavement a constant companion. For most people, food was short, meat a luxury, and at times the grain-seed had to be eaten with awful consequences for the next year. Before brick and tile replaced vermin-bearing wood or mud and daub and thatch, man's habitation was a breeder of diseases. Medical knowledge was very primitive. Aspirins and anaesthetics were unknown before the nineteenth century. Previously tooth-ache had to be endured stoically, or with the aid of laudanum or alcohol if they could be afforded; and if the tooth had to be pulled out, the operation was done without aneasthetics. So were amputations and other operations. Some surgeons in the armed forces carried a mallet as part of their professional kit, to knock out any patient struggling too much under the knife. Of those who survived the shock of an operation, three out of four were killed later by gangrene, blood-poisoning or other complications. In the past, how much cruelty to children was the result of a parent's nerves tormented by pain? How many enemies did sufferers from gall-stones make by their irascibility? How much did malnutrition, discomfort, fear of pain, starvation and early death pockmark the quality of life?

Industrialization joined to scientific, medical and technological discoveries has brought a far better life to many in the West. Instead of homeward plodding his weary way, the ploughman goes by bicycle or bus. The modern Mother Hubbard finding the cupboard bare goes to a supermarket or cornerstore. Oliver Twists today are given more. The wounded on the battlefield are not robbed, stripped of their clothes, and left to die, but are given plasma and lifted by helicopter to hospital. Contemporary Western people can be, and are, more humane as well as longer-lived, less fearful and brutish than their ancestors. Despite nuclear bombs and atrocities, Madison Avenue and materialism, modern progress has in most significant ways been kind. It is impossible to deny that we are, at the moment, much better off than our ancestors, even when they were gentry or aristocrats. And we owe this equally to both sides of the Dual Revolution—the French and the Industrial.

Nevertheless, each Industrial Revolution brings hurt, suffering, loss, fearful dislocation. Its victims far outnumber those of a French Revolution. Periods of transition are always painful to state and society. They are, as it were, society's adolescence with all its instability, insecurity, quarrels with parents, rudeness, clumsiness, wild oats, as well as its adventures, discoveries, idealism, romance, and discovery of independence.

In pre-industrial society, people accepted all the world's many imperfections and ills as natural and eternal. As *Ecclesiastes* put it with compassionate resignation: 'The thing that hath been, it is that which shall be; and that which is done is that which shall be done; and there is no new thing under the sun.' The pace of change was very slow and so there were very few adolescent troubles.

2

Slowness of change was indeed one of the four basic characteristics of European, pre-industrial, traditional society. The other three were that society was agrarian; that it was hierarchical; and that it had a *Weltanschauung*, a life-view or world-picture, compounded of Religion and Reason. This is to simplify; traditional societies of course varied from time to time and place to place. But, by and large, these four characteristics were basic to all, and certainly basic to the German society which was uprooted by industrialism.

Slowness of change is too obvious to need more than passing demonstration. Until the coming of the railway, the speed of travel on land had not increased since Roman times; in fact it was probably slower than on Roman roads. The rule of the seasons and

31

lack of communications between villages and towns encouraged it; the interests of rulers ensured it. The German of the 1860s would find much more in common with his countryman of ten centuries earlier than with a German of a century later, or, come to that, half a century later.

Traditional society was agrarian. Agriculture employed by far the majority of people, and land was the prime source of wealth. Commerce was important, but secondary, as is shown by the paucity of shops and the humble retail trade in as advanced a city as Paris before the 1830s and 1840s. Workshops were small and extremely primitive by modern standards. There were large cities—Berlin, London, Paris, Vienna and St Petersburg—but they were not industrial centres so much as commercial clearing-houses and administrative centres, the location of royal courts, halls of justice, and government offices. There were busy ports like Hamburg and Bristol, but they depended on commerce rather than manufacturing. Country towns had only a few thousand inhabitants, and were more or less dwarf copies of the city, without the royal court, grand society, great wealth, and sophis-tication.

In the countryside villages had little contact with each other, not much with the nearest town, and practically none with the capital city. Friedrich Paulsen, born in rural Germany and later a distinguished scientist, stresses in his autobiography the isolation of mid-nineteenth-century country people and the self-contained life of their village. Isolation came from the economy being largely of a subsistence kind, the primitive state of roads especially in winter, the expense of overland transport before the coming of railways and good waterways in the nineteenth century, and the understandable lack of a regular cheap postal service in a land where all but a few were illiterate. Many villagers never in their life ventured more than a few miles from their homes, and many women (Paulsen recalls) never set eyes on a town.

One important trait of this agrarian society was the 'extended family', where, unlike the twentieth-century 'nuclear-family', employees lived as well as worked in their master's house. Children —or, at least, sons—tended to marry late, having to wait to hive off until the father could afford to set up his son on his own or give his daughter a dowry. Married children rarely lived with their parents, unless their spouse had died. In the master's house, servants, apprentices, and other employees lived and worked, almost as members of the family.

Traditional society was aristocratic and hierarchical. A few owned the bulk of the wealth and alone possessed power. This was a God-given fact of life, generally accepted by high and low. The monarch was, in one sense, a person set apart with special powers, rights and duties. He was, so to speak, the keystone of traditional society. Nevertheless, he was of the same stock as the aristocracy; he was the highest aristocrat, different in degree but not in kind. It might be that if this keystone was pulled away, all else would fall; but the arch would also collapse if other stones were removed. All were interdependent and interconnected, particularly at the top of society. The literal meaning of the word 'monarchy', rule by one person, had probably never been reality; in fact, rule was dispersed through society.

Aristocratic power depended greatly on possession of most of the wealth. But it also depended heavily on two other near-monopolies less often stressed by historians. Aristocrats supplied all the senior officers and most of the junior ones in the armed forces. Whilst this gave them considerable power *vis-à-vis* the monarchy, it also meant that in practice they controlled law and order, until urbanization demanded the invention of professional police forces in the nineteenth century. As a consequence, aristocrats dispensed absolute justice in their own courts on their own lands, as well as holding special rights in other law courts.

Their other near-monopoly was education. Except for churchmen and a small middle class, only aristocrats could read and write. In our age of universal literacy in the West, it is hard to grasp what illiteracy entailed: how difficult or even impossible it was for an illiterate to command troops, manage an estate or business, be a churchman, or a representative in Parliament or its local counterpart. The best way to mount the social ladder was by acquiring not money, but literacy. The Church was the classic ladder with peasant lads picked for their brains, taught to read and write, and able to die a Bishop. Another outstanding ladder was the eighteenth-century Prussian civil service, where Hohenzollern kings found it good strategy in their running battles with overmighty aristocrats to open a career to literate talents. The French *noblesse de robe* (the administrative aristocracy distinct from the *noblesse d'epée*, the aristocracy of birth and army) was a similar

33

social ladder, a device of Richelieu which anticipated the Hohen-zollerns' civil service by a century. In Russia it was possible for a civil servant who rose to a high rank to obtain nobility: Lenin's father was one. There was in traditional society an aristocratic title in every schoolboy's satchel.

The limited extent of literacy and the isolation of rural inhabi-tants meant that the literate, educated section really constituted 'the nation', since they were the only men ever to come together on more than a local basis to consider the interests of the whole community. The illiterate, uneducated and isolated had to rely on their educated, wealthy, powerful betters for representation of his local interests in any wider context of country, province or nation. So, as late as the nineteenth century, their betters thought it justifiable to see and talk of themselves as 'the people', 'the state', 'the nation', and to debate the 'rights and representation of the people' as though these referred only to themselves. And the illiterate did not dissent. Hierarchy—and the observance of 'degree, priority and place'—were based on palpable realities, of which wealth was only one.

Traditional society had a *Weltanschauung*, a world-picture, composed of Religion and Reason, which helped give meaning to the order of state and society. In our scientific age, Religion and Reason often seem like oil and water. In the traditional world, few found it hard to blend them, or not to worry if they did not seem to blend. After all, most people—even the educated—have always easily carried in their minds unconnected, even contradic-tory, points of view, opinions, prejudices. Persons who insist on their philosophy being consistent, their world picture being an integrated whole, have always been rare.

Besides giving spiritual consolation to souls in jeopardy, the Church provided intellectual support for authority as one of its prime functions. It explained and justified a hierarchical, aristo-cratic society in which each person had his defined place; why obedience was owed to superiors, to the law, and to morality; and why the poor are always with us. The simple—over-simple—answer was that God so created and ordained it; but the full answer had to be more complex and sophisticated to satisfy those with brains, scepticism and contra-suggestibility.

Every person—man, woman and child, high and low—was supposed to be brought up in Church. Except for the city rabble,

34

this assumption was fact for almost all. One duty of each priest or minister was to teach his flock a catechism which included promises to submit to the order of society and to the state of life into which it pleased God to call them. Damnation was the promised wages of the sin of breaking such promises, although, no doubt, some did not bother overmuch about the prospect of collecting wages which seemingly lay so far in the future.

There were, however, sanctions other than spiritual to translate the catechism's theory into fact. The parishioner obeyed his landlord for fear of eviction as well as for fear of his immortal soul. Crude fear of sanctions was buttressed by the dependence of the lowly on the high and mighty, who could afford help in pestilence, fire, flood or famine, and whose favours and patronage could assist a well-behaved man or his children to improve their lot. Usually, such patronage was the only way of rising in life.

The priest or minister was the link between the common man and the gentry and aristocracy. He translated their pleas for help. He imparted government edicts and explained news of the great world outside; before the day of universal literacy or radio, the pulpit was the only mass medium to reach the common man. The local clergyman was a formidable figure to cross. In Germany the country *Pfarrer*, or minister, often superintended the election of the village *Vogt*, or head police official, and together they were responsible for most administrative matters including poor relief. The minister was the government's confidential agent, reporting on villagers. He was the village registrar of births, marriages, deaths, orphans, bastards, homeless families, the blind, deaf, dumb and maimed. He conducted the census and listed recruits to the army, and superintended and examined local schools. He presided over the district's ecclesiastical court dealing with moral offences which could carry gaol sentences. Clearly, his activities were not limited to the seventh day of rest nor to the realm of the spiritual.

Church and aristocracy were helped, in maintaining law and morality and the stability of society, by the smallness of villages and country towns. They had their own voluntary security service, for everyone knew everyone else's business and all the gossip, sooner rather than later, reached the clerical or aristocratic ear. The clerical remedy was Hellfire, refusal of the sacraments, or less spiritual weapons. Recent French and English research has shown

35

that the ceaseless campaign to preserve sexual morality—perhaps the hardest of all morality to maintain—was much more of a success than books like *Tom Jones* and *Fanny Hill* suggest. Perhaps the sexuality of such books was wish-fulfilment rather than reflections of reality.

Traditional society with these four basic characteristics had existed in Europe for centuries or, some would say, millennia. In France the Revolution of 1789 had overthrown the *ancien régime* but after 1815 French society was still basically traditional. In 1815 England was the only land where Industrial Revolution had commenced its destruction, but even there only the façade had been removed. The full power of the steam from James Watt's kettle was only just beginning to shape a new society and—less spectacular but certainly no less important—destroy an old society and all its values.

3

German industrialization started slowly in the first half of the nineteenth century, gathered impetus from Bismarck's unification, and was moving at breakneck speed in the generation before 1914. By 1910, Germany was Europe's leading iron and steel producer, although less than 40 years earlier her output had been a mere fifth of the United Kingdom's. In 1847, Germany had a tiny mercantile fleet of 8,944 gross registered tons; in 1913 she could boast 2,098 ships with 4,380,000 tons. Between 1872 and 1913 German exports more than quadrupled and her imports almost tripled. In new industries like the manufacture of chemicals, electrical goods and cars Germany became a world leader. In the course of little more than a generation before 1914 Germany was transformed from an agrarian society to a modern, highly efficient, industrialized and urbanized nation, a strong challenger of England's long and proud position as 'the workshop of the world'.

German industrialization was marked by a concentration of large-scale units of production and distribution on a scale unknown in England. Businesses carried on by the extended family in the home became more and more of an anachronism. Their place was usurped by factories, joint-stock companies, department and chain-stores. The growth of joint-stock companies was phenomenal: between 1851 and 1871 only 205 were created; between 1871 and 1874, the number was 857. Department and chain-stores overshadowed and withered the small shop-keeper. *Kartels*, a method of industrial concentration, especially developed in Germany, multiplied: in 1875, there were less than 10, in 1885 about 90, and in 1905 there were 366. World War One and the inflation of 1922–3 further culled small businesses and proliferated large units.

Perhaps the most important concentration brought by industrialization was in cities. In 1875, about a third of the population lived in towns; by 1910, two-thirds did. In 1871, Germany had only eight towns with a population over 100,000; in 1890, she had 26; in 1905, there were 41 over 100,000, eleven over 250,000 and five over 500,000. Berlin grew alarmingly fast, its population soaring from 180,000 in 1800 to a million in 1877 and two million in 1905. By 1900, Berlin had the reputation of being the biggest tenement city in the world and its tenement buildings which spread desolately through many suburbs were regarded as the worst-built in the world.

The Jehu-like speed of industrialization helped drive German traditional society to destruction. Factories supplanted domestic industries. Steam power outmoded sailing ships. The whistle of the railway train was heard daily in the countryside, opening up wider markets for farmers and peasants, and taking their sons off to the bright lights and new jobs in the city. Once there, the peasant could walk along streets lit at night by gas and later electricity; he could ride in electric trams, dodge motor-cars, gape at buildings towering higher and higher and boasting wider and wider areas of glass as steel and reinforced concrete made new construction techniques possible and as lifts solved one of the skyscraper's problems. He could be excited by the news and scan the advertisements in the new cheap popular press. After 1888, he could ride into the country on bicycles equipped with the newly invented pneumatic tyre, taking his sweetheart with him if he had a bicycle built for two. Woman's life was radically altered by a cluster of new inventions: the sewing-machine, type-writer, tinned food, refrigeration, cheap factory-produced soap, sealed roads diminishing dust, vacuum cleaners, contraceptives. Compulsory elementary education sent them to school, either as pupil or teacher. A police force and street-lighting allowed them out in the evening unescorted, a necessity to a woman employed outside the home. By the twentieth century,

D

37

planes travelled in the sky and submarines below the sea. Radio had been invented. The telegraph and telephone were becoming commonplace. Medicine, science and the arts were revolutionized —and revolutionizing. A new world was created in a few bewildering years.

Industrialization showered many benefits on Germans. Besides international power, prestige and wealth, it brought a general rise in the standard of living, as was revealingly indicated by the increased consumption of sugar and textiles and meat. Shops displayed a much wider and cheaper selection of goods, and even poor homes contained more factory-produced household articles. There was more comfort and opportunities, less pain and poverty for many. Diversification of the economy created a wider range of jobs. Health improved; infant mortality plummeted; life expectancy rose steadily. Women were less home-tied and shackled to the cradle and kitchen sink, and the leisure of men also increased. Mass schooling produced a literate, though not necessarily an educated, community. New mass media put newspapers on the breakfast table, popular weeklies in the hands of schoolboys and commuters, radio in the home after World War One, all sowing knowledge of a wider world, however scrappy, superficial and garbled that knowledge might be. The cinema offered vicarious romance and adventure, and, occasionally, useful information. It would be idle and silly to deny that the Industrial Revolution brought to many a richer life—in more senses of the word than the obvious.

For others, however, it opened up a Pandora's box of ills. Industrialized man lost that strong sense of community, coherence and stability that characterized traditional society. City life could be all too lonely, anonymous, rickety. Morality lost many of its former sanctions, as mobility between suburbs and cities provided refuge for the transgressor. Gentry and pastor had little hold over the slum-dweller, and civil servants emasculated the power of the clergyman as they took over his non-clerical functions. In the city, there could be no real homogeneity. A man could easily come to feel like an isolated atom. His family might provide warmth and comfort; but, conversely, a family could mean brutal husbands and parents, nagging wives, screaming babies, hungry, whining children, adolescents defying parents with the Dutch courage of wages of their own. To rural dwellers migrating to the factories

and slums, the city must often have seemed as it did to Shelley:
'Hell is a city much like London.'

4

The working man was the most obvious victim of industrialization.
Whether his standard of living rose in the long run is a subject on
which economic historians delight to disagree. To the working
man, however, living from day to day, it was only the short run
that mattered, and he did not need Lord Keynes to tell him that
'in the long run we shall all be dead'. Without doubt, many
working men did suffer. They bore the psychological pain of
uprooting themselves from the countryside and facing the unfamiliar regularity of the working-hours in a factory, shop or
office, and the monotony of the machine, selling over the counter
or clerical work. Wages were low, sometimes barely enough for
subsistence when the loneliness of city life and an income beyond
parental control encouraged early marriage, or living together, and
the many children that soon followed. Rents were high, and the
rush to the cities proved an Eldorado to jerry-builders and
rack-renters.

Degeneration of morals, and morale, could be escaped; but it
took considerable energy, courage, or idealism. Those with
enough of these qualities, combined with political interests, could
join the Social Democratic Party and, as Philip Scheidemann
relates in his memoirs, roam the countryside and towns and slums
on party work, discovering purpose in life. They could find
adventure, too, in the days of repressive legislation, in organizing
branches, distributing party literature, making speeches in
sympathetic inns or homes, eventually achieving the status of a
Reichstag deputy. But Scheidemanns were rare. Many were
called, but few even wanted to be chosen. In 1913 there were only
three million trade unionists; well over half of the workers joined
no union at all. The ordinary working man would vote Social
Democrat and some would join the party; but their political
consciences sat lightly on them and politics were at most a peri-
pheral and spasmodic activity. For very few in Germany—as
elsewhere, then and since—was politics a way of life providing an
ethos with moral imperatives.

The Social Democratic Party tried hard to foster such an ethos
by building up a network of political, educational, cultural,

sporting and benefit clubs. Their main clientèle, however, too often came from younger workers who usually joined for the non-political activities, just as many young people belong to a church nowadays because it owns tennis-courts or a dance-hall. Older married men preferred the warmth of the kitchen after work, and continued paying party dues against the day they would fall sick, lose their job, or need cheap and decent burial.

Much of this state of affairs is overlooked by historians living and working solely in the rarified atmosphere of archives, libraries and book-lined studies. The history of any institution is almost invariably written from the point of view of the upper echelons, since it is inevitably they who provide the raw material for docu-ment-dominated historians. Working-class institutions are no exception, so that almost all their professional chroniclers give an impression (no doubt genuinely felt by themselves) of political bustle, purpose and enthusiasm throughout the whole body of workers. Labour leaders, their noses forcibly rubbed in the real world, have suffered from few of the illusions cherished by academic historians of working-class movements, and have known that the political interest of most of those who vote for them is merely skin-deep.

Religion may have been intended, in Marx's famous phrase, as 'an opiate for the masses'. Most of them, however, were in fact never addicts. Many a peasant trekking to the city relapsed from religion almost as soon as the village steeple was out of sight. Most of the city-born working men were pagans from birth through parental apathy or through the inability of the church to supply enough clergymen for suburbs spreading so swiftly. If parents taught them Christianity in childhood, adolescence could bring antagonism to religion in migrant circumstances, a notorious breeding ground of antagonism between first and second genera-tions. In Germany, the situation differed little from that which Disraeli is reputed to have described when the Archbishop of Canterbury mourned that the Church was losing the working people in the cities. 'Your Grace,' Disraeli observed, 'it never has had them.'

Most working men were a-political, irreligious, and ill-educated, though through no fault of their own. They spent their scant leisure hours in sleeping off exhausting work, drinking bouts, hobbies, beating their wife or children, or similar simple pleasures.

It was enough of an effort to survive and work from day to day with an occasional outlet for cheap and almost effortless gratification. A moral void like this in most working men proved no real danger to the German Empire. Bismarck's constitution and the Imperial régime restricted their power. Even in 1912 when the Social Democratic Party was the largest in the Reichstag, the government had no difficulty in carrying on without its co-operation. In any event, rising prosperity and the government's provision of new social services drew the Social Democratic Party's fangs. By the twentieth century it might still have a revolutionary and Marxist bark, but its bite was revisionist and reforming. When war came in August 1914, the Social Democrats put patriotism before party politics and voted almost en bloc for the government. However, after the war, Germany's politics were envenomed by economic catastrophes. After the accession of Hitler to power, the moral void in so many, including working men, was to prove poisonous—literally so to millions of exterminated Jews and Slavs.

5

Demoralization was not confined to working men. Besides manual workers, the Industrial Revolution needed—and mass education provided—millions of clerks, petty officials, shop-assistants and teachers. Between 1882 and 1907, white-collar workers multiplied nearly six times. They liked to think of themselves as completely distinct from the working man and as belonging to the *Mittelstand*, a German term often loosely translated as 'middle class' but literally meaning 'middle estate'. Traditionally, German society had been organized around *Stände*, estates, rather than classes: the *Adelstand*, or nobility; *Bauerstand*, or peasantry; and *Bürgerstand*, or middle estate. When industrialization produced new forms of the lower order, a workman's estate, *Arbeiterstand*, was invented and added to the other three. The word *Mittelstand* until at least World War Two meant more than an income group comparable to the lower middle class. It contained concepts of status and caste. A *Stand*, or estate, was regarded by German conservatives—and most of the *Mittelstand* was conservative—as a group defined by equality of social status and occupation, by approximately equal property and income, and by possession of rights not enjoyed by others. The last criterion is essential, even if by the turn of the century the rights existed more in the minds of members of a *Stand* than in the statute books. Not only the landed aristocracy, the officer corps, the clergy, but also the artisan, the small merchant, and petty official felt entitled to certain privileges by virtue of belonging to his *Stand*. In Germany, unlike in England where the pace of the Industrial Revolution was slower, much of the caste system survived alongside a growing class system. World War One and the economic catastrophes of the inflation of 1922-3 and the depression after 1929 wiped out most remnants of caste, and consequently impelled many of the *Mittelstand* towards the Nazis who promised to restore and defend their status.

Economically the *Mittelstand* were more akin to the working man than to the employer and property-owners who more usually connote the middle class. Most of the *Mittelstand* were employees, owning hardly any property. Their salaries were often less than the wages of a workman. They lived usually on an economic knife-edge. Their homes were dingy and shoddily furnished. Their savings were so meagre that another baby or a sustained bout of sickness could quickly consume them. They were more at the mercy of their employer than was a workman, since such trade unions as existed among them were weaker than the working-men's: lower middle-class groups always have difficulty in banding together for effective political action because of their position between capital and labour and because of the immensely varied nature of their social and economic interests.

Because members of the *Mittelstand* could so easily be squeezed through the eye of a needle into what they regarded as a working-class Hell, they were obsessed with status, with social distinctiveness. Although they might be impoverished, they fought to the last against being proletarianized. Their social status and place in the caste system were typified by obeisance to patriotism, *Kultur*, respectability, thrift, hard work, and Sunday church. They were symbolized by a bowler hat instead of a cloth cap and a celluloid collar and tie instead of a muffler; in colloquial German a white-collar worker is *Stehkragen-Prolet*, starched-collar proletarian, a contemptuous epitaph often on the tongue of trade unionists. When the inflation of 1922-3 and the Depression after 1929 cost many of them their savings and livelihood so that they were willy-nilly proletarianized and deprived of their social status, they were vote

42

fodder for the Nazis. On the other hand not all the *Mittelstand* were proletarianized by depression. Many were fortunate enough to preserve their job and social status—or even to increase the latter when plummeting prices considerably raised the real value of salaries. These were so alarmed by the threat of 'Red Revolution' that they, too, slid easily to the extreme right.

These nervous little men of the *Mittelstand* were often as hurt by the new industrial capitalism as the working men whose sufferings have been the dominant theme of the study of Industrial Revolutions. Their cities were the homeground of this dynamic industrial capitalism, nurturing a spirit of competition and self-advancement in place of the co-operation and community of tradition. In the pre-industrial times, employees had often enjoyed a paternalistic relationship with employers; there were so few in each household and they ate and slept as well as worked there. The Industrial Revolution, however, shrunk family businesses and they became rare in the city. In the rising department stores and even in the corner draper's or corn chandler's shop, assistants had to compete against each other and there was no paternalism between manager and clerk, shop-walker and shop-assistant. Any member of the rank-and-file was easily expendable as new recruits flooded into the cities. An employer or manager found no difficulty in forgetting that the labourer on the office stool was worthy of his hire, and the clerk often did have to go from business-house to business-house in agonizing search of new employment.

Competition and individualism suited the gifted, the energetic, the personable, the unscrupulous, and the lucky. But what of those without special talents or luck? The clerk with many years' service but few brains could be dismissed because of a new technological device: the adding machine developed commercially between 1872 and 1882; the mimeograph and dictating machine, both invented in 1887; carbon paper which began to be applied to type-writing in the 1890s. Cheaper female employees could supplant male bread-winners. A department store, consumers' co-operative or chain-store could ruin a small retailer and throw his assistants out of work. Artisans and handicraftsmen could not compete with factories except in the production of a few kinds of articles. The *Mittelstand* members felt all the more bitter about such possibilities or actual happenings, because modern capitalism was mysterious and its workings were quite incomprehensible;

43

they did not understand what was dictating their fate. Because of an event on a German stock exchange or in a foreign city hundreds of miles away, the little man might lose his livelihood, his savings, and his mortgaged home, however respectable, thrifty, honest, hard-working, and obsequious to his superiors and customers he had been. Many of the *Mittelstand* came to distrust, fear and hate modern capitalism and industrial civilization.

So did many farmers and peasants, victims of a capitalism spreading over the countryside, invading the farm, determining prices, and deciding whether they made a profit, they had to go to the moneylender, or were driven into the ranks of the agricultural labourer. The trend to large-scale agriculture squeezed out the small farmer. Factories mass-producing cheaper articles deprived the peasant's family of the money earned by domestic industry in the times that the irregular business of farming had always left fallow.

The *Mittelstand* had no obvious political home. It was hard, probably impossible, for it to combine in a political party of its own because of its very diverse economic and social interests. Conservatives, dominated by the upper classes, had little sympathy for clerks, minor officials, shop-assistants, peasants, and artisans, and little to offer them but praise of *Mittelstand* moral virtues. Unlike in England, German upper-class conservatives were too secure in their control of the Imperial régime to need to woo *Mittelstand* voters, and where the Weimar régime strongly suggested this need, there were other competing right-wing parties with offers more attractive to the *Mittelstand*. Socialists wrote the *Mittelstand* off as doomed by the iron laws of Marxism prophesying inevitable immiseration and proletarianization for all but a rapidly contracting capitalist upper class. In any event, Socialism was obviously repulsive to the *Mittelstand* as a working-man's egalitarian movement. Liberalism was only a little less repulsive, with its gospel of capitalist *laissez-faire*, individualism and competition. German Liberalism's political record was not magnetic. Historically it was associated with foreigners and failures. Initially, some Germans had welcomed the Liberalism brought in the baggage-trains of the French Revolutionaries and Napoleon, but French domination and exploitation induced disillusion. Thirty years later, the failures of the 1848 Revolutions dimmed Liberalism's refurbished lustre. After another 20 years, the victorious sound of the gunfire at the Prussian triumphs over the Austrians at Sadowa in 1866 and over the French at Sedan in 1870 effectively drowned the grumbling of many liberal consciences, schizophrenically split between the urgings of nationalism and constitutionalism. After 1870, Bismarck's skill stemmed liberal advances and further fragmented an already-split party. In the Weimar period, Liberal moderation stood no chance against the extremism hot-housed by economic and political chaos.

In Industrial Revolution England, Liberalism had provided a comfortable enough haven for the rising middle classes. But industrialization in England was at first effected mostly through small economic units, usually family businesses and not by the large-scale units that characterized German industrialization. Too, Liberalism in England had a flying start, since until 1867 only large property-owners were enfranchised and many of the social ills brought by industrialization had been overcome before the days of mass suffrage. Significantly, even in England, Liberalism —at least as a political party—went to the wall in the twentieth-century mass age.

The German *Mittelstand* abhorred the Parliamentarianism and political party system so beloved by Liberals. They feared these would eventually redistribute power and privilege; would accelerate social mobility and break down caste and class barriers; and would abolish the *Standesgesellschaft*, or estate society, on which rested their status and sense of distinctiveness. The sorry record in Weimar Germany of democratic Parliamentarianism and the political party system confirmed their fears and magnified their abhorrence. They were, therefore, easy prey for ideologies expressing as bitter and frustrated an anti-capitalism as Marxism and Socialism did for many workers. However, whilst workers extravagantly looked forward to a future egalitarian Elysium, the dissatisfied members of the *Mittelstand* morbidly longed for the golden pastoral age they dreamed existed before industrial complexity despoiled simple innocence. They forgot too easily what happened to Lot's wife because she insisted on looking backwards.

Many were eager recruits for 'revolutionary conservatism'. This was neither an organized party nor movement until the days of National Socialism. It was revolutionary since it wished to abolish industrialism and capitalism, and it was conservative since it wished to return to the orderly communities of the pre-industrial

45

world. Its most popular prophets before Hitler were Paul de Lagarde (1827–91), Julius Langbehn (1851–1907) and Arthur Möller van den Bruck (1876–1925). Their books sold by the tens of thousands and were read by many more. Lagarde wanted to replace industrial society with an agrarian trading economy and handicraft production; this goal neccessitated the conquest of *Mitteleuropa* so that space could be found to break up the great urban masses and to reconstitute traditional and hierarchical village communities. In *Deutsche Schriften* (*German Writings*) Lagarde proclaimed: 'What will be cast into the molten metal to make the bell of the future toll . . . is to be found behind the plough and in the woods, by the anvil in a solitary smithy; it fights our battles and grows our corn.' Langbehn's *Rembrandt als Erzieher* (*Rembrandt as Artist*) was a diatribe against modern civilization and ran through 40 printings in 1890, the year of its publication. Möller van den Bruck in *Das Dritte Reich* (*The Third Empire*), written in 1923, exhorted Germans to replace 'reason by faith, the individual by the community, disintegration by union, "progress" by evolution'. Class consciousness needed replacing by nation consciousness and materialism by self-sacrifice. All three writers sought to eradicate the sordid present and recapture an idealized past. They have been aptly called 'cultural Luddites'. Nazi propagandists plundered their books, and the Socialism included in the title of the Nazi party was that of the *Gemeinschaft*, or community, as blueprinted by Lagarde, Langbehn and Möller van den Bruck. Brought up on a diet of such books, many of the *Mittelstand* could easily digest Nazi propaganda.

Lagarde, Langbehn and Möller van den Bruck were extremists. Nevertheless, it would be exaggerating to suggest that all the *Mittelstand* were so badly off that they clutched at extremists' remedies. The Industrial Revolution had lifted many of them up. New businesses needed new clerks; expanding civil services called for more officials; growing prosperity meant more shops and advertisements for new shop assistants and promotions for old. Many a village lad must have ended his career a respected civil servant or bank manager or factory employer. Wilhelmine Germany was by and large prosperous and this kept the canker from becoming malignant. But what if prosperity ended, the economy contracted disastrously, the political and social system broke down? *That* was the condition of Weimar Germany by 1930.

6

Like many of the *Mittelstand,* aristocrats had cause to regret industrialization. An Industrial Revolution, almost by definition, challenges aristocratic predominance. Late in the nineteenth century a new rich class rose in Germany—industrialists like Krupp and Siemens, shipowners like Ballinn, businessmen like Walther Rathenau. Early in the twentieth century, German industry was being increasingly staffed by graduates of *Handelschochschulen,* schools of business and commerce with university standing. There were not enough aristocratic sons to staff all the top positions in the many new or expanding professions even if all of them had had the necessary ability or willingness to enter business.

Many aristocratic families continued to stand apart from the new world, content to carry on their landed estates or send their sons into crack regiments or high positions in the bureaucracy. They could stem the flood of *parvenus* a little by ensuring that none but the conservatively-minded entered the Prussian civil service and by maintaining a monopoly of the appointments of officers in the best regiments. Yet, even in the Army some of less than aristocratic blood had to be admitted as officers; the Southern states showed a distressing tendency to appoint bourgeois officers —something the Prussian nobility could not prevent since constitutionally each state appointed its own officers though Prussia, through the Kaiser, commanded the German army as a whole.

Other aristocrats had the good sense not to play Canute to an inevitable tide. In 1878 and 1879 Bismarck had engineered a political liaison between the landed aristocracy and the big industrialists by means of a bargain from which each obtained protective tariffs. Although the landed aristocracy still despised industry and although the industrialists disliked agricultural tariffs which raised food prices and wages, they both knew that an alliance was necessary if Liberalism and, even worse, Socialism were to be contained. Connections were made between some Junkers and *nouveaux riches.* As in England, aristocratic parents often could not resist the handsome dowries which accompanied the marriage of a son to the daughter of a wealthy merchant or industrialist. The marriage traffic was not nearly so heavy in Industrial Revolution Germany as in England where there was no large army and, until the end of the nineteenth century, no large bureaucracy to provide plentiful posts for aristocratic sons. So, in Germany much more of the caste system persisted, although by 1914 the aristocracy no longer held exclusive power.

Politically, even before 1914 the traditional caste system had to be adulterated. But a strong flavour remained. Constitutionally, the Empire was an unstable compound of federation, autocracy and constitutional monarchy. Formal executive authority was in the hand of the states represented in the *Bundesrat*, the upper house. The *Bundesrat* presented legislation to the *Reichstag*, the lower house, for its decision, and the *Bundesrat* issued the regulations to implement the legislation. The laws were usually drawn up by the Chancellor and his state secretaries and both he and they were responsible not to the *Reichstag* but to the Kaiser. The *Reichstag* could reject the budget; but its financial powers were more limited than those of the House of Commons. In practice, it did not control the purse-strings and could not easily force a change of government through its financial powers. Also, an important part of government funds came from indirect taxes which were to all intents and purposes beyond the *Riechstag's* control.

Prussia had a double political control. It had enough votes in the *Bundesrat* to dominate it. And, except in the Caprivi Chancellorship (1890–4), the Imperial Chancellor was also Minister-President of Prussia responsible to the Kaiser who was King of Prussia. Upper-class predominance in the Prussian *Landtag*, or lower house, was ensured by a three-class vote: the electorate was divided into three classes according to property qualifications and each class elected a third of the deputies. The Prussian representation to the Imperial *Bundesrat* was chosen by these deputies. So the Prussian upper classes controlled the Imperial Parliamentary system, which was no true Parliamentary system. Lower-class power remained insignificant even when the Social Democratic Party's votes rose from 123,975 in 1871 to four and a quarter million in 1912, and its deputies from 2 to 110 (the largest single party representation) in the same period. The *Reichstag* was (to use Lassalle's phrase) no more than 'a fig-leaf for absolutism'.

This absolutism was a casualty of World War One. Total war necessitated total mobilization of the whole population either marching as soldiers or working in war industries. Force could not achieve this alone, and the upper classes had to learn to work with trade unionists. By 1916, the Hindenburg-Ludendorff
48

military dictatorship transformed the Kaiser into a mere Imperial figure-head. Revolution followed defeat in 1918 and ended absolutism. In Weimar Germany, the upper classes still exercised an influence disproportionate to their numbers through their positions in the bureaucracy, judiciary, *Reichswehr* and universities. But their monopoly of political power was no more.

If before 1914 the aristocracy retained most of their political power in alliance with industry's leaders, they were losing it in the cultural domain. Education—of a sort—spread downwards to the lower classes, and the middle classes successfully challenged the aristocratic monopoly of higher education. Nowhere else were so many Ph.D.s produced as in Germany. German book production jumped to 19,000 in 1890. Popular cheap editions such as the Tauchnitz series of translations and the *Reclam Universal Bibliothek* put Europe's books within reach of mass pockets. Newspapers and weeklies multiplied, the *Berliner Illustrierte* attaining before the war a circulation of nearly two million. Mass literacy created a new mass 'culture'; it also enabled new non-aristocratic educated Germans to climb to the top of the ladder of the old culture.

In traditional society, the aristocracy dominated fashions and tastes. Before industrialization the outside of an aristocratic home had been well-proportioned but plain and the interior was more lavishly decorated as if the aristocrat's first concern was with the 'insider' rather than the 'outsider'. The new rich were entirely different and wished to make an outward display of their wealth to all and sundry by ornate façades decorated with a mass of architectural frills and furbelows easily produced in the machine age. Craftsmanship, sense of proportion, and good taste were lost in an orgy of what Thorstein Veblen called 'conspicuous consumption', the need of the *nouveaux riches* to display their wealth—and worth —by spending money on useless objects and ornamentation. The greater the wealth, the greater the ostentation; and the greater the ostentation, the greater the kudos.

Control of other arts was snatched from aristocratic hands. Aristocratic theatres had been small and intimate, well-suited to a conventionalized drama of sophistication and wit. The admittance of middle-class and plebeian audiences enlarged theatres and called for a ranting style of acting, melodrama, and for the spectacle which machinery could supply *ad infinitum*—and *ad absurdum*

49

—and which only an exceptional producer like Max Reinhardt could manage with good taste. Aristocratic order had previously been reflected in the theatre by the classical unities as it had been by tonality in music, chronology in the novel, and perspective in painting. All these were departed from more and more in the twentieth century as the creative arts were freed from the shackles of aristocratic patronage.

Painters were in the vanguard. They ceased to be the servants of upper-class patrons and either degenerated into mass-producers of 'Stags at Bay' and civic portraiture or found a new patronage in a painterly élite of mixed class with a devouring interest in artistic experiment. The painter, not the patron, now was able to dictate taste. Artists like Braque, Cézanne, Klee, Manet, Monet, Picasso, van Gogh followed their own bents. Breaking loose from traditional modes they sought new insights and explored relationships between shapes, lines, colours, rather than confining themselves to formal representations. New esoteric movements were born, thrived and perished: Impressionism, Post-Impressionism, Expressionism, Fauvism, Cubism, Dadaism, Surrealism. *Avant-garde* dealers prospered as middlemen between the painter and the new patron who, however wealthy, was humble before the artist in a way the aristocratic patron had never been. Germany had its famous art-dealers: Cassirer and Walden in Berlin, Thaunhauser and Gaspari in Munich, Flechtheim in Düsseldorf. They encouraged coteries and art-groups like *Die Brücke (The Bridge)* in Munich, and these, in turn, gave birth to influential new periodicals like *Pan* and *Der Sturm* in Berlin and *Die Fackel (The Torch)* in Vienna. The painter who was interested in real art had become his own master. A price had to be paid for this freedom: the retreat of the artist and art-lover—and of the cultured generally—into narrowing circles of *cognoscenti* separated by an ever-widening gap from a philistine mass public; the problem of 'the two cultures' existed then on this level as well as on the general level. But the art-lover and cultured were well content to pay this price. They revelled in their new-found freedom in Weimar Germany as much as anywhere else, to the disgust of conventionally-minded Germans, notably the Nazis. The conventionally minded saw the cultural experimentation and ferment there as yet another sign of the disintegration of the stable, traditional, morality-bound world and contemptuously dismissed the fact that Germany between

1919 and 1933 was an outstanding object of admiration to the cultured European, however much of a political and economic failure it was.

Hierarchy's hold on the family structure as well as on the arts was hard hit by the Industrial Revolution. The 'extended' family was reduced to the 'nuclear' family of only parents and children as factories, department stores and joint-stock companies took employees from the family household. Even the bonds between parent and child were weakened. The traditional bonds had been those of dependence. A son would enter the family business, work on the family farm, learn the family craft. If he did not follow in the paternal economic footsteps he needed his father's financial aid or recommendation to a friend or patron to enter on a new livelihood. A daughter could free herself from the family shackles only by marriage, for which she usually needed a dowry and her father's permission. Industrialization loosened this dependence as schools and professions multiplied and family businesses declined. Even daughters could find work beyond the family threshold. In childhood school interposed between parent and child; in adolescence, youth movements took a growing number of German youths away from homes in the evenings, at weekends and on holidays. The state increasingly regulated the child's health and upbringing, infringing traditional parental prerogatives. Although even in Weimar Germany the point had not been reached where (as the title of an American book seriously contended in the 1920s) 'The Child is Always Right', children were becoming persons in their own right, not mere chattels or appendages of parents. In a family quarrel the father no longer held the trump card of dependence over the child with a job away from the home. As the growing child discovered his or her new freedom the old family *mores* and morality declined. Industrialization helped free those 'lesser breeds', women and children; here, as in other parts of the hierarchical society, it swept away old and tried codes. The trenches of 1914–18 made youths men before their time, and munitions factories and other war work gave young girls an early independence. In the slumps of the 1920s and early 1930s, young people were usually the first to lose their jobs, and, hanging around street-corners or Nazi halls, they naturally blamed the older generation for the economic and political mess of Weimar Germany and complained about how the sins of fathers are visited on the children. Forgetting that their fathers had been compelled to eat sour grapes, many young Nazi teeth were set on edge.

7

The traditional *Weltanschauung*, or world picture, based on Religion and Reason, was hardly likely to survive the changes wrought by industrialization. The dechristening of modern times took place in the cities. The spread of literacy and education not only brought people into contact with anti-religious ideas, it also abolished the leading role of the preaching clergyman as the only interpreter between the illiterate majority and the political, technical and educated élite. In the cities there was none of the compulsion to religion that existed in the countryside and small towns. Absence from pews no longer brought notoriety and penal sanctions. Once migrants to the city found—or thought they found —that the god of their fathers did nothing either to protect them from starvation, unemployment, rack-renting, and other forms of exploitation, or to prevent their children becoming delinquent, husbands drinking or gambling away wages, wives being unfaithful, the Lord God no longer seemed almighty. So, the masses came to say, as Brecht realistically put it in *Die Dreigroschenoper* ('The Threepenny Opera'), 'Grub comes first, morality only afterwards.'

The cities grew so fast that the Churches could not keep pace. Church building fell far behind; finances declined with falling congregations; and every year it was harder to find new recruits to the lowly-paid ministry in competition with the new, expanding, and more lucrative other professions. The Churches could not minister properly to those still wanting to be Christians, let alone attempt to convert those who were pagan through ignorance, backsliding, sloth or hostility.

In better educated suburbs the Churches were also plagued by strong intellectual criticism and scepticism. Scholars of Biblical texts, geologists, and Darwinist evolutionists cast doubt on the validity of the Bible, or, at least, on its literal truth. In 1890, Sir James Frazer started publishing his epoch-making and much-translated *Golden Bough* which highlighted the study of comparative religions, cast into shadow Christianity's uniqueness, and brought into the limelight the trend away from absolutes and towards relativism. Religion was punctured by the pens of psychologists like Freud and social thinkers like the Marxists, interpreting religious belief as mere rationalization, a veil for what were often less worthy motives. After World War One religion was further deflated by the philosophy of the logical positivists and their descendants insisting that all metaphysical questions and systems were strictly speaking meaningless. By then, philosophers, sociologists and psychologists were not needed to teach such lessons to many; World War One and the economic cataclysms of the inflation of 1922-3 and the Great Depression after 1929 left so much in rubble, not only buildings and businesses but also belief in any form of meaning. In the sludge and slaughter of the trenches it was hard for belief in God to survive in the hearts and minds of many soldiers and of the wives and parents whose loved ones died there.

The best literature was not friendly to Christianity. Virtually no writer or poet of note in the German Empire or the Weimar Republic held Christian convictions, and even in Catholic Austria the poet, Georg Trakl, was the only outstanding Christian imaginative writer. The Expressionist movement was extremely hostile to religion and thrived in Weimar Germany. The Churches did not have intellectual guns of heavy enough calibre to reply effectively. The counter-attacks of fine-minded theologians like Karl Barth and Paul Tillich in the 1920s and 1930s did not achieve any general advances until after World War Two. For all too many the language of Christianity came to have a hollow sound, fit only for festive or funereal occasions.

Even the Christianity of most of those who sat more or less regularly in Sunday pews and put their ten *Pfennig* piece in the collection plate was a mere veneer, a blind observance compelled by an expiring traditional society, or a shrewd form of after-life assurance, or a soothing source of sentimental sanctity, or an outward sign of *Mittelstand* respectability. Many of the young preferred to sleep in, or tramp the countryside with the *Wandervögel* youth movement rather than attend Sunday morning service, and to take their girl out instead of attending evening service; most of the heads bowed in prayer were grey and bald. For most Germans religion was no longer an authentic, deep-seated, fervent faith; it could not help much in a profound spiritual and moral crisis; it could not provide spiritual anchors in the storm-tossed seas of Weimar Germany; it could not rival the evangelism of rising Nazism. For too many Germans, the power and the glory had gone from religion; for others it had never come. Religion's accompanying pillar, Reason, upholding the traditional order, was also cracking. The trend towards irrationalism in the second half of the nineteenth century, which had characterized phases of the Romantic movement, was strengthened by several outstanding thinkers of whom Schopenhauer, Darwin, Dostoevsky, Nietzsche and Freud were probably the most important. The importance of Schopenhauer and his insistence that the real world was ruled by will and only the apparent world was ruled by Reason, lay in his influence on later intellectuals such as Nietzsche and Thomas Mann. Darwin unintentionally assisted the growth of irrationalism by demonstrating that the struggle for survival was the prime motive of behaviour. Dostoevsky's world throbs painfully on the edge of utter despair, complete spiritual confusion and collective insanity because—as Dostoevsky knew by the intuition he prized so greatly—the world's heart was gravely diseased by false beliefs resting on Reason: individualism, liberalism, scepticism, atheism, the deification of man, heathen tribal nationalism, egalitarianism. The only cure he knew was the leap into the dark of an irrational religion. Religion was derided by Nietzsche; 'God is dead', he proclaimed. Dead, too, for him were all the traditional beliefs, and the human will alone gave meaning to life. Like Schopenhauer before him and Dilthey at the same time and Bergson a little later, he wanted a return from the cloying conventions of a false civilization to something profound, primeval, primordial. Freud, the Columbus of the unconscious, discovered a whole new continent of the human mind which shook faith in Reason as much as Columbus had challenged faith in the world's flatness.

Riding the wave of irrationalism, the German publishing firm of Eugen Diederichs in Jena began in the years before 1914 to publish works by irrationalists, ancient and modern: translations of Sören Kierkegaard and of Bergson; books on German and other mythologies, on Oriental beliefs, and on the Russian 'soul'; and modern editions of the great German mystics from Johannes Eckhart to Jakob Böhme who claimed that life's realities could only be experienced, not described or analysed rationally. In the 1920s Möller van den Bruck popularized translations of Dostoevsky. Twentieth-century painters sought to depict the inner meaning of things rather than the external world. Poets plunged into what Rilke called the *Weltinnenraum*, the world's inner space.

Science contributed to the confusion as well as to the progress of society. The twentieth century witnessed a scientific revolution greater than that of the seventeenth century, puzzling as well as profiting the ordinary person. Einstein's theory of relativity was a radical restatement of the meaning of space and time, based on the impossibility of determining absolutes. His ideas lapped over into other academic and mundane streams of thought. In a relative world, what could remain absolute? Einstein was only one of many scientists transforming the whole character of science. Where once scientists had known certainties they now knew only probabilities. Where once they were sure truth was objective, they now realized it could only be subjective. To many scientists this revolution was exciting, stimulating and exhilarating; but to the ordinary person the new ideas seeping down were more often disturbing and dislocating.

The wave of irrationalism was whipped up by other prevailing winds. The growing complexity of industrial and cultural life made it increasingly impossible for even the educated to comprehend more than a few aspects of life. Specialization was ousting even the gifted amateur. Intellectuals helped little. '*Le trahison des clercs*' has been a popular charge of treason against intellectuals ever since Julien Benda wrote his indictment more than a generation ago. Intellectuals (the indictment runs), by withdrawing into their specialist ivory towers and by refusing to beat out a well-worn path between their towers and the mundane market-place, betray the everyday world which looks to them for guidance. But what else could the scientist, engineer, historian, artist, poet, musician do but withdraw as their fields became more narrow? The problem of 'the two cultures' had been urgent long before C. P. Snow popularized it; indeed, in confining himself to only two cultures he was over-simplifying the issue. The inclination of intellectuals towards the ivory tower has been aggravated by the incomprehension of the general public of specialized subjects and by their contempt for the artist and poet.

Aristotle was scornful at the expense of the expert and remarked that the wearer knows better than the cobbler where the shoe pinches. Yet, although he wrote this in his *Politics* (which is still a textbook in universities), how right is his view in regard to mass man when the fit of modern society is in question? How can mass man be expected to understand rationally the intricacies of a national budget, or of foreign policy, or of educational systems? He has to take them or leave them—vote on them—by irrational faith or prejudice. Politicians and the masters of the mass media soon realized this and exploited passions, sentimentality, hatred and impulses, all to the detriment of Reason. Universal suffrage and universal education assisted the birth of a mass society which discarded, lacked, or did not know the kind of ethical, religious and rational standards that helped guide aristocratic societies, sometimes well, sometimes not so well. It was no use—it still is no use—expecting mass man to be rational, or humane and calm in a crisis. The great majority of voters have had no proper chance to obtain an adequate education, learn reason, acquire human values. Sentimentality about the virtues of the 'noble working man' may gratify modern intellectuals as sentimentality about the virtues of 'the noble savage' gratified Rousseauist intellectuals in the eighteenth century. But it is entirely beside the point; and is no good reason for obscuring the incapacity of most voters for sensible political decisions. The ignorant voter is a fact of political life and as yet no contraceptive is in sight.

8

In the years immediately before 1914 many voices complained that there was something rotten in the state of Germany. One main fear was for national unity, less than 50 years old. Political parties were accused of forgetting national interests and concentrating on *Interessenpolitik*, the politics of particular interests, and their tactics were stigmatized as *Kuhhandelhung*, or log-rolling. The general tone of leading writers was corrosively critical. Thomas Mann's brother, Heinrich, was only one of many indicting Wilhelmine society. In *Professor Unrat*, published in 1905 and after the war filmed as 'The Blue Angel' with Emil Jannings and Marlene Dietrich as stars, Heinrich Mann exposed the thinness of the veneer of *Mittelstand* respectability. In 1914 he published the first volume of his trilogy, *Das Kaiserreich*; this first instalment, *Der Untertan*, bitterly condemned state officialdom. Rilke began his *Duineser Elegen* in 1912 by repudiating the scientific materialistic age which destroyed individual creativity. In a much cruder style revolutionary conservatives continued their nostalgic invective, and were, not surprisingly, much more read than Rilke's sensitive but convoluted poems. Acute observers were alarmed by the proliferation of freakish nostrums claiming to cure society's ills: theosophism, spiritualism, Nordic 'religions', sun worship, nature mysticism, vegetarianism, racism, plans for Utopian settlements at home or abroad; each attracted dedicated sects turning contemptuous and frustrated backs on the conventional *mores* of Wilhelmine Germany. Even the *Wandervögel* and other youth movements seemed—at least to the older generation—a repudiation of existing conventions. To many, most Germans seemed like sheep to have gone astray.

The intense feeling of unity, brought by the outbreak of war on 1 August 1914, gave a great sense of relief. The Kaiser's declaration on the first day of war that there were no more political parties, only Germans, and the *Reichstag's* almost unanimous declaration of a political truce, were rapturously welcomed. German enthusiasm for the war, like that of the populations of the other belligerents, was based on ignorance of the new nature of war. They all believed that the war was certain to be short, over by Christmas at the latest. The universal opinion was that modern complicated industrial economies could not possibly sustain a long war. The Russo-Japanese War of 1904–5 encouraged this opinion, since both participants had been driven to peace by the threat of economic exhaustion. Best-sellers like Norman Angell's *The Great Illusion* popularized the opinion in Britain and wherever it was translated; history appeared to confirm the opinion since all the European wars since 1815 had been short. The contrary evidence of the American Civil War between 1861 and 1865 was easily discounted; it had been an amateur's war, and a civil war, and so was the exception proving the rule. The German Schlieffen Plan for general war, involving the violation of Belgian neutrality, was founded precisely on this belief in the impossibility of a long war; the military planners were convinced that the only way for Germany to win a war was by a strategy which alone permitted a devastatingly swift march on Paris. Had the High Commands and the statesmen of Europe been aware that the war would be long, they would not have embarked on it so lightly—if at all.

Accordingly, Hitler was not the only one overcome with the emotion he describes in *Mein Kampf* when the news of war was announced. The historian, Meinecke, considered war would

57

fortunately reunite a disintegrating Germany. His view was shared by writers like Stefan Zweig, Thomas Mann, Carl Zuckmayer and Rilke, none of them given to mass hysteria or rabid nationalism. Ernst Jünger was typical of young Germans in regarding war as a cleansing force bringing that *Aufbruck*, or awakening, which had been enthusiastically and endlessly discussed around the camp fires of the *Wandervögel*. This enthusiasm for the war was not confined to Germans. In every major European country, most people hoped that the sword would cut the ropeful of Gordian knots tied by modern industrialized society.

9

It turned out otherwise. Sir George Grey's melancholy words, as he stood at dawn at the window of the Foreign Office of which he was the political head, that the lights were going out all over Europe and would not be relit in his time, became much more true of Germany than any other country. The idealism and romanticism and optimism did not survive in the mechanized soullessness of modern, mass war. Instead of being short and cheap, the war was agonizingly long and terribly expensive in wealth—and lives. Some ten million men of all the belligerents, one in five of all those who fought, were killed in the war, and more than twice that number were maimed, many for life. By the end of the war more than two-thirds of the 39 million men mobilized by France, Russia, Austria and Germany, and over a third of the 14 million mobilized by Britain and Italy had been killed, wounded or captured. All the wars of the previous century, from the Napoleonic Wars to 1914, had cost less than four and a half million lives, not half the toll of World War One. Germany lost nearly two million dead. The French calculated that between August 1914 and February 1917 one Frenchman was killed every single minute.

For front line soldiers the war was a shocking experience. They were surrounded by death, suffering, maiming. Rats were everywhere growing sleek on the bloated corpses, lying unburied in No Man's Land or hanging on the barbed wire entanglements within sight of the trenches. Dead bodies were used to build and rebuild the sandbagged trench parapets and were often uncovered by exploding enemy shells. The screams of the badly-wounded men lying in No Man's Land, unable to move or to be rescued, rang insupportably in their comrades' ears until it seemed kinder to put them out of their agony with a rifle shot or machine-gun burst. The countryside was stark, stripped by high-explosive of all vegetation and all colour except the dusty browns of uni-forms and mud or dust, and the red of Flanders poppies, and blood. Outside the trenches there was no life apart from attacks over the top and the rat multitudes. A few naked skeletons of trees gave a nightmare impression. An occasional bird sang in the un-natural devastation; a butterfly brought back unbearably memories of home, peace and carefree childhood. The shells screamed and thundered over; the bullets struck down bodies, and there were 7,000 casualties every day. Each heavy attack left behind the usual contribution of greyish corpses between the lines, putrefying and stinking, and lying not in gallant or heroic postures but in grotesque or grimacing horror. The survivors still had comrades, the urge to avoid death, the hope of leave or of a wound severe enough to end the agony of the trenches but not bad enough to completely cripple them; little else mattered. Men do not endure experiences like these without suffering deep after-effects. Disillusion crept in; belief in God and Reason shrivelled; and sense and beauty and love went out of their world. These qualities went out of the world for Germans more than for others because they were de-feated.

In Germany suffering on the home front was much greater than in England or France. By 1918 textiles were so short in Germany that bandages for the troops had to be made of paper. Food supplies were so short that turnips became a staple diet: turnip 'bread', turnip 'meat', even turnip 'coffee'. One measure of domestic food shortages was that in the last-hope great German offensive which began in the West in March 1918, many local attacks petered out as ravenous German soldiers stayed to plunder captured Allied food-dumps; and their officers could not stop them. In German cities during the unusually rigorous winters of 1917–18 and 1918–19 many women and children died of mal-nutrition or the diseases which it aggravated. With the inflation of prices the rich grew richer and the poor grew hungrier. The dreaded telegraph-boy knocked on doors, bringing bereavement. Family life suffered whilst the father was at the front and the mother was out on war work. One Nazi party member recalled in the '30s that he and his friends had only occasional glimpses of their mother in the evening and that even then she was prevented from devoting herself to the children by the need to do the shopping and housework after being in a munitions factory all day. The inevitable exhaustion, the irritable snapping at the children or the absence of parents prevented the cultivation of family love and ties. The children grew up amid privation, and hungered for food—and affection. And by 11 November 1918 all the suffering was known to have been in vain.

10

Defeat was shattering. The German High Command throughout the war had artificially buoyed up morale by keeping out of the communiqués any news of setbacks. And to Germans 1918 had seemed the year of hope: early that year Russia and Rumania had been forced to sue for peace, and in the spring and summer the successes of the German offensive in the West daily brought Paris and victory closer. But the hope was only a mirage. By August the German army had met its 'Black Day' and within only three months the soldiers had been swept back to the frontier and an Armistice had had to be signed. Two days before, on 9 November 1918, revolution had broken out and the Hohenzollern Empire was overthrown.

The revolutionaries hoped for a lenient peace by exchanging Wilhelmine autocracy for Wilsonian democracy. They were soon disillusioned. Despite British war-time propaganda that the Allies were fighting the Kaiser and not the German people, and despite Wilson's 14 Points proclaiming a new world of national self-determination and peace and goodwill among nations, the Germans were forced to sign the vindictive Versailles Treaty on 28 June 1919, five years to the day after the assassination at Serajevo that had sparked the war.

By the Versailles *Diktat* Germany had to sign a humiliating confession of war guilt; she lost 13 per cent of the *Reich's* area containing 26 per cent of her coal reserves, 68 per cent of her zinc, 75 per cent of her iron ore as well as other substantial economic assets; she lost all her colonies. The reparations in money and in kind were far heavier than Germany had imposed on France in 1871; those reparations had amounted to only 3 per cent of France's wealth, but in 1919 Germany had to promise to pay 38 per cent of her wealth. These exactions struck hard at the German economy, deprived by the war of all the foreign investments which had previously done much to keep her solvent.

Versailles also performed major surgery on the German defences. The Rhineland was demilitarized, so that French invasion could at any time be a mere parade. Germany was permitted only 100,000 troops equipped only with light arms and light field guns; heavy artillery, planes and tanks were prohibited; the General Staff and Military Academy, together the nerve-centre of the military system, were to be dissolved; all armament factories were to be scrapped, except a single one for each permissible type of equipment; all preparations for a secret mobilization, such as the keeping of registers of trained military personnel, were strictly forbidden; Germany had to agree to constant Allied surveillance to ensure the keeping of these treaty provisions. So emasculated an army was scarcely adequate to act effectively as the last line of defence of law and order at home in a crisis of civil disorder. It was incapable of defence even against a minor power like Poland.

The impositon of such a peace with dishonour seemed necessary to the Allied peoples inflamed to hate and fear by the severe sacrifices and overheated propaganda of total war. They took literally Benjamin Franklin's statement that there is no such thing as a bad peace and ignored the more realistic warnings of John Maynard Keynes that the economic consequences of the peace would be disastrous to the victors as well as the vanquished. Keynes believed in sticking to his economic last; otherwise, he might well have warned of the political consequences in the same vein. By dictating the Versailles Treaty and refusing in the inter-war years to modify it amicably, the Allied statesmen inflicted on Germany a running sore which nationalist demagogues like Hitler found all too easy to turn poisonous and which permanently enfeebled Weimar democracy between 1919 and 1933. On the unloved weakling of the democracy inaugurated at Weimar rested any hope of arresting the already deep demoralization of German society.

II

Democracy failed. On 29 March 1930 Parliamentary democracy was abandoned and the Chancellor, Brüning, resorted to dicta-torial government through Presidential decree. In the prevailing circumstances democracy had no chance of success. In fact, it is not nearly so surprising that it failed as that it lasted as long as it did. Historians of Germany between 1919 and 1933 ask the wrong question when they pose the problem of Weimar democracy's failure; they should be questioning why it endured at all, given its legacy of dislocation caused by industrialization, defeat in war, the overthrow of the Empire, and the Versailles Treaty, and given that in its brief life it suffered so chronically from deep political and social rifts, a multiplicity of parties, mass demagogy, a runaway inflation in 1922–3 which radically redistributed wealth, and a series of depressions culminating in the Great Depression after 1929 which, though it benefited many who had a permanent income and job, brought extreme poverty and misery to other millions. That English-speaking historians ask the wrong question is really no puzzle: they are parochially obsessed with the notion that democracy is the natural form of political life and any departure from it indicates a disease needing diagnosis. But that European historians, more accustomed to the prevalence of autocracy, confine themselves so much to the wrong question is puzzling. Perhaps they have been brain-washed by the potent twentieth-century belief that democracy is virtue and it is falls from virtue that need explanation; the historical social worker needs calling in only in cases of delinquency: normality has few or no historians. Certainly some European historians before 1945 did ask the more appropriate question; but then Fascism was not almost universally regarded as a vice. Now that Fascism is seen as a vice by all but a very few perhaps it is not to be wondered at that so many European historians have been impelled along a Damascus road to a blinding conversion making them amazed that everyone does not see the democratic light.

The multiple causes of the fate of Weimar democracy are no concern of this book. What matters here is the further dislocation of society and the growing demoralization of more and more Germans. Failure to achieve stable, secure and sound government, and economic cataclysms culminating in the worst depression the industrial world had ever experienced, gave Germans no opportunity to recover from the devastating shocks already sustained. Weimar Germans would have laughed with ironic bitterness at Milton's claim that 'peace hath her victories/No less renowned than war'. After 1919 Germany had none of the good fortune of nineteenth-century Industrial Revolution England; there, the wars of 1793–1815 had not touched most of the population; and victory, unparalleled prestige abroad, an expanding Empire, continued peace and prosperity without the incubus of a mass franchise, all took the edge off the problems of industrialization. Englishmen had time and opportunity to adapt their values and institutions slowly, peaceably, and healthily. In Germany, the ills, with which rapid industrialization and urbanization infected many, became an epidemic as the chronically ailing Weimar system tottered from crisis to crisis and the plagues of inflation in 1922–3 and depression decimated the economy. Values that had survived 1919 wasted away, rotted and putrefied.

Many of the *Mittelstand* were proletarianized as the inflation of 1922–3 destroyed their savings and the depression deprived them of their livelihood. The six million unemployed and the twice as many more on part-time by the winter of 1932 included many clerks, shop assistants and small retailers whose businesses were ruined when their customers had no money but a dole that progressively decreased as their period of unemployment increased. Those who could now obtain a labouring job could now count themselves lucky. Millions of unemployed hung around street-corners, cursing the government and the Weimar system, and finding their only relief from boredom in street-brawls between Nazi SA storm-troopers, Communist Red Front fighters, and Socialist *Reichsbanner* members. Many unemployed joined one or other of these organizations to avoid pointless inactivity or to obtain a cheap meal at the soup-kitchens each organization maintained to attract members and voters. A political meeting or rally gave zest to an otherwise empty life; uniforms and banners gave a sense of belonging somewhere; and warmth could be found in a crowded hall or a vigorously marching procession. Hans Fallada could aptly entitle his contemporary novel *Little Man, What Now?* His little man was too demoralized to find any answer.

The extent of the demoralization was demonstrated in two ways; by the support the extremist parties won; and by the circumstances in which Hitler was appointed Chancellor. On the extreme left, the Communist vote rose to six million in the election of November 1932, mostly working class. The Nazis gained more widespread support, swelling their vote to 13 million in 1932. The Nazi core was from the *Mittelstand*, to whom Nazi anti-capitalism, anti-semitism, anti-democracy and fervent nationalism had a traditional appeal. The Nazis also won many peasant voters, facing ruin or foreclosure. Many university students sympathized with the Nazis, some from an idealistic nationalism encouraged by university teachers who were almost all politically on the right. Other students became Nazis for materialist reasons: there was a surplus of university graduates even before the Depression of 1929, and hard-earned professional qualifications could not be turned to economic and social advantage. Further support came from the working class, notably those who retained their jobs and feared a Red revolution. This working-class support for the Nazis is indicated by the rise in the number of those who went to the polls, four million more in 1930 than in 1928, and a further two million in 1932. Big Nazi gains came from these additional voters. Some of them were young people previously not entitled to vote, but many came from the hitherto politically apathetic, and these predomate in the lower class.

Some assistance was given to the Nazis by bankers and industrialists. But it came from relatively few; most stood aloof. Moreover, those that did give support mostly did so as a form of political insurance: they subsidized all the main parties in the manner of their kind in most countries. This was unwillingly demonstrated by the war crimes trials of leading industrialists after 1945. Upper-class Nazi supporters were also found in the army, although army support came almost entirely among junior officers and the rank-and-file. This upper-class support has been grossly exaggerated by left-wing historians, keen on the scent of a capitalist conspiracy against democracy and 'the working class'. Yet, although the tale of a capitalist conspiracy in favour of Nazism is a myth, the existence of some upper-class support indicates how the demoralization of German society had spread upwards as well as downwards when wild demagogy, street-brawls, the whipping up of venomous hate, and political murders could be overlooked by educated and sophisticated Germans.

Such widespread support inevitably meant a cacophony of conflicting Nazi promises. Some were absurd; one story, perhaps apocryphal but certainly credible, is of one Nazi speaker proclaiming that Germany did not want the present bread prices, nor higher ones, nor lower ones, but, instead, National Socialist bread prices. Yet, the Nazis only took to extremes what is common to all large political parties in mass democracy: the need to be many things to many people. There are too many voters in a democracy floating on tides of whim, prejudices and ignorance; and, unhappily for democracy, very few voters seek consistency or even sense in electoral programmes and propaganda, or examine with any care the whole programme. Most hear only what they want to hear; logic is defeated by catch cries. When mass man is demoralized in acute, fever-pitch crisis, the defeat becomes an utter rout. Although this is not a valid argument for dictatorship, mass man's incapacity for democracy and his willingness to abandon it all too easily in a crisis is a sad but undeniable fact. T.S. Eliot's rueful conclusion that human kind cannot bear very much reality was borne out to the full by German history.

12

The dangerous demoralization of German society in the winter of 1932–3 is demonstrated by Hitler's appointment on 30 January 1933 as Chancellor leading a coalition of the Nazi Party and the Nationalist Party. By the beginning of 1933 the politicians were practically bankrupt in expedients for forming a viable government. There were five main political parties in the *Reichstag*: the Nazis, the Communists, the Socialists, the Nationalist Party and the Catholic Centre to which was allied the Bavarian People's Party. Bitter and sometimes venomous mistrust and hatred divided these parties and forbade any form of coalition having a majority. The election of November 1932 gave the Nazis 196 seats, the Communists exactly 100, the Socialists 121 seats, the Centre with its Bavarian ally 90 seats and the Nationalist Party 51 seats. After Brüning's fall from power, each of the parties, except the Socialists, had seriously entertained the idea of forming a coalition with the Nazis, but every attempt had failed through Hitler's insistence on the Chancellorship and special powers for himself. The November elections gave the extremist Nazis and Communists together 296 of the 583 seats, slightly over half the total. Increasing this majority against democracy, were the Nationalists' 51 seats, which meant that almost 60 per cent of the electors had turned down their thumbs on the Weimar system. Minority government by presidential decree since 1930 had not solved the economic crisis whether the Chancellor was Brüning from 1930 to mid-1932, or von Papen until December 1932, or von Schleicher until the closing days of January 1933. National confidence continued to decline. Schleicher's efforts to split the Nazis had failed; but even had he succeeded, his hopes for a coalition between the left-wing Nazis and the trade unions would have foundered on the rocklike refusal of most of the trade unionists to follow his course. Hindenburg had refused to use his prestige as President and hero of World War One to set up a military dictatorship, rightly fearing it would cause civil war. In late 1932 a slight easing of the depression raised some hopes, but January 1933 saw a renewed worsening. It is sometimes argued that had Hitler been kept from power a little longer, the depression would have lifted and his votes dropped further than they had between the elections of July and November 1932; but the experience of England and the U.S.A. shows that relief from the depression would have taken years, not months, in that pre-Keynesian (or pre-Hitler) age. Both those countries had forcible governments enjoying large majorities; their societies were much less demoralized than Germany's; and their nations had been united much longer than 63 years. In Germany, the final days of January 1933 were the time when the decision whether to cross the Rubicon had to be made. Caesar crossed his Rubicon in 49 B.C. knowing he would precipitate civil war in Italy; Hindenburg crossed his Rubicon on 30 January 1933 hoping to prevent civil war in Germany.

Hindenburg's crossing has not found the support among historians that Caesar's has. Yet, with Nazi support so widespread, the country so critically demoralized, democracy a patent failure, and the worst not necessarily past, is it as surprising as historians have insisted that Hitler was called to power? Moreover, was it as reprehensible as all respectable historians have implicitly or explicitly judged it to be—unless it is true that Weimar Germany was still a democracy until 30 January 1933, and unless it neces-sarily follows that it is reprehensible to supersede democracy by dictatorship? A cogent case can be put that it was neither as surprising nor as reprehensible as is commonly and unquestion-ingly believed, and that the King-makers (or, at least, most of them) acted from good or sincere motives.

It is true that a Presidential cabal, and not the majority of electors, made the decision to appoint Hitler and his coalition cabinet to power. This action has been stigmatized as a disgraceful intrigue or back-stairs manœuvre. Was it, however, any more an intrigue or back-stairs manœuvre to be condemned than has happened elsewhere without outraged voices being universally raised? How much of a back-stairs intrigue were the manœuvrings during World War One which ousted Asquith as Britain's Prime Minister in favour of Lloyd George? How many French Cabinets in the Third and Fourth Republics have been caballed into power? How many American Presidents have owed their elevation to intrigues, not perhaps on the back stairs, but in 'smoke-filled back rooms'?

The difference is that in Germany dictatorship was the outcome. Is it an all-important difference? In fact, German democracy had ended in mid-1930 and there already *had been* dictatorship through Presidential powers before Hitler's appointment; Hindenburg offered no more than this on 30 January 1933 and it was agreed that elections should follow as quickly as possible to restore government through a majority in the *Reichstag*. Dictatorship through Presidential powers was constitutionally permissible to tide over a crisis and then restore democracy; but in January 1933 there seemed to many shrewd observers no chance of revivifying the democratic Lazarus. Hindenburg and many others thought it best for Hitler to come to power constitutionally rather than by the violence threatened by the restive Nazi SA storm-troopers; and by late January he had come round to the view that it was constitutionally improper to keep from power the leader of the largest party with a chance to form a coalition majority government of national concentration which would restore confidence and overcome the national crisis. His view was shared by the former Chancellor Brüning who was certainly no admirer of the Nazis and who, by no stretch of the imagination could be called senile, slow of mind, or an opponent of democracy, as Hindenburg often has been called. Some democrats argue that it is proper in a democracy to give Communists power when they are the largest party, despite the indisputable fact that destruction of democracy would inevitably follow, something the Communists make no bones about promising before the event. Fortunately for the peace of mind of these democrats the occasion has not yet arisen in the case of Communists. If it does it will call into question the whole principle of majority rule, and no clear-cut or commonly agreed answer will be forthcoming. Since the question remains as yet an academic one, it is perhaps fair to wonder whether in the eyes of these democrats what is sauce for the Communist goose is *not* sauce for the Nazi gander.

The emergency powers entrusted to Hitler at the end of January 1933 were dictatorial but were not as extreme as those that were born of the hysteria caused by the *Reichstag* being set on fire on 27 February, or as extreme as those entrusted to Hitler in the Enabling Act of 23 March by all the parties in the new *Reichstag* except the Social Democrats. Were those emergency powers obtained by Hitler on 30 January so unlike those wielded by Franklin D. Roosevelt in his famous 100 days in the same year? Were they so unlike those given to the National Government in Britain in 1931 when it went to the electorate asking simply for a 'Doctor's Mandate', obtaining it by an overwhelming majority?

One difference was that Hitler, unlike Roosevelt or Ramsay MacDonald, had never concealed his abhorrence of democracy and his intention to abolish it as soon as power was his. Yet, the majority of German electors, and Hindenburg and his confederates, had also unmistakably shown their dislike of democracy and liking for autocracy, and they were as yet unaware of the brutal uses to which Hitler put his emergency powers as soon as he secured power on 30 January. A democrat may be saddened by the distrust and dislike of democracy shown by the majority of Germans, including their leaders; but he has no evidence to equate the distrust and dislike with a trust in, and liking for, Nazism. Hindenburg and *all* the electors had been born, and most of them had spent their youth, under the autocratic *Kaiserreich* which by 1933 had assumed an aura of a golden age when compared with the Slough of Despond into which Weimar democracy had sunk. And, there did not appear any democratic way of extricating Germany from that slough.

Hindenburg and his associates were wrong to put their trust in Hitler, as the events of 1933–45 affirmed. But it is easy to be wise after the event. In 1933 no one—not even Hitler himself, and certainly not Hindenburg and his advisers with their aristocratic ignorance of gutter politics—could have imagined the horror to come. In January 1933, anyone predicting a fraction of the awfulness of the 12 years of Nazi rule would have been laughed to scorn. In fact, many of those around the President believed that Hitler was not nearly so radical as he often seemed; he gave the appearance of not being the wild man so many of his followers were, and he was commonly considered a moderating influence on the revolutionary elements among the Nazis. Many sensible and shrewd Germans—and foreigners—thought that power would bring a sense of responsibility to Hitler and his Nazis; history offered many examples of radicals and wild men being tamed by the responsibilities of power. On the other hand, there were those who felt sure that the Nazis would prove so incompetent at governing, especially in such a crisis, that Hitler would be forced to resign from power in a few months. Wels, the chairman of the Social Democratic Party, told Hindenburg that Hitler ought to be appointed to power so that he could ruin himself, and Wels' view was shared by other Social Democrats including Schumacher and Breitscheidt, neither of whom lacked political acumen.

Hindenburg and his advisers had other apparently good reasons for their decision. Whether Hitler's power would tame or ruin him, they did not intend to allow his power to be uncircumscribed. Promises had been extracted from Hitler to respect the rights of the President, the *Reichstag* and the Press. Moreover, in the Cabinet of eleven members there were only two other Nazis besides Hitler; Göring was Minister without Portfolio and was considered a moderate man perhaps because of his upper-class origin and his fine war record; and Frick was Minister of the Interior and was regarded as colourless and rather weak. Hindenburg insisted on personally appointing the Minister of Defence and chose General Werner von Blomberg; he was not unsympathetic to the Nazis but was convinced that his first loyalty was to the Field-Marshal President. Control of the *Reichswehr* through a President, still an idol to many officers and men, and through a non-Nazi Minister, seemed adequate protection against any attempt by the para-military SA to force through a revolution. Hindenburg also insisted on controlling the appointment of the Foreign Minister and of overseas officials; in this way, a respectable foreign policy should be possible. Freiherr von Neurath, an equable career diplomat of conservative opinion, was made Foreign Minister. The Nationalist Party coalition partner held all three of the economic ministries, seemingly all-important Cabinet posts in the crisis of depression. The Minister of Labour was Seldte who was leader of the *Stahlhelm*, the Nationalist Party's para-military organization of veterans with Hindenburg as patron. The vital Ministry of Economy and Ministry of Food and Agriculture, both in the

Reich and in the Prussian governments, were in the hands of the Nationalist Party leader, Hugenberg. He might well consider his power impregnable since not only was he responsible for control of the economy but also he owned a considerable part of the Press and an even greater part of the film industry. The other ministries were held by non-party officials. Göring held the Prussian Ministry of Interior as well as his Reich Cabinet post; but since von Papen, in addition to being Reich Vice-Chancellor, was head of the Prussian government, Göring should be under control. All in all, the Nazis in the Cabinet seemed sufficiently hobbled.

If, however, Hitler kicked over the Cabinet traces, Hindenburg had the Presidential power to dismiss him whenever he pleased. The President showed no particular liking for the Nazis and had always been cold to Hitler; but the President's advisers warily insisted that Hitler agree never to see Hindenburg without von Papen being present; the Vice-Chancellor was a close friend of Hindenburg and was given the task of countering the possibility of the President's becoming subject to the personal magnetism and persuasiveness Hitler possessed. At the time it was not realized how easily and quickly Hindenburg would fall victim to the charm that Hitler could radiate at will, or how Hindenburg would be impressed by the respect the new Chancellor displayed as an old soldier to the Field-Marshal. The unexpected result was that very soon Hindenburg permitted Hitler to visit him unaccompanied by von Papen, and to gain such an ascendancy over him that he ceased to interfere in anything Hitler proposed except when it concerned the *Reichswehr*. He was, after all, an old man, born the year before the 1848 Revolution.

Other important safeguards against Hitler were not realized. Hugenberg was so busy dealing with the economic crisis that he was unable to find time to exercise any decisive influence in the Cabinet, and Hitler found no difficulty in excluding him at the end of June 1933. Seldte, the other Nationalist Minister, was soon magnetized by Hitler's power and persuasiveness. A more vital miscalculation was the underestimation of the political significance of a Ministry of the Interior, held by Nazis both in the Reich and in Prussia. The Minister of the Interior controlled the police and so could prevent—or encourage—Nazi brutality against political opponents. But this miscalculation is excusable; it took the lessons taught by the Nazis, and later by the Communists after

70

1945, for people to learn that the Ministry of the Interior is the Trojan horse for those bent on winning their siege of state and society.

Trust in all these precautions was unavoidable, for what was the alternative to Hitler? In the not unlikely eventuality of the 85-year-old Hindenburg's death, it was certain that Hitler would overwhelmingly win the ensuing Presidential election. No national figure could rival his vote-getting capacity; there was no other Hindenburg with the laurels of 1914–18 to draw away votes from Hitler as had happened in the Presidential election of 1932. Hitler, as President, could then appoint a completely Nazi Cabinet and wreak his will unchecked.

Another unpleasant alternative was Red Revolution. It was in fact unlikely, especially since it is now known that Communist ideology—and Stalin who was master of Communists outside as well as inside Russia—ordained that Germany had to necessarily undergo its Nazi phase, since Fascism and Nazism were last-ditch stands of an expiring capitalism which would soon inevitably be overthrown by the inexorable Marxist laws of historical development. However, this was not common knowledge in 1933. The German Communists were gaining support; in November 1932 they advanced to 100 seats which meant that six million people had voted for Red Revolution. Our mental picture of depression, aided by the writings of historians, so dwells on mass unemployment, that we forget that many people retain their jobs in a depression and even improve their real income as prices dwindle and as houses, businesses and consumer articles can be bought extraordinarily cheaply by these who still have money. Such people's fear of Red Revolution and dispossession is naturally magnified in a depression. The Communist Party was openly revolutionary and its bogey-power to frighten was strong in Europe in the 1920s and 1930s; Germans had been scared in the winter of 1918–19 by the Communist threat, especially in Bavaria, and again in 1923, especially in Saxony, Thuringia and Hamburg. The thought that six million Communist sympathizers formed only a minority of German electors could be countered by a reminder that the Communists had won power in Russia even though they were in a decided minority. November 1917 was less than 16 years away from January 1933.

Insurrection could be feared not only from the Communists but also from the Nazis if they were denied power. Compelling evidence exists that the SA and SS, numbering over half a million, were ready to storm the gates of power for Hitler if they were not opened from within. Evidence also exists showing that Hitler had great difficulty in restraining them. By January 1933, Nazi governments controlling the state police were already in power in the states of Anhalt, Brunswick, Hessen, Thuringia, Mecklenburg and Oldenburg. The peasants and farmers were strong Nazi supporters in Silesia, Saxony, Brandenburg, Pomerania and East and West Prussia, and could cut off food supplies to Berlin and other cities.

The question whether the *Reichswehr* could quell a Nazi rising was perturbing. If the *Reichswehr* were united, probably the Nazis could be defeated. But many junior officers were Nazi sympathizers although almost none of the generals were. Junior officers idealistically glimpsed a Nazi government restoring German prestige; materialistically, they were dazzled by a Nazi-expanded *Reichswehr* offering succulent opportunities for promotion; in an army limited to 100,000 promotion was painfully slow—too slow to allow many to marry, and too slow for the wives of those married. The police could not be relied on any more than the *Reichswehr*; a considerable number of them had been converted, and Nazi Ministers controlling the police in Nazi-dominated states had infiltrated old comrades into the ranks and into key posts.

Insurrection by either the Nazis or the Communists on their own was not the worst fear. Much more frightening was the possibility of civil war if one or other started a rising or widespread civil disorder. A general strike might develop, hampering troop movements by rail. In November 1932 the Nazis and Communists had joined in an unholy alliance and brought about a strike of the transport workers in Berlin. Consequently, the *Ministeramt*, the political department of the Defence Ministry, had undertaken a detailed study of the ability of the *Reichswehr* to quell civil war. The study was carried out by means of a war game, under the direction of Lieutenant-Colonel Ott. The participants included representatives from each of the military districts, representatives of the Ministry of the Interior, and representatives of the police. The outcome induced extreme pessimism, although the *Reichswehr* command naturally did not refuse to attempt the restoration of law and order if the worst happened.

Ott's report on his war game has had a very bad press from historians—with the exception of Robert O'Neill, significantly a professional soldier as well as an historian, although even he does not appreciate its full significance. The report has been derided by almost all historians or written off as part of the chicanery of Schleicher to push the Cabinet into a military dictatorship under himself. In fact, it is the Ott report that is realistic, and not the historians. They have forgotten that the *Reichswehr* was limited to 100,000 men, inadequately armed and necessarily spread very thinly in garrisons throughout Germany. A general strike would immobilize the railways and make it very difficult to move troops quickly enough to trouble-spots because the *Reichswehr* had very few motor vehicles. If a decision were taken to anticipate a general strike and move troops as a precautionary measure, this might precipitate the trouble feared.

As a last straw, Poland might well take advantage of internal unrest in Germany to seize the still disputed border areas. At this time, Pilsudski, the Polish dictator, had ordered an extraordinary concentration of troops in the Polish Corridor and in areas on the East Prussian border. Historians, with memories of September 1939 in mind, might despise the power of the Polish army; Germans in 1933 could not. The *Reichswehr* then was completely outmatched by the Polish army, which had about 40 divisions against the *Reichswehr's* 10 divisions. The Poles had tanks and heavy artillery and planes, all entirely denied to the *Reichswehr* by the Treaty of Versailles. It would be difficult, probably impossible, for the *Reichswehr* to combat successfully either extensive civil disorder or a Polish attack. If both happened together, the assumption that the *Reichswehr* could not succeed was absolutely reasonable.

Civil war might easily be precipitated by one other possibility; the appointment of a coalition government of von Papen and Hugenberg. Von Papen was extremely unpopular and Hugenberg's support was small. General von Hammerstein, Commander-in Chief of the army, was one of several shrewd observers who considered a von Papen-Hugenberg coalition could spark a civil war. Von Hammerstein was an extremely able man and it is a tribute to his fine intelligence and great ability that he was the only lazy man to become the army's Commander-in-Chief. Von Hammerstein loathed the Nazis; but his opinion of the *Reichswehr's* inability to cope with the distinct possibility of civil war or a Polish attack, or both at the same time, was the same as Ott's report. In the circumstances he chose what he considered would be the lesser of the two evils, and on 26 January 1933 he advised the President to appoint Hitler. He emphasized that the troops could not be relied on to fire on the Nazis. Hindenburg, who disliked von Hammerstein, pondered other solutions, but without success. On 30 January 1933 he appointed Hitler Chancellor, hoping that Hitler—and Germany —could be kept in order. The die was cast. It precipitated not civil war but events infinitely more terrible.

Some historians have laid the blame for Hitler's coming to power on the *Reichswehr* or the capitalists who expected to use him as their catspaw; after all, army men and capitalists are popular and ready-made villains amongst intellectuals. Nietzsche's foresight was more profound than those historians' hindsight. Before the nineteenth century was over, he had said that the morality of the common man had triumphed and that morality already was herd morality. He might have described even more accurately the plight of Germans in and after 1933 had he spoken not of morality but of a-morality—or a moral void.

Hitler's appointment to power seemed to many Germans not a moral void but the exact opposite, a promise of national regeneration. In the evening of 30 January 1933 Nazi storm-troopers and members of other Nazi organizations were joined by their Nationalist counterparts, the members of the *Stahlhelm*, and marched in an intoxicating torchlight procession through Berlin from the *Siegesallee* to the *Wilhelmstrasse* to parade past the new Chancellor at the window of the Chancellery in the *Wilhelmplatz* and past the old President standing at a nearby window. As they marched through the Brandenburg Gate thousands of spectators, bareheaded in the cold winter night, joyfully sang '*Deutschland über Alles*' and the Nazi Horst Wessel 'hymn'. The marching men shouted out at intervals '*Deutschland! Erwache!*', 'Germany! awake!'; or '*Tod allen Feinden*', 'Death to all enemies'; or '*Juda! verrecke!*', 'Jewry, kick the bucket!' Spectators groaned and moaned in excited sympathy. The procession passed Hitler at his window with his arm outstretched in the Nazi salute. He stood between Göring on one side and Heinrich Himmler, leader of the SS, on the other. Long after the procession had gone by, the crowd stayed in the *Wilhelmplatz* looking up at the Chancellery window and chanting '*Heil!*' and

'*Reichs-kanz-ler Hitler*' and 'Füh-rer—we're call-ing-you'. These were the hollow men, the stuffed men, leaning together in the wasteland of their lives. That night's behaviour proved Nietzsche all too right.

3   Absolute Power

I

LIBERTY IS RARELY RAVISHED, it is often seduced. Hitler's was
the seducer's gradual method. It took six months for him to become an effective dictator; it took years for his power to become
totalitarian. The process was aided because liberty is not merely a
matter of constitutional freedom. Few Germans in the early years
of the new régime felt deprived by the loss of such freedoms. Most
Germans preferred the freedoms brought by rapid reduction of
unemployment, regaining of national prestige, and the feeling that
life had purpose again. Most Germans preferred the freedom from
political beatings and killings on the street that Hitler conferred
after his election victory of 5 March 1933; they did not realize
that he had merely transferred open violence to less public places.
Workers willingly traded civil liberties, which seemed to them little
more than scraps of paper, for freedom to receive a wage packet
each week; or to move out of an overcrowded slum to one of the
new houses or flats erected by the Nazi housing programme; or to
have meat, cigarettes and beer, new clothes for their children, or
new furniture to replace the pillage of the depression. Industrialists
preferred the freedom to see the profits pouring from factory
chimneys. Farmers preferred the freedom to till their land without
threat of foreclosure or ruinous crop prices. Army officers preferred
the freedom of promotion, and privates the freedom of becoming
an N.C.O. Thugs preferred the freedom to taunt and beat up left-
wingers and Jews, to pay off personal grudges. Most Germans
eagerly traded civil liberties for the news of foreign-policy
triumphs.

    Hitler freed Germany of the Versailles *Diktat*, re-occupied the
Rhineland in 1936, accomplished the union with Austria in March
1938, and restored the Sudeten Germans to the Reich in the
Munich triumph in October 1938. Consequently had he held free
elections any time between 1934 and 1942, he would without
doubt have gained a decisive majority.

Had he died early in 1939, or the autumn of 1940, he would have been acclaimed by most Germans—and by many historians inside and outside Germany—as one of his country's greatest statesmen fit to stand beside Bismarck. His dictatorial methods, his brutal use of force, his dubious diplomacy may have been condemned; but they would not have tipped the scales against his achievements except in the judgment of a simon-pure democrat. Had he died early in 1939 he could not have been labelled 'totalitarian' according to any proper definition of that word so loosely and vaguely mouthed nowadays.

Before 1939, in the usual manner of the seducer, Hitler mixed force with blandishments, gifts and promises of respectability. His use of force was not great in peacetime compared with the awful terror sired by his total war. This may sound incredible when it is recalled that SA men and Göring's Prussian political police were arresting political opponents in the early months of January 1933, beating them up in disused factories and cellars deep enough to muffle the thuds of blows and screams of pain, and sending them to improvised concentration camps at Oranienburg or Dachau. It may sound incredible when it is recalled that the Gestapo and SS steadily strengthened their power in peacetime, and that force helped accomplish Hitler's foreign policy triumphs. Yet, for all that, the use of force was small in relation to that habitually associated with Hitler. It was more on the scale associated with Mussolini between 1922 and 1940, or with Franco since 1939, or with the dictators who have mushroomed in ex-colonial Asia and Africa since 1945. It is a little-known fact that in September 1939 there were only six main concentration camps and a few more minor ones in *Germany*, imprisoning in all about 30,000 inmates.* Many more than 30,000—although almost certainly not as many as 100,000—had been through the Hell of the concentration camps. Most of them emerged after short sentences into terrorized silence and political passivity, or into exile where their terrible

---

* True, the number of camps and inmates inside and outside Germany rose rapidly when Hitler acquired Austria and Czechoslovakia after March 1938. But it is worth remembering that this rise occurred more than five years after Hitler became Chancellor, and that, according to a Gestapo secret report, the number of inmates in April 1939 was 162,734, most of them in new camps in Austria and Czechoslovakia.

tales were rarely believed; some were murdered and left the camp only in urns of ashes delivered to their next-of-kin; the remainder stayed. There were, it hardly needs saying, too many camps and some 30,000 inmates too many, for any truly civilized person to stomach. Nevertheless, the statistics are nowhere near the hundreds of thousands with which pre-war Germany is so often credited. Those huge numbers were the product of total war and the totalitarian inhumanity it hot-housed.

The master architect, Hitler, executed his grand design by easy stages either because he wished to arouse the least possible opposition in important circles at home and abroad, or because he had no clear and constant idea of his plans. Necessity protracts revolution despite all appearances to the contrary, since a revolution is the violent overthrow of an existing régime *and* its replacement by a new one. The seventeenth-century English Revolution is not regarded by some historians as completed until as late as 1688 when the Stuart régime was finally overthrown and a new one founded. And when did the Russian Communist Revolution end? Hitler accomplished his revolutionary overthrow of the existing régime and its replacement not on 30 January 1933, but in the following years, and the nature of the new régime changed considerably between 1933 and 1945. Hitler's sharp political sense proclaimed the value of hastening slowly.

Germany could not be Nazified in a trice despite all Goebbels' able and energetic efforts and Hitler's nominal powers to make whatever laws he pleased. Propaganda is not a government mint which stamps a people in an instant. Nor are a Chancellor's powers on paper really powers in practice. As Machiavelli long ago wisely pointed out, a successful despot must win willing support as well as unwilling submission, and neither can be won without lengthy and careful perseverance. A dictator in his early days needs to steer between a multitude of Scyllas and Charybdises, and he cannot entirely ignore the siren voices of public opinion and powerful pressure groups not yet turned into enthralled or cowed choirs. Only an emergency enables him to deafen his men with the wax of propaganda and of police terror, and, tying himself to an ideological mast, to odyssey on to totalitarianism.

Ironically the gradualness of the growth of Hitler's power, and of his capacity for inhumanity, helped take Germans further into a moral void. It is often forgotten that the gates of Hell are much more frequently entered by small steps than by giant strides. 'Indeed', wrote C. S. Lewis, 'the safest road to Hell is the gradual one—the gentle slope, soft underfoot, without sudden turnings, without milestones, without signposts.' At first the return of prosperity and the Führer's successes in foreign policy made the going soft underfoot for Germans. Most Germans did not realize how easily and inevitably Hell on earth can be created for themselves as well as others through abnegation of political self-responsibility, through deafness and blindness to the need to cultivate humane attitudes, and through the official encouragement of inhumanity. In fact, they could not realize it; a very inadequate upbringing and human weaknesses prevented the realization, which, in any case, was much harder to attain in the poverty-ridden world of the centuries before 1939 than it is in the affluence of the post-war Western world. Those Germans who did realize it between 1933 and 1939 were too powerless and too few. Most Germans were rendered unwatchful not simply by the incessant police and propaganda that dimmed their minds, but also by the damnable legacy of the mass atomization occurring between the Industrial Revolution and 1933—and by their human condition of fallibility. It is a trite saying that the price of liberty is eternal vigilance, but the events before 1939 in Germany show how true a saying it is.

A totalitarian régime does not intend only destruction and degradation; it intends also saving society, or the world, by radical reconstruction so that what it regards as 'the good life' can be lived according to the righteous doctrine laid down in its dogmatic total ideology. Unhappily the way of the saviour has never been easy especially for the squeamish, tolerant or humane. When the saviour has power, the way has usually led, sooner rather than later, to resort to the whip, the sword, the stake or the execution-axe, and to the search for sanctity in the torture-chamber, the concentration camp, the mass-grave, or the gas-oven. Totalitarian power relies not only on the inhumane indifference, brutality, and sadism of the demoralized, but also on the equally, if not more, inhumane moral imperatives of thorough-going altruism. Beware the march of ideals.

2

There have been too few totalitarian régimes as yet for totalitarianism to be precisely categorized. Totalitarian dictatorship and

79

autocracy was unknown to the world before the 1930s. True, it bears certain resemblances to the European autocracies of the seventeenth, eighteenth and nineteenth centuries, and even more to the Eastern despotisms which have existed since the centuries before Christ. However, the totalitarianism in Nazi Germany, Fascist Italy and Communist Russia and China could not have come into being without the technological developments of the last 100 years or so. Industrialization, urbanization, modern communications—heavy traffic roads, railways, airplanes, radio, telephones, newspapers, cheap books, films—are among the most important. So, too, are modern civil services with up-to-date filing systems and bureaucratic organizations, scientifically equipped police forces and armies, and universal literacy. All of these, and more, enable the long arm of government to stretch into almost every corner of the state. This was not possible even 50 years ago when local citadels of power still limited the power of a central government, because they were buttressed and moated by poor communications, a low level of literacy, the decentralization of the economy, and strongly-held beliefs in the rights of the individual. One obvious example of this is the inability of governments a century ago to institute and operate a complex, modern system of taxation. The simple equation ran: cannot read and write = cannot fill in tax forms = no modern taxation system. Without a modern tax system no totalitarian government and no democratic government could finance the manifold activities it now undertakes. It is no accident that the growth of modern executive government is contemporaneous with the vast technological developments of modern times, and that the invention of totalitarianism has come at the same time. The hammer and sickle are obsolete as symbols of the Russian state; much more to the point would be the police-squad car and the electrical filing machine.

Yet, despite its newness, totalitarianism is distinguishable. In their pioneering *Totalitarian Dictatorship and Autocracy*, Carl J. Friedrich and Zbigniew K. Brzezinski examined Fascist Italy, Nazi Germany and Communist Russia and suggested that there are six basic features which are generally recognizable as common to totalitarian dictatorships. The six interrelated traits are: first, a single party typically led by one man; second, ideology; third, a monopoly of communications; fourth a terroristic police force; fifth, a monopoly of weapons; and sixth, a centrally directed

80

economy. For a totalitarian state to be distinguished, all six traits need to be present together. The presence of some without the others does not necessarily indicate totalitarianism, although it might suggest totalitarian tendencies. For instance, several obviously-democratic states maintain a monopoly of weapons and a centrally directed economy. Again, a number of old-fashioned despotic states (such as contemporary Egypt, Spain and Portugal) possess a terroristic police force and a monopoly of weapons but clearly could not be called totalitarian. On the other hand, each of the six traits making up the totalitarian syndrome do not have to be present in full measure. A state may still be totalitarian although it falls somewhat short of the model. For instance, Mussolini never completely subjected the Catholic Church, although he compelled it to compromise; even Hitler was wary enough not to attack the Churches in Germany openly and directly; and Stalin permitted some toleration of the Churches in Russia. Hence, none of the three classic examples of totalitarianism had a complete monopoly of the means of communication. Similarly, not even Stalin could achieve total central direction of the economy; some decentralization and freedom, however exiguous, was naturally necessary. Nevertheless, it would be as silly to insist on the perfect working of the model for a state to be called totalitarian as to refuse the title of democracy 'to the U.S.A. and Britain because they do not exemplify perfect democracy. It is all a matter of degree, but there can be no doubt that well above the cutting-line are Fascist Italy, Nazi Germany, Communist Russia, and now Communist China.

Totalitarian régimes have become practicable in the twentieth century because of modern political changes, notably those caused by the introduction of a mass suffrage. The possible pernicious effects of these changes were not at all obvious until the lessons were tragically taught by Hitler and Stalin. So, perhaps Germans and Russians are to be forgiven somewhat for falling under the sway of Nazism and Communism without realizing most of the likely consequences. Hitler and Stalin were among the very first to understand that modern mass man is clay to the twentieth-century political potter and they exploited the realization ruthlessly knowing that, in their circumstances, nothing succeeds like excess.

The mass party dates from the late nineteenth century. In a democracy, universal suffrage demands mass parties to win and hold power; in a dictatorship, although universal suffrage becomes largely meaningless even in plebiscites, and although there are no other parties to challenge the ruling party, the mass party may be needed to obtain power, and is certainly necessary for the régime's purpose to penetrate the population as far as possible. Before the late nineteenth century, the relative stability and élitism of an oligarchic system of government or of an old-fashioned despotism ensured that parties should be only temporary, amorphous and mercurial; they were more worthy of the name of fluid factions, breaking up and coagulating in different form and personnel as short-lived political issues rose and disappeared. But in a modern society, whether democratic or dictatorial, the necessity to provide social services makes parties long-lasting and, in the modern phrase, monolithic. The creation and continuation of a mass party is assisted by universal literacy, modern office systems, a popular press, films and radio, and, since World War Two, television. Universal education and literacy are needed in totalitarian dictatorships and democracies not only to provide an adequate reservoir of educated talent to staff bureaucracies, but also to enable the public to read, understand, and complete the forms and carry on the correspondence which are the life-blood of bureaucracy. The single party in a totalitarian state is a vast bureaucratic machine, taking over or supervising normal civil service functions as well as carrying out its own regimenting functions. By comparison, even the nineteenth-century bureaucracies of Russia and Prussia were puny dwarfs.

Totalitarian ideology is also the fruit of modern mass society. Some observers of totalitarian dictatorship, including Friedrich and Brzezinski, contend that a totalitarian ideology is a reasonably coherent body of ideas concerned with the radical destruction of existing society and its equally radical reconstruction in accord with a very different blueprint. But Hannah Arendt, in *The Origins of Totalitarianism*, is much nearer the mark in insisting that a totalitarian ideology is not a coherent body of ideas but, rather, a logical extension of an overriding simple—or over-simplified— idea. Such a logical process seems to the totalitarian ideologist to fit very well into his pseudo-scientific belief in the inevitable laws of Nature or History. The laws of Nature laid down for the Nazi the all-importance of the idea of race; the laws of History lay down for the Communist the all-importance of the idea of class. All else springs from the one idea, and coherence cannot be expected.

It is a mistake to equate a totalitarian ideology with a political theory, and to expect in it the qualities of coherence, rationality, and carefully geared detail to be found in the political theories of such as Plato, Aquinas, Hobbes, or Mill. Political theories and ideologies do not belong to the same species, and thus similarities are superficial and misleading. It is not important in the twentieth century—except to some highly educated minds—that ideologies should be intellectually respectable in the manner demanded before the birth of mass man. Intellectually respectable coherence, consistency, and careful reasoning may be important to university-trained minds, but they do not move the masses in the marketplace, or in the Nuremberg or Red Square rallies.

What mass man wants is a sense of certainty in a world that seems uncertain. He wants a sense of meaning where meaning seems lost. He wants hope in a miasma of bleak hopelessness. A totalitarian ideology offers what those living in a moral void want. It can offer what they want, not only through force and persuasion, but also through lack of effective competitors. The codes that once served an aristocratic, middle-class, or religious society have been too undermined in mass society to stem the flood of totalitarian ideology. And totalitarian terror widens the moral void by terror and by keeping society in a state of uncertain flux by war, forced industrialization and collectivization, and mass purges so that the sense of certainty, hope, and meaning never quite fills the moral void. In this way, a totalitarian system provides 'justification' for its own existence and ideology. Total terror breeds total loneliness; total loneliness enables total power.

Totalitarian ideology is armed with an apparatus of pseudo-science. What is more important, however, is that the simple primary idea is 'revealed', somewhat in the sense that religion was revealed for many medieval believers, and, in fact, for many religious people since the Middle Ages. In an ideology, revelation derives from the laws of Race or History as interpreted by the Nazi or Communist leaders, and it has the force and appeal of a revivalist religion. *Mystique* is as vital as *politique*.

The revealed law divides people into two kinds: Aryan and non-Aryan; proletarian and capitalist; and in each case one is a higher form of life than the other. The community is divided into insiders

83

and outsiders, those who belong and those who do not. Those who do not belong may have to be liquidated, or, at best, permanently condemned to serve as hewers of wood and drawers of water, because they are inferior, beyond redemption. Nevertheless, because the revealed law lays down that their state beyond the pale is natural, they often do not excite in the totalitarian mind the hate aroused by insiders who refuse to see the light or who slip back from righteousness. Betraying the race, the *Volk*, the class is the deadliest of the totalitarian cardinal sins.

Anything that does not fit into these simple ideas is totally wrong, unscientific, unreal. Both Nazism and Communism build up their own 'reality', which to non-believers is utterly unreal, even literally fantastic. Both, moreover, see their reality threatened by enemies conspiring against the revealed truth and the effort to achieve 'the good life'. Both adhere to a conspiracy theory which, to the non-believers, seems, to put it mildly, paranoiac.

The threat from the Elders of Zion or from Wall Street, together with a revealed knowledge of 'truth' necessitates inquisition and intrusion into every aspect of a subject's life through the agency of the propaganda machine and terrorist police. Propaganda and police are closely interwoven; terror controls communication, which communicates, amongst other things, terror. Propaganda and terror are, in a very real sense, two sides of one coin. Wrong action springs from wrong thought, or from the wrong nature of a Jew or capitalist, and it is most economically dealt with at source. The police must detect wrong thought; propaganda must correct it or the police must eradicate it, whereupon propaganda must replace it. The police terror is the modern inquisition, and must, in the interests of the class or the race, be permitted to see into the soul of every person. Not only does heresy weaken the state in the face of its internal and external enemies, it is not in the true interests of the heretic. Better be burned at the stake than live in mortal sin, which can so easily taint others. The righteous must root out unrighteousness ruthlessly, eradicate sin without weak squeamishness, cleanse pitilessly the world of capitalist sin and Jewish pestilence and Slav peril. A Hell on earth must be created to incline the flock to heaven. In the words of Orwell's *1984*, hate *is* love.

The totalitarian would rather have blood on his hands than water like Pilate. Because no humane person can fail to feel pity for those

84

who suffered under Pontius Pilate or totalitarian dictators, it is all
too easy to assume that the choice between blood and water is not
the only one, and that those who prefer blood must be immoral.
Nevertheless, the moral person has sometimes to choose blood
because there is no other choice. For instance, those who chose
after 1939 to kill in the war against Nazi Germany, or those
Germans who chose to try to assassinate Hitler, can hardly be
called immoral because of the choice they made. Like truth,
morality is rarely pure and never simple; and a moral person often
has no option but to commit the lesser evil. Although this is no
justification of totalitarian behaviour, it does suggest that totalitarians, although they are not humane, are still human.

The righteous totalitarian contends that force and violence are
necessary, and are justified on the grounds of being cruel to be kind,
giving people their rightful place, or keeping them in it, to create
maximum happiness and minimum conflict; forcing people to be
free; preventing people acting against their own interests which
they cannot understand, but their rulers can; and such sophistical
arguments. It is true that those who have felt the police lash,
especially if their race was Jewish or Slav, have rarely been treated
to such sermons. Despite the 'philosophy' of terror-makers like
Himmler, and despite the appalling slogans over the entrance gates
to concentration camps announcing at Auschwitz that 'Work makes
free' or at Buchenwald 'To Each his Own', the Nazi and Communist terror-machines acted with a ruthless crudity, and, in the
case of the majority of their servants, with little rationalizing
thought. Yet, there was always a surrounding atmosphere of
'justification'.

The revealed ideology has its priests: the SS and the members
of the Communist party. And it has its high priests: the leader and
his propaganda servants. The leader was almost deified by his
propagandists in his own life-time, all advances being attributed
to him and the power to perform miracles believed to be his.
Propaganda helps turn ideology into a quasi-religion. Communism
under Stalin had its patron saints and gospels according to St
Marx, Engels, Lenin and Stalin; Nazism under Hitler had its
patron saints and gospels according to Houston Stewart Chamberlain, Richard Wagner, Alfred Rosenberg and Hitler. Communism,
in Stalin's heyday, had its Holy Land of Russia with its new Rome
in Moscow, its Vatican in the Kremlin and its St Peter's Square in

the Red Square; Nazism, in Hitler's heyday, had its Promised Land of Greater Germany, its Chosen People, its Moses to lead them into a land flowing with milk and honey and its Philistines to smite hip and thigh. Nazism and Communism have their quasi-religious symbols: the crooked cross of the swastika and the SS runes, the hammer and sickle. Both have their hymns: the Horst Wessel song and the Internationale. The Nazis had their cere-monies of worship: the Nuremberg Rallies and the consecration of virgin party banners by dipping them in the sacred flag carried in Hitler's abortive *putsch* in 1923 which was hallowed by the blood of the martyrs who fell under fire. The Communist Con-gresses are mistakenly equated with a mockery of western par-liamentary processes; rather, they are church-like gatherings, to worship and gather believers together to strengthen their faith. Congresses in Stalin's time, and later, had their appointed moments when the congregation, in effect, genuflected and gave responses. A study of them shows that the bursts of applause are not spontaneous, but follow a remarkably uniform, ordained pat-tern; speeches are ritually punctuated at appropriate intervals with ever-increasing acclaim, ending with 'Prolonged stormy applause. Enthusiastic acclamation in the hall. All rise.'

Modern developments enabled the propaganda machine to broadcast the totalitarian 'truth'. Universal education, a mass press, films, radio had all been invented before 1914, but they matured only in the twentieth century. A cheap radio set became possible only in the 1920s, but advancing technology had created a mass press as soon as universal literacy gave birth to a mass public: the telephone and telegraph collected and disseminated news quickly; the rotary press turned out millions of copies of newspapers every single day; a national railway system, motor vans and bicycles delivered newspapers to breakfast tables and evening armchairs all over the country; industrialization force-fed the mass advertiser that made the mass press profitable.

The terroristic police was also fathered by new technology. The telephone, telegraph, type-writer, microphone, radio, multiple filing systems, automatic weapons and the squad cars are as essential to the terroristic police as the man in the Gestapo or N.K.V.D. uniform.

The fifth of the traits composing the totalitarian syndrome is the government's monopoly of armaments. In modern times when the main military weapons are expensive, mechanized pieces of equipment costing thousands of dollars, the ruling régime has an immense advantage over its subjects. Once, when amongst the main weapons were swords and shot-guns, the citizen could possess arms which were not completely unequal to those carried by the soldier in uniform. But, nowadays, even if it were legal, what citizen could afford a bazooka, house a tank in his garage, or possess a bomber?

A central control and direction of the economy is the sixth characteristic of a totalitarian régime. It is perhaps the least uniform feature of modern totalitarian states; but even when they cannot, or do not choose, to go into business management themselves, they cannot function without effective powers of taxation and economic intervention. These powers are given them as much by the immense increase in national wealth and vastly improved communications, both brought by industrialization. Charles I of England and Louis XVI of France were not the only rulers to find that an empty Treasury was an insuperable obstacle to absolute government. Had Strafford and Laud in Charles I's reign been able to wield the powers of control over a rich economy that are available to modern governments, then they and the king could have afforded a standing army that would have made possible an extension of the eleven years' tyranny which lasted from 1629 to 1640. Though the king was poor, the country was rich enough to afford a standing army; and the crucial problem was how to tap the riches in days when literacy was low and 'civil services' primitive. George III found that there were many Hampdens in the American colonies who knew that control of taxation was a central government's Achilles heel. R. W. Southern in his brilliant, deep-probing *The Making of the Middle Ages* points out that in medieval Europe 'even in the most favourable geographical conditions, man's technical equipment was so primitive that this helplessness before Nature—which added to his misery in one way—saved him from the misery of organized tyranny. There was a mercifully large gap between the will to rule and the powers to do so, and it may be that bad roads and an intractable soil contributed more to the fashioning of familiar liberties than any other factor at this time.'

In the contemporary world, Communist Russia (before China fell to Mao Tse-tung's Communists) has developed the most 'total' control of the economy. Nazi Germany never approached efficient total control, even at the height of the war. Indeed, until Speer took over the direction of the economy in 1942, Nazi Germany did not exercise as great a control over finance, industry and commerce as did the war-time government of Britain. In Mussolini's Italy, government control of the economy was even less complete than in Hitler's Germany. Yet in both—though more in Germany than in Italy—the state had control and direction where it really wanted it, and where it seemed to the rulers essential; and the state could, and did, extend it where and when it wished. Such autonomy as capitalists had consisted of what Karl Wittfogel in *Oriental Despotism* has aptly called 'irrelevant freedoms'. Under the Eastern despotisms, which were nearer to totalitarianism than anything in pre-twentieth century Europe, villagers did have the freedoms to allot the village land or to try cases involving disputes between themselves. But these freedoms were 'irrelevant'; the village was always subject to the arbitrary decisions and taxes of the despot. It was similar for the capitalist in Nazi Germany at war. Totalitarianism does not necessitate state ownership of all the means of production and distribution, but, rather, a central control and direction of the economy.

'Totalitarianism', with its connotations of totalness, is perhaps not the most apt word for Hitler's Germany and Stalin's Russia, where really total control and brainwashing of the whole population was neither present nor even feasible. But to reject the word for these reasons in either case would be silly, and any polemical study refusing it validity in regard to either of those two countries on those grounds would be worthy of a title like *The Baby and the Bathwater*. 'Words', Thomas Hobbes observed, 'are wise men's counters, they do but reckon by them; but they are the money of fools.' No totalitarian régime is, after all, a perfect model in all respects. Nobody knows, for example, how many people in Communist Russia disapprove of the prevailing régime; but it is well known that many, notably among the peasants and those to whom religion still means much, do not actively support it. They endure both ideology and régime because they have to. Much the same was true in Nazi Germany before 1939. After that date, in the days of the Greater Reich, the majority of the non-German ruled were bitterly opposed to Nazism. This caused no concern to the Nazis on theoretical grounds since their ideology was one for the

Herrenvolk, and was not for general consumption by the *Unter-menschen*. Nor were the Nazis frantically bothered that there were 'civilized' Germans who never joined—or even voted for—the Nazi party, but did not much mind accepting the fruits of economic recovery, personal advancement, and European conquest. Similarly, in Russia the élite nature of the Communist party provides for different degrees of ideological fervour.

If however the word 'totalitarian' is unacceptable, another new term must be coined to distinguish those twentieth-century dictatorships from other despotisms. It is a grave mistake to suppose that the despotisms of Hitler and Stalin were first cousins to those of Napoleon I or Franco; they are not members of the same family at all. The supposition also does less than justice to Germans and Russians who assisted their totalitarian masters without realizing what tragedy modern times had in store.

3

Friedrich and Brzezinski in *Totalitarian Dictatorship and Autocracy* are not intent on dating when old-fashioned despotism became new totalitarianism in Russia, Germany and Italy, perhaps because, as political scientists, they prefer the snapshot to the moving picture which engrosses the historian concerned so much with change. Yet, their own criteria of totalitarianism, applied to the events of 1933 to 1945, show either that totalitarianism was hardly born before the war, although the embryo was there earlier, or that, if totalitarianism was present in theory, it was not in practice. Even had totalitarianism been Hitler's early wish, he was in no position before 1939 to consummate it.

The first of the totalitarian characteristics, a single-party state, existed in Nazi Germany after some six months—if it consists of no more than the abolition of all other parties, the acquisition of legal power by the single party leader to decree almost anything, and the setting-up of scaffolding to control or supervise state and society. But if it consists of the thorough permeation of state and society by the single party, it did not exist until much later.

For almost a month after 30 January 1933 Hitler was ringed around by restrictions and had only the Presidential powers through which to rule. It is true that the SA Storm-troopers assumed the freedom of the streets and the police rushed to ruth-lessly suppress left-wingers. However, Hitler's first month was fully occupied with getting into the saddle of everyday administration and preparing for the imminent election due on 5 March. German eyebrows were raised by SA violence; but most Germans were by now habituated to bloody election campaigns and, when they were not indifferent, could comfort themselves with the thought that only 'Reds' suffered, and that Hitler was a moderate and would soon whistle the SA to heel.

To heat-up the election campaign, Göring's Berlin police raided Karl Liebknecht House, the Communist headquarters, on 24 February, and secured what the Nazis called evidence of a red plot to overthrow the state. The 'evidence' was never published; but any doubts about its authenticity were stilled when, three days later, the Reichstag was set on fire and practically burnt out. Communists blamed Nazis, and Nazis blamed Communists; and 30 years later Fritz Tobias cogently argued that the act of arson was committed by the Dutchman who in the trial later in the year stubbornly insisted that he started the fire alone and solely for his own purposes. In February 1933, however, the Nazis successfully foisted the blame on to the Communists, and secured from the aged and scared President an emergency decree, under Article 48 of the Constitution, 'for the Protection of the People and the State'. The decree legalized restrictions on personal liberty far beyond the hitherto constitutionally-prescribed limits. Similar emergency decrees under Article 48 had been pressed into service in the troubled years before 1924 and after 1928, many of them signed by Ebert, the Socialist President until his death in 1925.

However, before 28 February 1933, emergency decrees had always included a paragraph from the war-time Protective Custody Act of 1916, which ruled that any person arrested must be heard before a court within 24 hours; that he was entitled to legal counsel with full access to relevant records; that he could appeal to a special board which was authorized to set him free at any time and which was the only authority which could keep him detained more than three months; and that if this board considered him unjustly arrested, it could award him financial compensation out of funds the government could not block. The decree of 28 February 1933 was the first emergency decree since 1916 which failed to include these safeguards.

This omission spelt the most dreadful consequences for those arrested by the Nazis. Hitler's police could arrest at will and detain indefinitely; they could refuse any legal defence to those arrested; they need not inform the relatives of anyone detained of his fate or even his whereabouts; they could use any violence they liked; they could prevent any communication between a prisoner and the outside world; they were not subject to any control by the courts. Anyone arrested was completely at the mercy of the police.

Before 28 February 1933, it was understood that the police should use emergency powers impartially. Göring completely abandoned this understanding, and ordered his police to apply the decree only to leftists. He also made it amply clear that it was good tactics to shoot first and ask questions afterwards, and that policemen slow on the trigger would be penalized. Hitler, however, misted the conscience of the President and people by assurances that the emergency powers would be only temporary and would be responsibly used to ward off the Red peril. In fact, the powers remained in force as long as the Nazi régime and were used with increasing immoral, although not illegal, irresponsibility.

Hitler needed positive powers to implement his will as well as the negative powers that the decree of 28 February 1933 gave him to prevent opposition. Positive powers, however, required a change in the Constitution, which could only be effected by a two-thirds majority of the *Reichstag*. The election of 5 March did not provide him with the necessary majority, although his coalition's bare majority was comfortably increased by the proscription of the 81 Communist deputies elected. A mixture of self-restraint, promises and threats that a Nazi revolution would be forced through by bloodshed if necessary, induced the *Reichstag* on 23 March 1933 to pass, by the requisite two-thirds majority, the Law for Removing the Distress of People and State. The Act gave the Chancellor unrestrained power to by-pass the *Reichstag* and to promulgate decrees deviating from the Constitution and coming into operation the day following publication. Although a clause limited these powers to a period of four years, the Act, renewed at appropriate intervals, died only with the Third Reich.

This Enabling Act and the decree of 28 February 1933 were the central pillars of Hitler's power. They allowed him to turn Germany into a one-party state and, ultimately, into a totalitarian despotism. In legal theory, to quote de Lolme's saying about the powers of the British Parliament, he could 'do anything except change a man into a woman'—and with the modern advances already made by medical science, possibly even de Lolme's qualification was obsolete. Since 1945 some have argued that Hitler's power was not altogether constitutional; but his power did not seem unconstitutional to Germans at the time. Even his opponents objected only to the moral spirit, not the legal letter of his laws.

Using the emergency powers granted on 28 February and 23 March 1933 Hitler was able to bring the governments of the *Länder*, or states, under central control, and, in effect, abolish the parliaments of the states. In May he merged the trade unions in the Nazi Labour Front. Since he legally could—and did—govern without recourse to the *Reichstag*, and since regional parliaments and trade unions were in practice ended, parties other than the Nazi party no longer had a *raison d'être*, and they went either into a more or less voluntary liquidation, like the Centre and Nationalist parties, or into enforced liquidation, like the Social Democratic Party. On 14 July 1933, the 144th anniversary of the fall of the Bastille, the Nazi party became the sole legal party. Although a clause in the Enabling Act ensured the continuance of the *Reichstag*, that body served no purpose except as a swastika-bedecked rostrum for Hitler's orations. Its original building having been burned down on 27 February, it met in the Kroll Opera House; and, due to its habit of acclaiming the Führer's speeches by singing patriotic and Nazi songs, the irreverent dubbed it the most expensive opera chorus in the world.

By the middle of the summer of 1933, Hitler had eradicated, neutralized, or won over potential opponents in the Cabinet. Hugenberg, the leader of the Nationalist Party was too immersed in his demanding duties as minister in charge of a depressed economy to maintain his political influence. He was given no support by Hindenburg and he was deserted by his fellow-Nationalist, Seldte, the Minister of Labour, who was won over by Hitler's magnetic charm. On 29 June 1933 Hugenberg threw in his hand and resigned in despair. Hitler replaced Franz von Papen as *Reich* Commissioner for Prussia in April 1933, handing his duties over to Göring. Von Papen's position as Vice-Chancellor became merely honorary, since nothing was entrusted to him and he had lost all influence with Hindenburg, who sunk into passivity under the weight of old age and declining health and under the spell of Hitler's respectful attitude of an old soldier to his Field-Marshal.

Nazis like Goebbels were brought into the Cabinet. Ministers, such as those controlling defence, foreign affairs and the economy, were given much what they wanted or were left alone. The Ministry of Justice was in compliant enough hands; and the control of the *Länder* by the *Reich* government enabled the extension of the Nazi police over all of Germany. A corporative state was instituted, binding every citizen, directly or indirectly, to a Nazi association. Within six months of coming to power, Hitler had become a single-party dictator of Germany. And *Gleichschaltung*, or co-ordination, had been established, though more in theory than in practice.

A year later, on the morning of 2 August 1934, Hindenburg died and it was immediately announced that the offices of President and Chancellor were merged in the person of Hitler. This was a political formality. No figure could have rivalled Hitler if a Presidential election had been held; and Hindenburg's senility and Hitler's energy had already put the main political institutions at the disposal of one party. Nevertheless, Hitler and the Nazis were still a long way short of total power. They still had to tread cautiously in dealing with the army, the Churches, and big business which was sheltered by Schacht, now in charge of the economy. Moreover, the neatly ruled lines of control of the corporative society by the Party had to be fleshed with reality. Efficient party officials had to be found and trained. Their control could only permeate slowly through to the lower everyday levels. For some years non-Nazis in, say, the schools or the judiciary had to be ignored, or by-passed. Indoctrination and total control were by their very nature slow in coming. A clean sweep of non-Nazis would have left the administration without experts and in a chaos that Hitler could not afford and did not want, at least while the unemployed still numbered millions and international triumphs had not yet laurelled his rule. Historians are too apt to be misled by paper charts of control which often indicate no more than intentions or claims. Like the writing of most history, such charts are often composed of the top people, by the top people, and for the top people.

War provided the opportunity for totalitarian regimentation. Yet, it was regimentation not by the Party, but by elements of it. The exigencies of total war and of a racialist policy, which became the dynamic driving force of the war and the régime, made some party men more equal than others. The SS, controlling the Gestapo and the extermination machine, became by far the most powerful party organization. Indeed, whilst Hitler was more and more obsessively preoccupied with the military side of the war, it became almost a state within a state. For all practical purposes, the SS cut itself adrift from the Party, so that *Gauleiter* complained that they were treated by Himmler's men as no more than petty officials or errand-boys, instead of the important figures their high party position warranted. In place of a neat administrative structure, tidily controlled by the Party, the Nazi régime became lopsided as enormous power accrued to a few men at the top near to Hitler: Himmler, Goebbels, Bormann, Speer and Sauckel. A similar phenomenon can be discerned in Stalin's Russia where the avalanches of forced industrialization and collectivization after 1928, the Great Purges of 1936–8, and war after 1941 overwhelmed control by the Communist party. Power passed from the Party Head Office to the Kremlin and Beria's headquarters. In both Communist Russia and Nazi Germany, the party did not hold the position of power it holds in the textbooks of political scientists; it was relegated to the rank of N.C.O., and the Sergeants' Mess became its natural habitat.

The power of a Himmler or a Beria grew under the aegis of the totalitarian dictator, and their power contributed to his totalitarianism. Hitler dominated the Nazi régime as completely as Stalin did the Communist régime. Potent leaders like Himmler and Göring bowed in obeisance before him; prominent civil servants quailed before him or were hypnotized by him; courageous, strong-willed generals entered his presence determined to tell him the truth that the war was lost, and left utterly convinced that their Führer was right and victory inevitable. Hitler overtopped all around him.

His character is an enigma. To call him a fool, a madman, a paranoiac, or any other over-simple name will satisfy only those who think that glib labels constitute explanations. Hitler was far too extraordinary a person for such superficial labelling. To call him mad, for instance, means that a new word would need coining for those unfortunate enough to be confined in asylums or padded cells. It is understandable that, in the heat, hate and haste of the war and the years immediately after, even eminent historians should have abused him as a charlatan, a sorcerer, a lunatic. Even such a highly intelligent historian as Sir Lewis Namier regarded

94

him as a mere illiterate of fifth-rate intelligence; but then Namier
was of Galician Jewish origin, and was easily given to anger and
irritation—issuing in such judgments when he wrote on contemporary history, although not when he worked on eighteenth-
century English or nineteenth-century European history. Alan
Bullock's judgment that Hitler was a diabolical adventurer, an
'intellectual cretin' moved solely by the lust for power and sheer
destruction is much less excusable. Similar, though less well-
expressed, judgments in standard textbooks on Nazi Germany
are hardly excusable at all. One cause of vituperation and slick
labelling masquerading as explanation of Hitler is obviously an
understandable abomination of Nazi atrociousness and a mystifi-
cation at the appalling dimensions of Nazi inhumanity. But another
cause may be no more than snobbishness about a man of such
humble origins. Hitler also suffers under the stigma of eventual
failure. Stalin, although he came from an even more lowly background, at least succeeded; and historians, by the nature of their
trade, tend to be success-snobs. Yet now that the heat and dust has
died down somewhat, it can be seen that glib or disgusted labelling
will not suffice to explain how a man with such a poor start in life
and such unpropitious opportunities achieved the amazing feats
he did. Nor will it suffice to explain a dozen thunderstruck years
of German—and European—history.

That Hitler had a powerful, first-rate intellect amounting to
genius, however loathsome, has been compellingly demonstrated
by H. R. Trevor-Roper in a brilliant essay which acts as an introduction to *Hitler's Secret Conversations 1941-1944*. The observa-
tions of hard-headed, shrewd, intelligent Germans support
Trevor-Roper's case. Hitler's Chief of Staff for a time, General
Halder, certainly no lover of Nazism and one of the most intelligent officers in the German High Command, considered Hitler
had an unusual power of intellect and an amazingly quick comprehension, although the exercise of these was marred by moral
and personality faults. Schacht, in peacetime Hitler's economic
manager and in wartime a member of the resistance, had no illusions about Hitler's great intellectual ability. Nor did Speer, who
was undoubtedly one of the most percipient of Hitler's ministers.
Perhaps, however, the opinions of those three men are to be dismissed because they are Germans. Yet, European and American
statesmen, whose careers show them to have been no mean judges

of intelligence, attest the same view of Hitler's intellectual capacities. To explain the judgment of such statesmen as springing merely from a right-wing capitalist plot or from a willingness to be duped because of fear of Communism, as do Franz Neumann in *Behemoth* and his flock of fellow-travellers, is to reveal a damagingly blinkered and myopic historical vision—if it can be called a 'historical vision' at all.

If the voices of human witnesses carry no weight, Hitler's achievements speak for themselves. No man of his origins and circumstances could have risen to power and accomplished what Hitler did if he had been an 'intellectual cretin'. Bullock asserts in the Epilogue to his biography that Hitler achieved nothing but destruction. He is looking through the wrong end of the chronological telescope viewing only the ruin of 1945, unable to see that many non-Nazi Germans who died a natural death before 1939 had good reason to thank Hitler for achieving for them a weekly wage and all it bought. Bullock's vision is further narrowed because he restricts the meaning of 'achievements' to ideas, which are furthermore, as the list in the Epilogue to his biography indicates, ideas that he regards as morally good. It is an all too common fault of intellectuals to overestimate the effect of ideas and underestimate the effect of practical things. After all, a manufacturer has eyes only for his own kind of wares.

Hitler's mediocre secondary school record and *Mein Kampf* are put on the witness stand as part of the prosecution case that he had a fifth-rate intellect. Yet, in primary school, Hitler was always at the top of his class. *Mein Kampf* is far from being the turgidly written and unintelligent book it is nearly always judged by non-Nazis. In places, it is brilliantly written with a vivid and athletic style. It shows a perceptive insight into politics in a mass society, an insight extraordinarily rare when Hitler wrote. It can fascinate and compel a reader who finds its political and moral principles totally alien and horrible. The usual charges of turgidness, unreadability and stupidity arouse the suspicion that those who utter them have either never read *Mein Kampf* or have read it only to confirm a judgment preconceived in a closed mind.

Bad men are not inevitably stupid. When Plato said that 'knowledge is virtue' he did not mean that intelligent men are automatically good, however pleasing the thought may have been to an intelligent intellectual like himself. Acton was not far wrong

96

when he asserted that 'all great men are bad men'. He would not have been in the least surprised that Hitler had a first-class intellect. It would have been much better for Germany—and the world—had Hitler been a fool, or a thug, or a charlatan, or a madman. A man who was any of these could not have accomplished what Hitler did.

In the many-faceted character of Hitler, one little-noted trait may have been of much greater importance than has been realized. There seems little doubt that throughout his life, Hitler was an inveterate daydreamer given to wish-fulfilment fantasies. In his boyhood the highly-romanticized stories of Karl May, the German G. A. Henty or Fennimore Cooper, and books on German legends and on heroism in war dominated his reading. As a boy he enjoyed playing at war, and always wanted to be the leader in these war-games. Growing-up did not evaporate Hitler's taste for this pastime. In his adolescence, he withdrew into himself, a withdrawal which may help explain his failure in secondary school, and which certainly would have encouraged his penchant for daydreaming beyond the normal extent of most adolescents. As a young man he isolated himself from all but one friend who proved a good listener to Hitler's fantasies of becoming a great architect replanning public buildings and whole cities. His failure to be accepted for training as an artist or an architect must have aggravated his sense of isolation where daydreams provided compensation for the world not accepting him. He fantasized a romantic attachment to a girl named Stephanie, inventing details of its progress although Stephanie, so far as she knew, never set eyes on him, let alone met him. When he went to Vienna before World War One, he bought a lottery ticket, and erected the most elaborate fantasies on how to spend the money he was certain he would win. When it did not win, he was unwarrantably enraged and disappointed. He soon became completely and voluntarily a total isolate. At this time, he seems to have had no relations with women, except possibly in his daydreams.

In World War One he was a model soldier but no comrade. Those who served with him remember an extremely withdrawn person, and photographs of him at the time show him as always slightly behind or apart from his companions and with a lone look on his face. War is probably the ultimate haven of the daydreamer. There he can perform heroic deeds and the miraculous can appear

97

reality. It is perhaps significant that Hitler served mostly as a runner carrying messages, a duty that would have kept him apart from his fellow soldiers much more than standing companionably with them in the trenches or going over the top in attacks with them; as a runner he would have spent most of his time on duty in the orderly room dug-out instead of yarning or playing cards in the dug-outs in which the ordinary soldier whiled away his time in between stand-to's and attacks. The sordidness and messiness of war, the unromantic, common coarseness of his fellow soldiers, and German defeat probably caused Hitler to withdraw further into himself. When he could wage his own war after 1939 he probably daydreamed it as a personal Karl May-Wagnerian epic, imagining that he himself could transform war into what, in his mind, was its properly heroic character. No doubt his early victories confirmed his over-romanticized picture, seeming to him to prove that what would have been fantasies to others were reality. When victory ebbed, he withdrew into even more isolation; his last open-air public appearance was in the summer of 1940 when he drove in an open car through the streets of Berlin after his return from triumph in Paris. After 1942, he made only very rare appearances before select audiences, spoke on the radio only very occasionally, and did not visit the front. His headquarters were aptly described by General Jodl at the Nuremberg Trial as 'a cross between a cloister and a concentration camp'. Increasing isolation took him even further from reality until in April 1945 he fantasized armies and victories out of the air and lost touch with it altogether.

In *Mein Kampf* Hitler romanticized his boyhood and youth by inventing stories to show himself more pitiable in harder circumstances than was true; for instance, he grossly exaggerated the severity and bad habits of his father, as well as his own poverty in Vienna. After World War One, he remained practically friendless, and the only Nazis with whom he used the intimate '*du*', or thou, form of address were Feder, a crank economist whom he came to know in the early 1920s, and Ernst Röhm, the SA leader. Hitler dropped Feder after the Nazi rise to power, and he had Röhm executed in the Blood Purge of 30 June 1934. The eminence of power naturally intensified Hitler's isolation, and his 'table-talk' with his entourage consisted not of conversation but of monologues marked by wish-fulfilment fantasies.

Hitler never lived an ordinary routine life after his youth. He neither kept regular hours nor ate regular meals. He seems rarely, if ever, to have engaged in the give-and-take of conversation, but would sit morosely silent at parties sometimes for hours or break into long, impassioned monologues in his harsh, but compelling, voice. Even more than Stalin, at the height of his power he remained ascetic, unostentatious in dress, and uncaring of wealth. His only luxury seems to have been cream cakes of which he was inordinately fond. He was not a womanizer. In his last years he formed some sort of attachment to Eva Braun, whom he married only hours before their joint suicide; but whether the attachment was an *affaire* into which sex entered no one knows. Possibly he was impotent. Felix Kersten asserts he was, and Kersten is usually a very reliable witness. Neither a German nor a Nazi, his skill as a masseur forged a bond with Himmler who suffered badly from stomach cramps and other pains Kersten could relieve. Because Himmler could not do without his massage, Kersten was able to save many Jewish lives and learn a number of state secrets. He claims that Himmler allowed him to see the file on Hitler's medical history, which revealed that Hitler was impotent and enjoyed orgasms whilst making his speeches. Speeches for him—and for many in his audience—were passionate outbursts of his fantasy life.

A prey to the isolating influences of his fantasizing nature and a daily life bereft of normal substitutes and satisfactions, Hitler increasingly lost touch with reality. And as his reality receded his daydreaming discarded all limits. The fantasist hates people because they do not live up to his illusionary expectations, and he blames them bitterly because reality strips substance from his delusions. Hitler had an immense talent for hate, and at one time or another spat out his hate for every section of society and for every country. In his final testament at the end of his life, he expressed hatred even for the German people and hoped they would perish in utter ruin; by then he had reached the ultimate destination of the incurable daydreamer: *Weltmacht oder Niedergang,* world power or complete ruin. It is true that his capacity for hate derived also from being an outsider who did not belong anywhere. He was an Austrian in Germany; he was a corporal who was not accepted into the officer ranks; he had been prevented from having a tertiary education and was not regarded by intellectuals as one of themselves; he had no profession except that of politician, a

99

profession generally looked down upon by Germans; he never found a safe, secure place in society—even as Führer his life and régime were always in peril; he had no family or friends, except Eva Braun; military defeat confirmed the refusal of the world to accept him. Being an outsider helped envenom him; but this isolation may have sprung largely, or wholly, from an inability to stop the boundless fantasies.

The fantasist does have advantages. He completely believes what he says as soon as he says it, however wide of the truth it is. This utter conviction that he is speaking the truth convinces all but the least impressionable. It also endows him with the ability to act superbly a variety of roles and to carry complete conviction in each of them because he himself believes he is not an actor but a real sincere person. Because so much of what Hitler said and did was inconsistent, he has frequently been marked down as a cynic, or an opportunist. Yet, if it is true that he was the victim of fantasies, it is more than probable that he sincerely believed in most, if not all, of what he said and did. He was not one person, but many persons: real, sincere, honest persons, since he had the fantasist's extraordinary facility for wholly forgetting or rationalizing anything that contradicted his current words and actions.

The fantasist has another advantage. Because the limits of reality are not real to him, he can conceive and carry out actions which seems to others impossible to accomplish. He can be the Superman, not of Nietzsche's books but of the comic-books. This gives him the opportunity to surprise and to confuse opponents by his astounding and seemingly incredible daring. When he holds Hitler's power, and when the circumstances are as propitious as they were in Europe between 1930 and 1940, truly amazing feats can be accomplished: appointment as Chancellor in 1933, the *Anschluss* with Austria and the Munich triumph in 1938, the Nazi-Communist Non-Aggression Pact in August 1939, the brilliant strategy which defeated France in 1940 and which was Hitler's own decision.

Yet such gifts usually turn sour and destroy their possessor. He is a shell to be filled by the moment instead of a person in his own right. He has no permanent principles or beliefs to anchor him to reality, except his belief in his own genius, which casts him further adrift from reality. Reality will catch him unawares and administer deep wounds to mind and ego. When he is not ordinary or has great power, others are also sorely hurt. Not only absolute power corrupted Hitler absolutely; his successes also corrupted absolutely by cementing his profound conviction that he could bring about miracles. For him nothing *failed* like success. Bullock imputes Hitler's successes and failures partly to his having no roots. But very probably Hitler did have deep roots—in his fantasies. Alienation from reality was his fatal flaw—as fatal as any found in classical tragedy. And for this reason Hitler—who is unpitied universally even by those who never suffered under him—deserves some compassion.

Hitler's gift for assuming so many diverse roles helps account for the confusions, inconsistencies, and extemporizing of Nazi administration. But other factors assisted; and its peculiarity in modern times to Nazi Germany has been greatly exaggerated, perhaps to forward the view that Hitler and his agents were mad, vicious or stupid. A similar condition occurred in Stalin's Russia. No doubt, both dictators appreciated the salutary maxim, divide and rule. Yet, an additional cause was the existence of a state of extraordinary crisis, starting in Russia with Stalin's industrial and agricultural revolution in 1928 and continuing through the purges, the war, and post-war reconstruction, and starting in Germany with war after 1939. A somewhat chaotic system of administration is common to all countries in total war. The many volumes of the British official history of both world wars reveal that democracies engaged in total war are not exempt from administrative confusion and muddle or from the building of private empires within an empire. The ruthless private empire-building of Nazi and Communist leaders can be compared to that of several British ministers besides Lloyd George and Lord Beaverbrook. Michael Foot's official history *The S.O.E. in France* has fast become a classic on how total war in a democracy can spawn competing or overlapping organizations which sometimes are not even aware of the existence of rivals in the same field. Great untidiness and waste—to put it mildly—are of the essence of total war, whether the protagonist is totalitarian dictatorship or democracy. If any liberal illusions about the inevitability of the inefficiency of tyranny survived Stalin's success despite the confusion and muddle that marked his régime, they should have been finally destroyed by the launching of the first Sputnik in 1957.

4

The illusive, extemporizing nature of Hitler's régime is largely reflected in Nazi ideology, the second of the six totalitarian traits. Before total war, Nazism was a *pot-pourri*. The racialism of Houston Stewart Chamberlain, Gobineau and others, and the nationalism of Treitschke, Spengler and others, jostled shoulders with the socialistic revolutionary conservatism of many members of the *Mittelstand*. Romantic ideas came from right-wing youth groups as well as from ex-soldiers like Ernst Jünger and Ernst von Reventlow, and were contradicted by the nihilism of *Freikorps* veterans like Schlageter, Erhardt, Schultz and Berthold who found psychological demobilization impossible, and by the corps of thugs who discovered pleasure in Nazi violence. Hitler could utter the gospel of anti-capitalism to workers and the gospel of profits to businessmen. Nazi ideology was virulently critical of so many things; but the variegated ideological bricks of differing sizes, shades and colours were successfully cemented together in the earlier days by insistence on righting the wrongs perpetrated by 'the Versailles criminals' and overthrowing 'their inefficient and immoral' Weimar régime. The slogan *'Gemeinnutz vor Eigennutz'*, 'the common weal before selfishness', covered a multitude of competing ideas and interests. Nazi negativism was its greatest strength where mass man felt lost in a fearful and chaotic world, from which he desperately wanted to escape.

Because it was so much of a rag-bag of inconsistent and incoherent ideas, Nazi ideology always draws derision from post-war historians and political scientists who forget both that mass man is not interested in the intellectual respectability of a party programme, and that democratic party programmes are fast becoming intellectually disreputable—if they ever were, or could be, anything else—from the compulsion in a two-party system to appeal to so many diverse sections of society.

The decibels of the derision are increased by another illusion of historians and political scientists: that Nazi ideology compares very unfavourably in intellectual respectability with Communist ideology. Yet, the Communist ideology propagated in Russia—and elsewhere, for that matter—is even more crude and vague, more inconsistent and incoherent than Nazi ideology. For instance, Marx, Engels and Lenin had written and spoken volumes criticizing and condemning capitalism, and 'proving' the inevitability of the proletarian revolution. They seem, however, to have thought very little, and they certainly wrote very little, in any but the vaguest way about the new society which was to replace capitalism. That which they did write was so utopian, so unrealistic, that it is impossible not to judge it sheer nonsense by open-eyed criteria. They considered that once the proletarian revolution had abolished private ownership of the means of production and distribution, there would be an end to classes, class-conflict, exploitation, crime and vice, and so everyone would be good, just, kind, peaceable, and in every way virtuous. Lenin, a brilliant politician but a mediocre intellect, tried to stem with a pamphleteering finger the flood of reality sweeping away the illusions of Elysian fields. Stalin, an even more brilliant politician and an even more mediocre intellect, attempted the same task. But they did not succeed, and they only increased the number of contradictions, illogicalities, inconsistencies, and unrealities, although they kept illusions alive by methods that can lay no more claim to intellectual respectability than those used by Hitler. Even Communist sympathizers nowadays despise Stalin's intellectual contribution to Communist theory—if it can be so called.

The delusion that Communist ideology is intellectually respectable springs from the belief that it can trace a direct line of intellectual descent from the John the Baptists of Communism, Marx and Engels. How absurd this belief is has been shown by a number of cool critics, notably John Plamenatz in *German Marxism and Russian Communism*. Russian Communism may claim Marx and Engels as ancestors, but it has certainly strayed from the ancestral traditions into entirely foreign lands and ways. Observing in his old age the direction the theory and practice of Marxism had taken, Marx bitterly said that he himself could no longer be called a Marxist; and were he and Engels to be reincarnated today, without doubt they would kill no fatted calf for the prodigal that is totalitarian, elitist, bourgeoisified Communism in Russia, China and elsewhere. Instead, they would indignantly reject the theory and practice of twentieth-century Communism as their brain-child.

The delusion of the intellectual respectability of Communism is fostered by other factors. One is the belief that Marx was a far-sighted, perceptive thinker. In fact, events since he wrote have conclusively proved that almost all his prophecies were wrong, and

103

that his analysis of capitalism in his own day was imperceptive and erroneous despite—or perhaps because of—his warm-hearted horror at the evils of capitalism. His heart may have been in the right place, but his head was in cloud-cuckoo-land.

A more important factor is the mystical hold of the concept of 'class' on social scientists in the twentieth century. Explanation of human behaviour in terms of 'class' is fortunately at last becoming subject to stringent and sensible criticism. Yet, whilst it ruled the intellectual roost and determined the causal pecking-order, it has had as strong and as misleading an influence as belief in the concept of 'race' had among intellectuals and others in the second half of the nineteenth century and in the early twentieth century when Nazi leaders were growing up. Those who jeer so derisively at the racial ideology of Nazis overlook that scholars like Galton, Wilhelm Schallmayer, Alfred Plötz, Otto Ammon and Alexander Tille seriously believed in the concept of 'race', and yet were of quite as large an intellectual calibre as any socialist scholar. The jeerers forget that those scholars had their Karl Marx in Charles Darwin, however unwilling he, like Marx, might have been to acknowledge most of the uses to which his work has been put. They do not realize that the political climate of those days was as favourable to the concept of 'race' as the political climate of the mid-twentieth century has been to the concept of 'class'. The British Empire in India, European dominance of other continents, and nationalism in Europe encouraged and needed the concept of 'race' as much as the crusade on behalf of poverty-stricken workers and subject colonial peoples encouraged and needed the concept of 'class'. Possibly, in a generation or so, the concept of 'class' will draw jeers from Western scholars as derisory as those nowadays excited by the concept of 'race'. More probably, responsible criticism will have revealed it as mere myth. For the sake of the proper study of mankind, it is a consummation devoutly to be wished.

Nazi ideology did not remain the early motley patchwork. Hitler gradually sewed together an ideological quilt of racialist colour. Although he always insisted that he had not ever abandoned the 25-Point Programme he had proclaimed in 1920, he in fact dropped one after another of its points. For instance, in June 1934 he abandoned the socialistic revolutionary conservatism of the small tradesman, petty official, artisan and peasant in favour of the socialistic nationalist *Gemeinschaft*, or sense of community, which

he equated with the German *Volk*. Between 1933 and 1939, however, his speeches concentrated as much on regeneration of the
nation and the economy and on the pernicious evils of democracy
and the Versailles *Diktat* as they did on race and anti-Semitism.
In fact, he gave them a greater stress.

Hitler's anti-Jewish policy* was implemented step by step to
avoid scandalizing many Germans as well as foreigners. Theodore
Abel's *Why Hitler Came to Power*, a careful investigation of 600
Nazi party members, shows that many Nazis freely admitted that
anti-Semitism weakened rather than strengthened the Nazi appeal.
Nazi publications after 1933 confirm Abel's findings: *Der Stürmer*,
the main Nazi Jew-baiting paper, complained on 30 November
1935 that too many Germans opposed or were lukewarm to anti-
Jewish measures; so did the *N.S. Parteikorrespondenz*, the official
party newsletter, on 22 August 1938, *Das Schwarze Korps*, the SS
paper, on 17 November 1938, and several regional party papers
between 1933 and 1939.

Organized legal action against Jews started on 7 April 1933 when
Jews were excluded from the civil service and most teaching posts.
However, the decree was relatively mild since it pensioned off
those dismissed at 80 per cent of their full normal salary. Gradually
entrance into the professions was closed to Jews; but it was not
until 1938 that those practising were excluded. In September 1935,
over two and a half years after Hitler came to power, the notorious
Nuremberg Laws ordained that Jews could no longer be citizens;
but the laws allowed them to remain members of the German state.
The laws also forbade mixed marriages and sexual intercourse
between Jew and German. Harassment rather than full-scale
attack continued until 1938. Then, Jews had to take the name of
Israel or Sarah, and have their passports and identity papers
stamped with the letter 'J'. On 9 November 1938 a 'spontaneous',
officially organized pogrom occurred after a young Jew had assas-
sinated a German Embassy official in Paris; Jewish synagogues
were burned down, damaged, defiled; Jewish shops and houses
were looted; many Jews were beaten up, some were killed, and
several thousands temporarily imprisoned in concentration camps.
The pogrom green-lighted a policy of more than harassment; a
spate of decrees forbade Jews to visit places of entertainment, hold

* The concentration camps and extermination policy will be considered in Chapter 4.

driving licences or own motor vehicles, possess property or valuables, and to live in any but Jewish areas. One East Prussian municipality forbade the service of Aryan-owned bulls to Jewish-owned cows, and elsewhere Jewish mothers were not permitted to wet-nurse Aryan babies.

Nevertheless no solid evidence has been discovered to show that, before total war, Hitler intended the extermination of the Jews. Other Nazis spoke of liquidation of the Jews before 1939. Hitler's first mention of the annihilation of the Jewish race was in a speech on 30 January 1939 celebrating the sixth anniversary of his appointment as Chancellor amidst the rumblings of menacing war. In his speech Hitler uttered a vague threat that if Jewry plunged Germany into another world war, the Jewish race would not triumph but would be annihilated. He did not say how or by whom. It is true that in *Mein Kampf*, written in the mid-1920s, he had stated that if 'at the beginning of the War twelve or fifteen thousand of these Hebrew corrupters of the people had been held under poison gas, as happened to hundreds of thousands of our very best German workers in the field, the sacrifice of millions at the front would not have been in vain'. These words have often been quoted by historians as witnessing Hitler's long-standing intention to exterminate the Jewish race; but their content and context clearly show that he had in mind those Jews whom he regarded as the 'Versailles and Weimar criminals who had stabbed Germany in the back' during the war. In any case, 15,000 Jews does not equal the Jewish race. Furthermore, it needs recalling that Hitler's mention of gassing Jews was not a prediction of the gas-chambers of Auschwitz and elsewhere, but, without doubt, a memory of himself being a victim of poison gas in 1918. Elsewhere in *Mein Kampf* Hitler says that he was 'oppressed' by the medieval pogroms against Jews and would not want them repeated. No reading of *Mein Kampf* can show that anywhere in his book does Hitler adumbrate, either explicitly or implicitly, the extermination of the Jews, however much it shows his fear and hatred of them. The statements to the contrary of so many historians are the product of either irresponsibility or failure to read *Mein Kampf*. That book is much too flimsy evidence that Hitler always intended the extermination of Jewry. Hatred sometimes leads to murder, but it by no means makes it inevitable.

Before 1934, Hitler told Rauschning (then a confidant of

Hitler's, though Hitler's enemy in exile when he wrote his books) that he had no intention of destroying the Jews because it was 'essential to have a tangible enemy, not merely an abstract one', and he adapted Voltaire's saying about God to state that if the Jew did not exist 'we should have to invent him'. Before 1939—perhaps even before 1941 when the policy of total extermination called by the Nazis 'the Final Solution' was finally decided upon—Nazi measures seem to have been designed to provide a scapegoat, to offer opportunities for loot and openings in professions where Jews were prominent, and to drive German Jews into exile after being despoiled of almost all their property. About half Germany's 600,000 Jews did flee. The others could not bring themselves to believe that worse and worse was to follow. The thought that they would be exterminated either never occurred to them or was incredible. After the war a wry saying about German Jews was current amongst surviving Jews: 'The pessimists went into exile; the optimists went into the gas-chambers.'

War made it possible to focus ideology on racialism. German victories in the first half of the war nourished the belief that *Herrenvolkismus* was feasible. Until 1941 shreds of respect for American public opinion caused hesitation. The declaration of war against the U.S.A. as well as Russia in 1941, involving world war to the death, made a burning of the remaining civilized boats seem possible, even imperative. It is surely no simple coincidence that the Wannsee Conference of 20 January 1942, where the details of the Final Solution were worked out, was convened only a few weeks after the Japanese attack on Pearl Harbour on 7 December 1941.

Racialism springs from many sources other than simply the eternal human urge to find scapegoats and to bolster egos. In Germany, and elsewhere, both the Catholic and Protestant Churches had a record of anti-Semitism going back to the early days of Christianity. Anti-Semitism welled up, too, from a Gentile sense of the difference of Jews. Resentment at the difference in others existed long before the 1950s and 1960s. 'The stranger at the gate' has long been an object of fear, whether he be homosexual or hippie, coloured or Jew.

In the Middle Ages, the Jew was forced into a distinctive economic category. He could not own land since he could not swear a Christian oath of fealty to his overlord: hence he lived

107

in towns, and by trades other than agriculture. Most Jews even in the twentieth century entered occupations where they could work with fellow-Jews, and so keep the Jewish Sabbath and religious holidays; this helped to segregate them from the rest of society. Gentiles in the twentieth century sharpened this sense of difference in their own minds by a stereotype of Jewish physical difference. In fact, the Jew is not a separate, marked, physical type; many Jews are indistinguishable from Gentiles, and in parts of Spain, Italy and Eastern Europe there are many blond, Aryan-looking Jews. However, the stereotype was a half-truth in twentieth-century Western Europe because at the end of the nineteenth century many Jews were driven by pogroms from Eastern Europe, where their families had lived for centuries. Most of these Jews had the characteristic swarthy skin and hooked nose inherited from the Arab Semitic peoples from whom they had originated.

Many of the poorer Jews driven West by Russian pogroms in the 1880s and 1890s undercut local labour in unskilled jobs, thereby inciting anti-Semitism in the urban poor. More intelligent and richer Jews flocked into the new professions created by industrialization and into those of the greatly expanded old professions where entrance was not denied by the aristocratic caste system. In Germany, the army, the civil service and the teaching profession put up bars against Jews; but banking, journalism, medicine and many others remained open. In the 1920s, the proportion of Jews in some professions was ten times as high as in the whole population. Jews were given an educational head-start on Gentiles by their religion which had always tried to ensure at least a skill in the three Rs even when the Gentile population was almost wholly illiterate. So, superior grounding in education and well-to-do professional fathers ensured that the proportion of Jews to Gentiles among university students was noticeably higher than in the total population. Anti-Semitism was already strong in German universities where it was fertilized by professors, the great majority of whom were nationalist conservatives; but it became rabid in the 1920s when there was a glut of graduates on the professional market even before the Depression. So, an understandable fear of competition from Jews among rich and poor Germans aggravated an unjustifiable view of Jews as a different kind of human beings. More and more Germans looked on Jews as strangers and wanted to lock the gates against them.

Hitler capitalized on this growing anti-Semitism, though in economic terms, his dividends could not be great. Even if every Jew was deprived of his job, less than one-tenth of the unemployed Germans would benefit. However, the catch-cry of the Jewish menace paid its way when depicted as a Jewish world conspiracy against Germany. 'Explanations' of many of the world evils as the result of a conspiracy were popular in the inter-war years. Many otherwise sensible people in the West believed that wars were the result solely of conspiracies by armament manufacturers. Extreme left-wing people who are amazed that anyone could believe in a Jewish conspiracy might pause to consider whether they themselves do not believe that the world's main ills are caused by a conspiracy of a few capitalists, or, to use the title of a book by an outstanding exponent of the 'conspiracy theory', C. Wright Mills, by a 'power elite' of a few hundred Americans. Also, those who are disgusted at anti-Semitism in German universities before 1933 might reflect how popular anti-Catholicism still is among their academic colleagues. Anti-Catholicism is the anti-Semitism of Western intellectuals.

Fear and hatred of Jews were equalled or surpassed among Germans by fear and hatred of Slavs. Few memories west of the Rhine now recall that the Nazi régime exterminated as many civilian Slavs as Jews. In *Mein Kampf* Hitler's race hatred was directed also at the Slav whose nationalism had threatened in his youth the privileged position of the German minority in the multi-racial Austrian Empire; by the time he wrote *Mein Kampf* the same nationalism had fragmented the Austrian Empire and impoverished German Austria. It is often forgotten that much of Germany lies east of the Elbe, uncomfortably confronting Slav Europe. Germans have feared and fought Slavs more than they have feared and fought Anglo-Saxons and Latins. Metternich said that Asia began on the Ringstrasse, one of Vienna's main streets; and Germans were always apprehensive of the peril from the vast mysterious hinterland to the East from which had emerged the hordes of Genghis Khan, the armies of the Turks, and the teeming Russian millions. On that side, Germany had no geographical defence: no wide rivers, high mountains or protective sea. The east wind, unimpeded by geographical obstacles, blew from the Urals right across Germany.

When Hitler's war took Germans into Poland and Russia, they

were disgusted by the low level at which Slav peasants lived. They conveniently overlooked that much Slav degradation was the product of the ruthless German occupation. Yet, it was as easy as it was convenient for the German recruit on the Eastern front to fail to realize that so much of the degradation of the Poles and Russians had a German trade-mark. He came east in, say, 1942 and no one told him that the appalling conditions he saw in peasant villages were not the natural condition of the Slav: in fact, Goebbels kept impressing on him the exact opposite.

On the Eastern front a war of the utmost hate was waged between two bitterly conflicting ideologies. No Queensberry rules applied. War in the West was tame in comparison: so tame, in fact, that Englishmen usually regard World War One, rather than World War Two, as the terrible traumatic holocaust of modern European history. They recall that in World War One their dead amounted to one million, whilst in World War Two, the combined total of British and American dead was only two-thirds of one million; they forget that 55 million people were killed in World War Two, and that Russia alone suffered 20 million dead, 11 million of them soldiers—Russia had more soldiers killed in World War Two than *all* the combatant countries combined had soldiers killed in World War One. The immense scale of the casualties on the Eastern front is an indication of the ferocity of the fighting there. One side's atrocities whelped the other's counter-atrocities, and, as always, inhumanity spiralled upwards until no way could be found of breaking out of the vicious spiral. Prisoners of both sides were shot on the spot, or tortured; they were beaten, forced-marched, starved, worked, all to death. West of the Rhine only German atrocities are recalled. Although this one-sided memory may deal out poetic justice, it cannot shrug off the undeniable fact that the multitude of Russian atrocities intensified German race-hatred and provided a grist of truth to Goebbels' propagandist mill.

Racialism is not simply a matter of Führer decrees, executive action, the law courts, economic organization and social prestige. Nor is it only explicable in the psychological or sociological jargon of 'guilt complexes', 'protection', 'aggression' or 'paranoia'. Racialism pervades the whole of social living, and bites deep into everyday life particularly in war. It is not only in Nuremberg Laws but also in the frightened Jew fawning to avoid the Storm-trooper's boot, and so, with awful irony, 'proving' to the Storm-trooper the truth of Hitler's contemptuous judgment of the spine-lessness of Jews. It is not only in the SS, but also in the lack of understanding of orders in a foreign language. It is not only in abstract racial theory, but also in a German officer walking through Kiev, sleek, well-shaven, visored-cap over his eyes, looking at dirty, ragged, emaciated inhabitants in a distant, almost unseeing way, as though they were no more than animals cluttering the streets. It is not only in *Mein Kampf*, but also in Slav slave-labour on the farm or in the kitchen, dodging work, stealing food, having sexual intercourse behind the barn, and looking surly at orders. It is not only in radio broadcasts, but in the Pole out after curfew, stabbing a German for his money, food or weapons, or pulling a German woman into a dark street, raping her, and then cutting her throat. It is not only in Eichmann at his desk, but also in the comrade on the Eastern front being captured and tortured in your hearing by Russians who needed no concentration camp SS men to teach them how to stake out your friend naked in a sub-zero temperature so that he died agonizingly, or how to push barbed-wire up his anus, or how to thrust his testicles into boiling water so that the skin peeled off. None of this, of course, excuses German racialism, but it does help make it understandable.

The poorer strata of a society are, not surprisingly, more liberal on economic issues; but when liberalism is defined in other ways such as civil liberties or racial equality, the reverse is true. Low status and fundamentalist or chiliastic ideology are highly cor-related. Some of the most important contributing factors to both these phenomena are low education, low participation in politi-cal or voluntary organizations of any type, little reading and less thought, monotonous or isolated occupations, economic insecurity, and habituation to authoritarian patterns in workshop and home. A low level of sophistication and a high degree of insecurity lead to an extremist view of politics. So it was with the poorer German who made up the bulk of the population and army. Proud of his Fatherland; afraid of the revolutionary menace of Communist Russia; fighting a war of extinction; jealous of those better off than himself; nursing since 1918 an almost Irish sense of injustice; brought up in schools whose educational achievements had always been trivial; indoctrinated by the Hitler Youth and by skilful propaganda; magnetized by a Führer amazingly triumphant in peace and war; lost in a chaos of meanings; atomized by a long series of cataclysms culminating in totalitarian rule, it is not surprising that many ordinary Germans should embrace the notion that God appointed them to a master race.

5

Totalitarian control of the communication media—the third trait of a totalitarian régime—was achieved only gradually and never completely. Goebbels won control of broadcasting and films with relative ease, although care had to be taken that too many helpings did not lessen the audience's appetite. Total control of the Press was much harder to achieve. Germany in 1932 published more newspapers than any other country, its daily and weekly newspapers numbering 4,703. Berlin alone had 20 dailies, Hamburg 10, Cologne and Stuttgart each 8, Frankfurt 6, and Leipzig 5. Provincial cities usually had 2 or 3 dailies, and there was scarcely a town that did not have its own local paper.

On 4 October 1933 Goebbels had promulgated his Editor's Law, which was intended to put the Press under the control of the state and party. Editors were now theoretically subject to control, but until the lengthy business of building up an efficient organization of control was complete, they could discover many loopholes through which to fire their own ammunition. Moreover, a certain amount of latitude had to be allowed to important papers to pander to the susceptibilities of foreigners; not until as late in the war as 1943 was the world-famous liberal *Frankfurter Zeitung* suppressed. The Catholic Press proved especially frustrating. Worse still was the growing tendency of newspaper readers to turn to the sports' page or to reports of the latest murder or sex-crimes as propaganda dulled news; the law of diminishing returns applies as much to propaganda as to economics. A worrying drop in circulation alarmed Goebbels, to whom a propaganda pipeline into every home was a necessity. The propaganda pouring down the pipelines must often have run to waste; studies of newspaper-reading habits in Western countries strongly suggest that very few people read leading articles, and most take a newspaper's political line with a large grain of salt.

War eased Goebbels' worries. It gave him a vice-like grip on the Press, and readers no longer skipped or skimmed official pronouncements. War news was avidly scanned, even after 1943 by those who understood that 'a strategic withdrawal to consolidate conquests' was Nazi journalese for a German defeat. People often read the newspapers even though they bought them primarily to burn in the grate when fuel was rationed, or to block up bomb-shattered windows.

Indoctrination of German youth was necessarily slow, and the shortness of Hitler's régime allowed Nazism to gain a hold by this means over only a fraction of the population. It took time to write, publish and distribute Nazified school textbooks. Control of the many suspect or lukewarm schoolteachers was not easy until the usual rabid war-time militarism of civilians came to Goebbels' assistance. Wholesale dismissals of unreliable schoolteachers would have made the educational system unworkable. Even Nazified teachers could not rely on their pupils hearing or retaining the messages they imparted: schoolchildren have a disconcerting ability to look as though they are paying attention when, in fact, their mind is elsewhere. In addition many subjects, especially the sciences, are not readily politically colourable. Historians make much of the publication by a Nazi university professor of a book called *German Physics*; but reading beyond the title and the short Nazi preface reveals that the contents consisted of what were perfectly respectable physics for that time. The Jew, Einstein, was anathema to Nazis; but his theories had not found a place in many European textbooks on physics in the 1930s and 1940s. True, German university and school teachers preached a creed of German superiority; but it scarcely differed from that preached in France, England, America or elsewhere. It is also true that intending university students had to pass a political examination; but lip-service comes easily to all but the honest, fanatical or contra-suggestible.

The number of members of Nazi youth movement rose more slowly than the Nazi leaders would have liked. Between the end of 1933 and 1935 it increased from two and a quarter to a little short of four million. In 1937 it stood at six million, and at the end of 1939 at seven and three-quarter million. The steeper increase after 1935 was largely due to membership being made compulsory for all boys over 10. Membership was not compulsory for girls, and, perhaps significantly, the *Bund Deutscher Mädel*, the League of German Girls, could boast less than half-a-million members at the end of 1939. For many young Germans, the Nazi

Youth Movement provided little more than a chance to wear a uniform, march with a band through the streets, ramble in the countryside or play games in their meeting-hall. Some must have joined voluntarily to get out of their parents' home. At meetings, apart from vague obeisances in the direction of the Führer, often there was little political activity unless the youth leader was a dedicated Nazi with sufficient personality to magnetize the attention of his group. Often the Nazi youth movement branch differed little from the one it superseded, except for a change in uniform and a new portrait on the wall. Of course the youth movement had numerous fanatics, and bits and pieces of propaganda dribbled into the minds of all but the dullest and worst listeners. It is, however, a travesty, based on very insufficient evidence and very little knowledge of the young, to suggest that all, or even most, members of the Hitler Youth were inevitably ardent Nazis, or grew up fanatical followers of the Führer. War naturally raised the political temperature in Hitler Youth meeting-places. In the final months of the war, Hitler Youth units fought with tenacity and ferocity alongside their elders. Yet, it is impossible to estimate how much they were motivated by Nazi ideology, how much by patriotism, how much by a natural liking for playing at being real soldiers.

In peacetime, the Nazi propaganda aces were their mass spectacles and their master-orators, Hitler and Goebbels. The leaders made a habit of speaking in the evenings, starting when the audience's mental faculties were dulled by work and ending too late for the audience to retire to coffee-house or beer-hall where critical faculties might return to life. Both Hitler and Goebbels had an intuitive command of audiences: both were outstanding virtuosos in knowing how to work themselves and their listeners to an unthinking pitch of mass excitement by the repetition of incantatory phrases to the point of hysteria. When Hitler spoke, men and women hissed the hate he invoked, groaned and sobbed to relieve the tension he aroused, and were galvanized by his spitting out of violent words like 'smash', 'traitor', 'fight' and 'blood'. His excitatory methods had the art which Germans call '*Fingerspitzengefühl*'—'finger-tip feeling'—devoid of the necessity for reasoned argument. After 1940, Hitler retired into seclusion and Goebbels made all the main speeches. But Hitler's magic at meetings was no longer needed; Germans were at the mercy of the urgent imperatives of a total war—and a totalitarian terroristic police. The war provided a propaganda impulse of its own; the police ensured that no rivals could communicate rival propaganda.

The German Churches, like the army, were citadels, and the Nazis had to capture or neutralize them if they were to have absolute power. A strong and militant Church might have fought successfully against the formidable battery of Nazi-controlled mass media, because it was itself one of the mass media. But the German Churches were weak, their morale sapped by industrialization, urbanization, materialism, and intellectuals' criticism and disbelief. Percipient churchmen knew how thin was the gloss of religious belief coating most German churchgoers. They knew that German Christians were Germans as well as Christians. They knew that the Churches were fighting with obsolete muskets against modern automatic weapons.

Even the most pugnacious souls faced formidable difficulties and dilemmas in the fight against Nazism. Before 1933, Catholic churchmen had forbidden members of their flock to join the Nazi party. Yet, what were they to do when the Nazis became the legally constituted temporal authority? The question of what is God's and what Caesar's has bedevilled Church–State relationships from the earliest days of Christianity. But how is a Christian to know what is Caesar's? How is he to know when the temporal authorities ordained by God act against God? When should he profess Christ and obey God rather than man?

The Lutheran churches are reputedly notorious for unquestioning obedience to the temporal authorities. The Lutheran attitude, however, differs little from the Catholic. True, the Lutheran Churches have never engaged in the outright battles with their temporal rulers that have, at times, marked the history of the Catholic Church in the Middle Ages; but, in modern times, the Catholic Church has fought only when a war of aggression has been launched against them, as when Bismarck declared war against Catholics in the *Kulturkampf* in the 1870s. Although Lutheran tradition—like Catholic tradition—has lacked consistency and uniformity in answering the question of the rightness of resistance, this is more evidence of the difficult complexity of the question and of the practical difficulties of resistance than of the lack of Christian courage in Lutherans. Luther himself has often been misrepresented, not least by his followers; the Augsburg Confession of 1530, although refusing to advocate any kind of revolt even against tyranny, does enjoin passive resistance against whatever is contrary to God's clear commandments. Unfortunately, however, God's commandments are rarely clear to mere man. For instance, the Fifth Commandment says 'Thou shalt not kill'; yet, the Church, God's representative on earth, has sanctified wars and crusades as well as the execution of criminals and heretics.

The complications of religious resistance to the Nazis were practical as well as theological. In Germany, unlike in England, non-conformist traditions offered no inspiring example. The Churches were Established; and the Sects, such as the Mennonites, Baptists and Jehovah's Witnesses, were foreign in origin and tiny in numbers, only about 150,000 in all in the 1930s. In 1933 most churchmen were deceived by Hitler and had no inkling of his real character and of the hideousness to come. True to form, Hitler moved guardedly against the Churches despite the urgings of anti-Christian advisers like Rosenberg and Bormann and his own contempt for Christianity. Churchmen were deceived. Writing after the war, Karl Barth, a strong anti-Nazi and a profound Christian thinker, wrote in *Eine Schweizer Stimme 1938 bis 1945*, 'A Swiss Voice, 1938 to 1945', that the Nazis had deserved to be given time and opportunity to prove themselves, and it was the duty of the Churches to remain neutral. The conclusion of a Concordat between the new Reich and the Papacy gave grounds for optimism especially since no Concordat had ever been concluded with the whole German state, the only ones existing being between the Papacy and certain of the *Land* governments. To Protestants, Hitler's institution of the office of *Reichsbischof* seemed to have advantages in the face of the separatism of the various Lutheran Churches and their need for a keystone representative in relations with the Reich government and foreign Churches. Although it quickly became clear that Hitler's intentions were not peaceable, Hitler concentrated his sniping in 1933 on the Churches in Prussia and left the south surprisingly alone. Goebbels radio propaganda avoided the subject of religion and eschewed anti-religious remarks, except, implicitly, by drumming on Teutonic mythology. Not until 1935 and 1936 were some Catholic monks and nuns arrested, and then the charges were currency offences and immorality, which, although trumped up, were, after all, within Caesar's province. The Students' Christian Movement was allowed to continue until July 1938; and only on 14 July 1939 was a Nazi party regulation passed forbidding clergymen and those closely connected with the Churches to be party members.

War allowed more ferocious Nazi attacks. Seminaries and religious schools were closed. Newspapers were ordered in March 1944 to use the word 'Providence' instead of 'God'. General Heinrichi was warned that his Christianity was incompatible with the aims of National Socialism, although he was not a party member. In 1940, however, Hitler bowed to religious outrage at his euthanasia programme. As late as 1942, a *Gauleiter* could still belong to a Church; and the army kept its chaplains until the end. Although hundreds of recalcitrant German pastors and priests were sent to concentration camps, the slow insidiousness of the attack helped lull opposition. A dramatic, all-out onslaught, such as Bismarck's *Kulturkampf* or the campaigns waged by some anti-clerical French governments against French Catholics, might have incited more opposition.

Other considerations, also, emasculated Christian opposition. Before 1933 the German Protestant Churches were not united: there was no organization like the post-1945 *E.K.i.D.* (Evangelical Church in Germany). In 1933 a variety of 28 *Landeskirchen*, or regional Churches, existed with shades of difference in theology and dogma, size and importance; some were entirely or predominantly Lutheran; others were 'Reformed'; a few were a mixture. All were loosely joined in the *Kirchenbund*; but this Church Union had been born only after World War One, and still suffered bad teething troubles. In 1933 the *Kirchenbund* was replaced by a Nazi-sponsored German Evangelical Church headed by a *Reichsbischof*. On the other hand, the Nazis encouraged further division by fostering the *Glaubensbewegung Deutscher Christen*, the German Christian Faith Movement, a group of militant Nazi churchmen attracted by anti-Semitism and the *Führer-Prinzip*. In 1933 the Movement boasted 3,000 of Germany's 17,000 Protestant pastors. This Protestant fifth column declined in later years, but it had served Hitler's purposes. However, unintentionally Hitler midwifed the courageous Confessional Church which held its first Synod at Barmen at the end of May 1934. The Confessional Church grew out of theological resistance to the German Christians and to Nazism, and its roll of honour included the names of famous resisters like Niemöller and Dietrich Bonhöffer, both of whom were sent to concentration camps. Niemöller survived, but

Bonhöffer was executed a few tragic days before the end of the war.

To know when, how, or even whether to resist was not easy for churchmen with active consciences. At the height of Nazi power Bonhöffer and a friend had to attend a Nazi function which was punctuated by many Hitler salutes. His friend was distressed to see Bonhöffer vigorously saluting with the rest. Bonhöffer said: 'Put up your arm! this thing isn't worth dying for.' Bonhöffer knew that the majority of pastors were politically neutral. Some, no doubt, kept neutral for fear of their own skins. A seat at each church service was always occupied by a Gestapo agent taking notes of clerical words straying from the strictly ecclesiastical path. After 1941 turbulent priests and pastors were coerced by measures increasing in severity by seven stages. The first was a warning; then, a fine; third, came a prohibition to preach; fourth, exile from the parish; fifth, an order to cease all clerical activities; sixth, short-term arrest; and seventh, *Schutzhaft*, or protective custody, a Gestapo euphemism for imprisonment in a concentration camp. It is glib and uncharitably casual to blame churchmen for preferring their own life to having to descend these seven rungs to a secular Hell.

Many brave churchmen chose neutrality for reasons other than fear of crucifixion by the Gestapo. Protestant clergy had given hostages to fortune by marrying and having children; and whilst profound admiration cannot possibly be withheld from the indomitable courage of a Pastor Schneider who suffered agonizingly before he died a tortured death in Buchenwald rather than submit to the Nazi demand to cease to minister to his flock, it is impossible to be certain he was right when he told his wife that his martyrdom would achieve more good for his six children than surrender to the Nazis. The Gestapo stopped any publicizing of the fate of men like him and the pall of silence covering his martyrdom prevented courageous opponents of the Nazis from drawing resolution from his example. On the other hand, when his martyrdom became known after the war, his self-sacrifice uplifted some post-war Germans and others. But how much did it achieve before 1945 in preventing or lessening Nazi Satanism?

Catholic priests devoted to celibacy had also given hostages to fortune. A clergyman's flock needs his spiritual ministrations, and Gestapo prohibition of such ministrations could mean that parishioners' souls could be imperilled, perhaps mortally. Often he could not be replaced even by a politically compliant minister. The order to cease parochial ministrations was so feared by the clergy that at least one Vicar-General implored Himmler to lift the ban on one priest and instead place him under short-term arrest. A brave yet wise churchman could recognize his dilemma when Nazi paganizing influence waxed where Christian influence waned. War worsened the dilemma. The German army needed chaplains, and the Nazi government placed many obstacles in the way of training new clergy. Of 18,047 Protestant ministers 6,687 were acting as army chaplains; and 1,022 theological students, candidates for the ministry, and religious assistants were in the Medical Corps. War created such a condition that in the homeland every third congregation lacked clerical ministrations, and in rural areas where pastors had to take over two or more congregations, every second congregation was without spiritual care. Ministers in Germany were overworked. Almost all young ministers were serving with the army, and only the elderly remained in Germany. Old age, fatigue, the deprivation of coal and petrol by war-time rationing, the exhaustion brought by the struggle against Nazism since 1933, the effects of Allied bombing, and the evacuation of civilians from bombed-out cities, took their toll on ministers and made it extremely hard, sometimes impossible, for them to cope with vital spiritual duties. Aware of these circumstances, only those who think superficially, or are viciously anti-clerical, or do not realize how all-important spiritual ministration is to the true Christian, can conclude that a churchman's duty to offer himself as a Christian martyr is obvious and clear-cut.

Would martyrdom have halted Nazism or toppled Hitler? Nazism was winning away Christians; the number of Christians was declining under the influence of additional forces; the religion of patriotism was often stronger than the religion of Christ particularly to those who did not understand Nurse Cavell's warning that 'patriotism is not enough' or did not realize that Dr Johnson's saying that 'patriotism is the last refuge of a scoundrel' was startlingly applicable to Hitler. The number of Catholic denominational schools fell between 1931 and 1938 from 15,256 to 9,639 through Nazi closures and lack of aspirants. War winnowed the remaining schools even more disastrously. Germans, after the manner of humankind, were well able to live with a jumble of

Christian and Nazi ideas in their minds. Before 1939, who knew which they would prefer if a choice had to be made? After 1939 the answer was obvious; Churches stood no chance of outbidding Nazism by calling a crusade against Nazism when the *Vaterland* and the *Heimat*, or homeland, meant to Germans so much more than their counterparts—if they existed in anything like the same intensity—meant to Englishmen, Americans, or even Frenchmen.

Open protests by churchmen would undoubtedly lose Church members forced to a choice. Some ministers might fear that their congregations and chances of promotion would fall together. More feared the consequences of driving Christians into a pagan wilderness, however righteous the Church's cause might be. The Church has to be preserved as intact as possible with as many members as possible for the day when tyranny ends. The Church is eternal; a Nazi tyranny is temporary. Decision in their dilemmas cannot have been easy for churchmen.

The refusal of Church leaders to raise the standard of revolt against Hitler does not need as explanation their fear of Communism. Fear of Communism did play its part: for a Christian—or anyone with a belief in humaneness—how real is the choice offered between the Tweedledum of Nazism and the Tweedledee of Communism?* Also, aside from his personal opinions and theological beliefs, the Church leader knew that fear of Communism only welded his flock to Nazi rule and minimized hope of insurrection. True, protests from German Church leaders stopped the euthanasia campaign waged by Hitler in 1939 and 1940 to liquidate Germans with diseases like tuberculosis and insanity. Protests, however, were not revolt; and, in any case, Hitler may have been influenced by the fear that Germans would not stomach the liquidation of fellow Germans, and by concern about reactions in the still neutral U.S.A. The fact that the euthanasia programme was kept as far as possible secret and that it was stopped immediately the secret was out, lends credence to this view. On the other hand, few Church leaders raised protests against the extermination of Jews and Slavs. Their silence may have been due to lack of knowledge of the extermination policy, which was a top Nazi secret. Or if Church leaders heard rumours they may have been, like many others, unable to believe such horrors. The anti-Nazi

* For further consideration of this question see Chapter 5.

Bishop Otto Dibelius said in 1955 that when he was told in 1942 of the ghastly policy and practices in extermination and concentration camps, he genuinely found it impossible to believe his informer. Hitler probably reckoned, with some justification, that most other Germans would not believe, or, if they did, that they would be less squeamish about the extermination of Jews and Slavs than of fellow Germans. In any case, the Gestapo functioned efficiently. Monsignor Bernard Lichtenberg, of St Hedwig's Cathedral in Berlin, protested loudly; he was arrested, imprisoned and died on his way to Dachau in 1943. No news of his protests or martyrdom appeared in the Press or on the radio.

A strong case can be—and has been—built up condemning the sins of omission of the German Churches under Nazi rule, and part of the case carries conviction. Much too often, however, the difficulties and dilemmas confronting churchmen have been overlooked or unrealized. It needs to be remembered that they too were human: subject, like laymen, to human frailties, driven, like laymen, to a compromise between evils as the best of an agonizing circumstance.

Such a circumstance confronted Pope Pius XII in his six years of agony in a personal Garden of Gethsemane where he had to choose what action he should take on the nailing of Jews to their cross. The character and motives of the Pope and the Catholic Church have been travestied and smeared with filth by Rolf Hochhutz's play *The Representative*, and ignorance is the most charitable explanation of why so many have accepted his indictment and buttressed it with further writings, some of which, like Saul Friedlander's *Pius XII and the Third Reich*, make hardly warrantable claims to be scholarly. Pius XII is arraigned on many charges: of being an admirer of Hitler and Nazism; of supporting Nazism as a bulwark against Communism; of being a callous Pilate who washed his hands of the Jews, of fearing for his own life, of refusing to excommunicate and anathematize Hitler and German Catholics, of preferring to protect the Church's investments rather than save Jewish lives.

Pius XII did not wash his hands of the fate of the Jews. Pinchas Lapide is a Jew who has made a balanced, well-evidenced study of the Pope's actions. Lapide used mainly Jewish sources, and neither asked for nor received any assistance from the Vatican. He proves beyond the doubt of any reasonable person that the Catholic

Church under Pius XII's guidance saved the lives of 860,000 Jews —or more than the combined total saved by all the other Churches, religious institutions and rescue organizations. He shows that many prominent, and ordinary, Jews have gratefully recognized Pius's humane contribution to Jewry, and that Israel has publicly and officially acknowledged it. The American Jewish conductor, Leonard Bernstein, on hearing of Pius's death in October 1958, prefaced a concert by the New York Philharmonic Orchestra by calling for a minute's silence to commemorate 'the passing of a very great man'. Letters to Israeli newspapers have suggested that a 'Pope Pius XII Forest' be planted in the Judaean hills 'to perpetuate fittingly the memory of the humane services rendered by the late pontiff to European Jewry'. Many in supposedly Christian Europe could learn a necessary lesson in Christian charity, and in the honest search for, and recognition of, truth, from Jewish Israel.

The Allied record of saving Jews compares shamefully with that of the Catholic Church under Pius XII. The governments of Roosevelt and Churchill refused to take any real action. Despite repeated requests from respected Jews and responsible Jewish bodies, they refused to bomb the crematoria incinerating Jews, an action which would have halted the death machinery for a time sufficient to save tens of thousands of Jewish lives. The British refusal quoted 'technical difficulties' for its refusal. Presumably, the lives of perhaps a hundred R.A.F. men were considered more valuable than the lives of 10,000 or more Jews. The British government refused to allow more than the usual small quota of Jews into Palestine, and was instrumental in turning back to certain death one ship loaded with Jews fleeing Nazism. In 1963 the U.S. State Department revealed that the British government expressed fear in 1943 lest the Germans change over from a policy of extermination of the Jews to one of extrusion thereby embarrassing other countries by flooding them with refugees. In 1944 Roosevelt helped block efforts of the U.S. Congress to help Jews find refuge in Palestine from the Nazi slaughter. Whilst the King of Denmark defied the Nazi occupation so that all but 52 of his country's 6,500 Jews were saved, and whilst the Finnish government, Nazi Germany's ally, saved all but four of Finland's 2,000 Jews, none of the democracies fighting, so they said, for humanity would give sanctuary to more than a handful of persecuted Jews. Hitler had allies in occupied Europe to help him in his policy of extermination; he also had, as allies in that policy, the Western Allies and Communist Russia. The Vatican was no ally of Hitler. It hid and protected thousands of Jews in monasteries, convents, other religious havens, and in the Vatican City itself.

The Pope did not publicly protest against the extermination of the Jews. Some good reasons existed for this omission. For instance, many Catholic dignitaries, especially in Poland, begged him not to speak out because protests only brought reprisals. Again in Holland in 1942 the Catholic bishops protested to the Nazi authorities against the deportation of the Jews, and, although they could not persuade the Nazi occupation authorities to stop them altogether, they did obtain a concession which exempted all Christianized Jews and all Jews in mixed marriages; when the Catholic Archbishop of Utrecht on the next Sunday denounced Nazi deportations, the reprieve was withdrawn, and the exempted Jews were deported to extermination. The Red Cross, dedicated to the alleviation of suffering, also did not protest against Hitler's atrocities because it justifiably feared that Hitler would stop its work of charity for prisoners of wars, many of whom owe their lives to the Red Cross parcels.

The assumption that, had Pius XII openly protested, Hitler would have been compelled to halt his extermination policy is facile. Pius knew the facts of German religious life as well as German churchmen did; he could have no hope that Catholic Germans, let alone Protestant Germans, would—or could—revolt against Hitler. He could have no expectations that they would even believe him. Equally facile is the claim that he could have saved the Jews by excommunicating Hitler and putting Germany under an Interdict. How often have excommunications and interdicts succeeded? In July 1949, the Papacy—perhaps smarting under the charge of a sin of omission between 1933 and 1945, and certainly aware of the growing strength of Communism in Italy—excommunicated all Communists and fellow-travellers. The Communists increased their vote in each succeeding election.

Pius was not a cold, callous man. He was reserved and shy. He was, however, extremely sensitive; probably his reserve and shyness were the product of his sensitivity. His warm-heartedness, well-developed sense of humour, charm, and tenderness are well attested by those who knew him intimately. The accusation that he feared death at Nazi hands, if he protested, is quickly dismissed by anyone aware of his courage. Pius had served many years in Germany before becoming Pope and had come to love Germany; but there is ample evidence that he loathed Nazism, in part because he *did* love Germany.

Anyone with a knowledge of the facts must agree that Pius was placed in an agonizing dilemma, and it cannot be doubted that he spent many long hours on his knees praying for guidance between 1939 and 1945. Even if it is judged that he chose wrongly, it has to be admitted that his was a terrible dilemma. He may have been, without meaning to be, a Peter for whom the cock crowed thrice; but, like Peter's predicament, his awful agony has to be appreciated. His—and the Church's—dilemma was part of the tragedy of the Jews.

6

The Nazi terroristic police—the fourth totalitarian trait—was really sired by total war, if 'terroristic' connotes the Hell of a Belsen, a Buchenwald, an Auschwitz. After 1939, Himmler out-Himmlered Himmler. In the years of peace his police were not appreciably worse than those of Franco or Castro, and probably Franco's concentration camps held in the mid-1960s as many inmates as Himmler's before 1939. No doubt Franco's secret police in the 1960s and Himmler's Gestapo before 1939 froze with fear many would-be opponents; but so did the secret police of both Napoleons and all the nineteenth-century Czars. To equate the Nazi secret police before the war with that during the war is to equate grey with black.

War, rabid racialism, and Himmler's energy accelerated the number of camps from the few that existed in 1939 to little short of 1,000 during the height of the war. At the Nuremberg trials, Höss, for some time commandant of Auschwitz, testified that there were over 900 camps in which inmates were worked or beaten to death or straightaway exterminated. Most camps were outside Germany, but several hundreds were on German soil. Although few Germans knew that extermination was the business of the camps, most heard enough to know that the way of the political transgressor is hard, and not at all the romantic adventurous business it sometimes appears to the liberal who counsels resistance from his suburban armchair. They had learnt that already before 1939. Although the lips of freed inmates were sealed by the threat of return to the camp if they revealed how they had been maltreated, enough information reached the public to arouse and keep alive fear. Lack of precise knowledge, not surprisingly, led to exaggerations of the extent and power of the police system.

Himmler had steadily dug his way to power. On Hitler's 46th birthday on 20 April 1934, Himmler united all the political police under his own control, and on 17 June 1936 he was made supreme commander of all German police. A network of espionage and information on unreliable Germans at home and abroad was patiently constructed at No. 8 Prinz Albrechtstrasse, formerly the Academy of Arts where the most famous fancy-dress balls had been held. Now at No. 8 the sound of threats and blows and screams replaced the music of Strauss and Lehar waltzes, and Berliners crossed the street rather than pass close by the Gestapo H.Q. The emergency decree of 28 February 1933 had given the Gestapo extremely wide arbitrary powers, but its actions were still being contested in the courts in 1935, although usually unsuccessfully. On 25 January 1938 the Gestapo was freed from any interference by judicial or administrative courts. However, some judges managed to preserve a few shreds of justice until as late as 1943. Then, Hitler savaged the judges, reorganized the Ministry of Justice, and compelled every judge to consult the Gestapo on the verdicts to be given and the sentences to be inflicted before ever the trial took place. For all practical purposes where politics entered in, judges became ventriloquist dummies.

In the war the political police became a totalitarian, terroristic system dominated by the black-uniformed SS. Tens of thousands of files were kept on suspects; no one knew who might be a Gestapo spy or informer; the Gestapo registered alphabetically the names and descriptions of all wanted men in a weekly blacklist; and a copy was sent to each police office in the Reich. The blacklist, and frequent, unexpected check-ups and road-blocks made it very hard for those wanted by the police to stay free.*

The failure of the plot to assassinate Hitler on 20 July 1944 brought police power to its apogee, if the ability to destroy lives

---

* The SS and the concentration camps will be discussed in the next chapter.

and spread terror is counted power. The police were a state within a state responsible to no other authority but a Führer too intent on moving armies to bother with purely domestic concerns. Police arrested at will; they condemned suspects at what amounted to a travesty of drum-head court-martials; in the final days they hung 'defeatists' and deserters on street lamp-posts and left the corpses dangling with warning notices tied to them; they executed prominent Resistance leaders, and sometimes their families, only days before Allied troops could arrive to liberate them. As far as was possible, in 1944 and 1945 terror had become total.

7

The failure to assassinate Hitler in 1944 pulled tight the noose of total control around the neck of the army. The plot had been directed from the Bendlerstrasse building housing the Army High Command in Germany, and the bomb had been planted at Hitler's headquarters in East Prussia by an army officer, Colonel Claus Schenck von Stauffenberg.

Control of the armed forces—the fifth of the totalitarian traits—is of the utmost importance to a totalitarian tyranny. No dictatorship—or, for that matter, no other form of government—can survive against the wish of its army. Much more than a Church, a united army is a potential island of resistance impregnably moated against its government's attacks and invincibly equipped to dethrone its government. The proliferation of military dictatorships in the underdeveloped parts of the world since 1945 is good, convincing evidence that a united army can easily be the King-maker. This was not news to students of history. In England before 1914, one reason why the ruling classes made concessions to the lower classes was that they had no real repressive armed forces at their disposal. There was no standing army; the police were not spread extensively over the country until late in the century. They were seldom armed except with batons; and the rank-and-file were all recruited from the class of the 'oppressed'. On the continent of Europe, on the other hand, governments did have standing armies as well as efficient police forces, and despotism could continue. It is no accident that it needed unsuccessful war, and the ensuing economic and administrative chaos, to destroy the allegiance of the armed forces and police, and allow the overthrow of the Romanoffs in Russia, the Habsburgs in

Austria-Hungary, the Hohenzollerns in Germany, and the Otto-mans in Turkey. The critical moment in Russia in February 1917 was when the army and police in Petrograd started to go over to the revolutionaries. In 1905-6 revolution had been defeated because army and police remained loyal to the Tsar. Similarly, in 1848 it was the professional armies that destroyed the revolutions that spread over Europe.

The nineteenth-century military machines were primitive com-pared with the technologically-developed resources at the disposal of the modern despotic or totalitarian government backed by its army. The sad truth is that no domestic revolution has succeeded against armed forces loyal to the government. What happened in Hungary in 1956 is a recent example of this. It took superior armed forces from outside to bring about the overthrow of Fascist Italy and Nazi Germany. Modern history offers little or no hope of success to domestic revolt against totalitarianism unless the armed forces desert or disintegrate.

War—or rather victories in the early years of the war—gave Hitler control of the German army. In 1933 and the years im-mediately following, he needed no more than the army's tolerance of his régime. An early attempt at gaining totalitarian control of the *Reichswehr* (or *Wehrmacht*, as it was later called), or a purge similar to Stalin's purge of the Red Army in 1937, were unneces-sary. In fact, if Hitler had attempted early totalitarian control of the army, he probably would have stirred up enough opposition and unity among the army leaders to topple his régime. However, he shrewdly refrained from hampering or annoying the army leaders until he was in a strong enough position to use the army for his own purposes despite opposition from within it. Various other factors also made the army docile: rearmament kept the Army High Command happy and too occupied to take a serious interest in politics; the restoration of German prestige filled them with as much patriotic pride as it did most other Germans; the army had immunity from the political police so that they were the only Germans at whose doorstep the Gestapo had to halt; the presence until 1938 of highly respected leaders like General Beck and General Fritsch was reassuring; the belief—perhaps a naïve one, and certainly, as matters turned out, a wrong one—that they held the ace of trumps made army leaders think that they could halt Hitler when they decided; a sense of honour kept doubters true to

127

the oath of allegiance they had sworn to Hitler. By the time they learned that Hitler had outmanœuvred them, victories in war naturally forged a strong bond of loyalty in soldiers to their country and government. When defeat followed defeat, it was a hard decision for a military man to elect to commit treason and to stab in the back a Germany threatened with conquest by Russian Communists.

The army's docility under Nazi rule, and the reasons for it, have been avidly misinterpreted by historians. A number of reasons account for this. One is that military history has been the Cinderella of historical studies ever since 'drum-and-fife' history, concentrating on diplomatic manœuvres and military campaigns, ceased to be popular at the beginning of the twentieth century, and economic, political, and social historians began to beat swords into ploughshares and to turn military chargers out to pasture, preferring to mount much more favoured hobby-horses. Military history has a place in very few historical courses at schools and universities. Habitually, history courses take the student up to the causes of, say, World War One, and then brazenly leap to the Treaty of Versailles, omitting any description or explanation of the actual war, except perhaps the domestic political machinations the war engendered. So the student and teacher is left oblivious of the traumatic effects of the war on soldiers and civilians, and of the character of armies and their leaders.

It is not altogether surprising that military history should be swamped by the wave of pacificist nausea at the horrors of war that has swept the Western world since 1918. That wave has been swelled by the atomic explosion over Hiroshima. There are, however, stranger reasons for the contemptuous neglect of military history. Almost all historians regard military men as not only blood-thirsty monsters, but also as oafs. For almost all historians, the soldier is even more of a villain than the businessman: the historian at least allows the businessman the virtue of having brains, however nefarious the uses to which he puts them. In actual fact, however, even in England and the U.S.A., the military profession has attracted some of the best minds in society. The Cardigans, Butlers, and Frenches are remembered in England; the Marlboroughs, Wellingtons, Montgomerys, and Alanbrookes are forgotten. The stupidity, crudity, and muddle of a Charge of the Light Brigade are recalled; the skill, subtlety, and organizational genius
128

of a D-Day are overlooked. Clemenceau's famous saying that 'war is too serious a business to be left to soldiers' badly needs alteration.

Only someone ignorant of generals could consider them naturally bloodthirsty. True, in the British navy in the eighteenth century, officers used to toast 'a long war and a bloody one'. But the glasses were filled as much by Dutch courage at the prospect of possible mutilation or death as by the wish to be promoted into dead men's shoes. In any case, those who drank the toast were junior officers. Certainly, in modern times, military commanders have usually gone to war with much heavier hearts than have the politicians and civilians who sent them to their business; military commanders are much more aware than politicians and civilians of the inevitable suffering and destruction of life that war brings. The fact that a commander has to send men to their deaths as cold-bloodedly as he can manage is not evidence of his callousness or blood-lust. If he allowed the thought of appalling casualties to prey on him he would suffer a nervous breakdown, or, at least, indecision, and the consequences of either would increase the suffering and slaughter. Wellington wept when he was shown the casualty list after Waterloo. He has by no means been unique among military commanders who have broken down in tears.

Military men, like policemen, are whipping-boys for civilians, especially those brought up in a democratic generation which rightly suspects the use of force. But society cannot exist without force in a world where men are not able to be perfect and always peaceful. This truth is essential to a proper assessment of why German generals accepted Hitler and Nazism. If generals are instinctively condemned, the human situations in which they are important cannot be soundly analysed.

In January 1933 military leaders accepted Hitler's appointment; some welcomed it. A variety of factors contributed to their attitude. Fear of civil war and Polish aggression played a part. So, too, did a shrewd suspicion, or conviction, that the junior ranks of the army were too riddled with Nazism to be trusted in any military attempt to stop Hitler. Others were sincerely moved by the mirage of a national arising that would obliterate the shame of the Versailles *Diktat*. Some soldiers were content to consider that what was good enough for Field-Marshal Hindenburg was good enough for Germany and its army. Yet others approved of Hitler whilst disapproving of Nazism. On the day after his appointment,

129

the new Chancellor unexpectedly appeared at the barracks of the Berlin regiment and addressed the soldiers moderately but invigoratingly. Von Hammerstein, the Commander-in-Chief of the army, invited Hitler to dinner at his home that night in company with the army leaders, and there Hitler spoke with a moderation that deeply impressed all. General Beck, who was later to lead plots against Hitler and be killed for his leading part in the assassination attempt of 20 July 1944, regarded Hitler in 1933 as moderate, and until as late as 1938 thought it possible to reform the régime by ridding the country of the Nazi Party and the Gestapo whilst retaining Hitler as head of the government. Nobody who knew Beck considered him lacking in intelligence, integrity, or decency. Another leading soldier, Erich von Manstein, at first approved of Hitler but not of the Nazis; no one knowing von Manstein could deny that he was a man of extraordinary intelligence and profound honour, even though he disliked democracy.

Many soldiers detested the Weimar régime as Socialist, and were willing to trade it for almost any other régime providing it was not communist. Hostility between *Reichswehr* and Social Democrats was mutual. Social Democrats made offensively clear their hatred of what they called 'militarism', and all but the most level-headed of them equated 'militarism' and *Reichswehr*.

The most general and important factor conditioning the attitude of army leaders to Hitler was probably political naïveté. The *Reichswehr* under the Weimar Republic was ordered by its commanders to rigidly eschew politics, although the commanders themselves did not always obey their own ruling. The Prussian officer code laid down that a good officer was concerned solely with his own military conduct and that of his men; the business of politics was not for him, but for civilians, and a soldier should stick to his military last, a view not peculiar to German soldiers. The autocracy of Bismarck and Wilhelm II had encouraged this view. Rearmament and the extraordinarily rapid expansion of the army, besides speaking a good word for Hitler, necessitated that army leaders throw themselves into their work with such enthusiasm and absorption that they had little or no time or energy for politics even if they had the inclination.

The German army commanders have been condemned for being '*Nur-Soldaten*', nothing but soldiers, for practising '*Vogelstrausspolitik*', head-in-the-sand politics, and for their conviction that their responsibility was to obey their political masters without question. It is true that Hitler was the beneficiary of this a-political attitude. But was it as stupid as post-war historians have insisted? After all, a chorus of British historians has berated the 58 British army officers who, in 'the Curragh Mutiny' in March 1914, took a political stand and resigned their commissions rather than obey the orders to coerce Protestant Ulster into union with Catholic Ireland. Again, historians indict generals like Haig in World War One for persistently playing a political hand in the conflict between soldiers and politicians, or, as it is irreverently known, the conflict between 'brasses' and 'frocks'. General MacArthur incurred opprobrium from historians by daring to join political battle with President Truman during the Korean War in the early 1950s. On the other hand, historians of World War Two have universally acclaimed Allied military leaders for refraining from meddling in politics. Apparently our military Levites—but not theirs—are entitled, even required, to pass politics by on the other side.

Should the German generals be censured for supporting Hitler's rearmament policy? Nowadays, most people deprecate the Treaty of Versailles. Their grounds for doing so are that it tore away too much territory from Germany, exacted excessive reparations, and thrust the blame for World War One down the German throat, all of which gave Hitler a stick to beat his way to power. The Treaty is rarely condemned for restricting Germany to an army so minuscule that it could not defend the country or restore order in the event of civil war. Many wise European statesmen in the 1930s, however, realized that the Treaty was indefensible for this reason, and accepted realistically Hitler's rearming although they did not like his methods. Only those who believed in total disarmament could expect a major European country to perpetually remain virtually defenceless.

The charge against German rearmament rests on three main grounds. The first, that it was *German* rearmament can be summarily dismissed. The second, that it was preparation for war, is more serious. None the less, there is no real evidence that, until the winter of 1937-8, the rearmament programme was anything but defensive in character. The army commanders certainly conceived it as defensive. For years after he came to power, Hitler permitted the General Staff to plan rearmament and strategy as they saw fit, without any other direction from him than that Germany should be brought to a level of military power equivalent to that of other leading countries. A third criticism of German rearmament is that it broke the Treaty of Versailles, a treaty which is now in disfavour.

The statistics of rearmament show that the policy was not menacing until 1938. Although there are minor discrepancies between, say, the memoirs of Hitler's Minister of Finance, Schwerin-Krosigk, *Es geschah in Deutschland (It happened in Germany)* and Burton H. Klein's *Germany's Economic Preparations for War*, general agreement exists that rearmament statistics leapt ominously only in 1938. Klein also demonstrates that civilian levels of consumption improved considerably during the same period. Contrary to the generally believed words of Göring that the German aim was guns *before* butter, German policy then was guns *and* butter.

Although Hitler, Göring and Goebbels made exaggerated boasts about the number of new German tanks and planes, and foreign statesmen believed them, the German army commanders had the true statistics on their desks, and considered that the figures did not add up to German aggression. The High Command moreover, concentrated its energies on plans for defensive war. True, it prepared plans for attacks on neighbouring countries; but this is part of the business of High Commands everywhere, and they fail in their duty if they do not have ready such plans. Attack is often the better part of defence, and plans of attack do not necessarily spell a war of aggression. Unless war is universally regarded as immoral and soldiers as criminals, it is as unfair to indict them on such a charge—it was done at the Nuremberg Trials—as it is to indict a businessman for planning to prevent his competitors outdoing him, or a politician for planning to win the next election.

Relatively few foreigners believed that Hitler's aim was aggressive war, despite the promulgation of the Four Year Plan on 9 September 1936, the bellicosity of Nazi speeches, the reoccupation of the Rhineland in 1936, the Anschluss with Austria, and the dismembering of Czechoslovakia in 1938 and 1939. Books like F. Sternberg's *Die Deutsche Kriegsstärke (The German War Establishment)* arguing that the German economy was already a war-time economy, were rarities in 1938 and were given little credence. Furthermore, the German High Command knew what foreigners did not know: that Hitler's foreign policy triumphs between 1936 and 1938 were accomplished with very meagre forces, and with much muddle and confusion amongst the troops. They also believed that only the British and French surrender at Munich in October 1938 saved the German army from having to display its weakness against the strong Czech defences on the mountainous Bohemian border. The High Command, also, knew that, before September 1939, Germans had less than 15 submarines capable of operating in the Atlantic. Such knowledge and beliefs inclined them the more to the view that aggressive war could not be envisaged, except by a reckless gambler. And they were not yet convinced that Hitler was a gambler reckless to the extent of drawing the sabre as well as rattling it. It is true that on 5 November 1937 Hitler disclosed to his War Minister, von Blomberg, to his Foreign Minister, von Neurath, and to the Commanders-in-Chief of the army (von Fritsch), the navy (Raeder), and the *Luftwaffe* (Göring) his highly secret intention to go to war by 1943 at the latest. But a few months after the conference, von Blomberg, von Fritsch and von Neurath were removed from their positions. The German High Command probably never heard of this conference earlier than the Nuremberg Trials.

Hitler's foreign policy had the appearance of a series of bluffs by an international gambler who held a weak military hand but trusted that his French and British opponents would throw in their hands because they were decadent democracies rattled by the pacificism of their public, by their memories of the awfulness of World War One, and by their fear that a second World War would extinguish civilization. Hitler's foreign policy may, in fact, have been one of bluff that led to war through overcalling. However, if it were otherwise and he did intend war to win *Lebensraum* in the East, hindsight now reveals that he relied on a method of war—the *Blitzkreig*, or short lightning war—that was completely unfamiliar to military and civilian minds educated in the lengthy war of 1914–18. Foreigners, deceived by Nazi boasts exaggerating German military strength, could think that Hitler was prepared to wage another World War One with a different outcome. German army leaders, aware of the true facts of German military strength, could not think the same when their minds ran in 1914–18 ruts. Only a tiny minority of German soldiers understood that a new kind of war was feasible. Guderian and von Manstein did; but they were looked on as rogue elephants by their colleagues, and the High Command saw to it that they held unimportant posts until

K

Hitler made protégés and prodigies of them. The General Staff can be convicted of military backwardness; yet, they stand in the dock in good company. Who of the Allied generals in 1939 was not preparing to fight the next war on the lines of the last war? Who of them, except a very junior General de Gaulle, did not ridicule the warnings of Liddell Hart, Fuller and Guderian himself that the nature of war had radically changed? Who of them appreciated the new military methods that those far-sighted military thinkers proposed and explained time and again with heart-breaking failure?

The political naïveté of the German army commanders is the most charitable excuse advanced by most historians to explain how Hitler gradually obtained control over the armed forces. It will not serve, however, as adequate explanation of the army commanders' behaviour when Hitler executed the Blood Purge of 30 June 1934. In this purge, Ernst Röhm, the leader of the Nazi paramilitary SA, and scores of other prominent SA men, were summarily liquidated. One main motive for the Purge was that Röhm was insistently pressing for the amalgamation of the SA and *Reichswehr* in a 'people's army', to be led, not surprisingly, by Röhm. Obviously, the *Reichswehr* bitterly opposed Röhm's plans and benefited by the elimination of this threat to its professional and semi-autonomous status. These obvious facts, joined to the common belief that military men will stop at nothing however discreditable, have led many historians to accuse the army commanders of complicity in the crime. Other less severe historians have condemned them of passivity when they should have acted to stop the crime.

The charge of complicity is based on one piece of 'evidence'. In *The Nemesis of Power*, J. W. Wheeler-Bennett states that a secret pact was made in April 1934 between Hitler and his Minister of War, von Blomberg, on board the cruiser *Deutschland*. The terms of the *Deutschland* Pact were said to be liquidation of the SA leaders by Hitler, thus leaving the army a clear field, in return for the army's support of Hitler as the successor to President Hindenburg who was clearly nearing death. General von Fritsch and Admiral Raeder, Commander-in-Chief respectively of the army and navy, were said to have participated in the Pact. Ever since Wheeler-Bennett wrote in 1953 his scathing—and at times inaccurate—attack on the German generals, the story of the *Deutschland* Pact has been uncritically accepted and repeated by almost all historians. The story is, however, based solely on an unsubstantiated claim in the *White Paper on the Executions of the 30th June*. This was published in 1935 in Paris by a number of German left-wing political refugees and is scarcely more than a polemical, political pamphlet. Its author is unknown and therefore cannot be questioned on his sources of information. Dr Robert J. O'Neill in *The German Army and the Nazi Party 1933–1939* has subjected the claim that there was a *Deutschland* Pact to scrupulously careful and balanced examination. He has concluded that there is no real evidence that it ever existed.

The charge that the *Reichswehr* stood by passively whilst Himmler's SS did the army's dirty work is equally flimsily based, although this has not prevented its uncritical acceptance. Dr O'Neill—the exception again—has pertinently asked why the army should be expected to stop the Purge and so help the defence forces of Germany falling into the hands of Röhm and the SA, who were universally regarded at the time as the most radical Nazis. Moreover—and Dr O'Neill has overlooked these points—the Nazi top leaders planned the Purge in the utmost secrecy, and Hitler did not take the final decision to order it until the day before. True, the army commanders were aware that Hitler intended dealing with the threat from Röhm and the SA, who wanted radical social as well as military changes. The order on 25 June to put the army in a state of alert must have warned them. There is, nevertheless, not a single piece of tangible evidence that the army commanders had any inkling of the violent and bloody methods Hitler was to use on 30 June. Slaughter was not the only possible way to checkmate Röhm. Also, it was the duty of the Commander-in-Chief to put the army in a state of alert, if, as he was led to believe, Röhm was planning a *putsch*. No evidence has been discovered that the army leaders only pretended to believe in the possibility of an SA *putsch*. If the army leaders genuinely believed in a possible SA *putsch*, they had no justification for questioning the Chancellor's right to take necessary steps to prevent it. Indeed, the exact opposite holds: it was their duty not to question his right, but to assist it by putting the army in a state of alert and preparing further proper measures.

Once the executions of SA men started, it was, of course, theoretically feasible for the army to step in and stop the use of such barbaric methods. However, the whole Purge took place so swiftly that any action by the army would have been extremely

135

difficult. In any case, was the army to risk precipitating a civil war, especially one where they would have had to join the SA against the legally constituted authorities?

Finally, historians have assumed that an SA *putsch* was a figment of the imagination of Hitler, Göring and Himmler, deliberately conjured up to 'justify' the elimination of SA rivals. Yet, compelling evidence can be culled, even from the scoffing pages of Bullock, that the SA was very much aware that a showdown with Hitler was imminent, and that, in fact, the SA wanted such a showdown. It does not seem to have occurred to any historian that the holiday Röhm gave his SA just before the Purge may well have been, not proof of Röhm's peaceableness as historians assert dogmatically, but, instead, a ruse to lull Hitler into a false sense of security so that he had the army stand down from its state of alert, thereby giving the SA a much better chance to launch its *putsch* later in June or in July. Röhm was an experienced tactician and almost as bold a gambler as Hitler. He certainly was not the simpleton implied in most accounts of the Blood Purge.

If, on the other hand, the threat of an SA *putsch* was myth, and if the army leaders were politically naïve to believe in its reality, so were a multitude of others, many of them shrewd, level-headed men. If the army leaders were politically naïve, that surely is the most severe charge which can be brought against them for their behaviour in June 1934.

The army leaders certainly did display a measure of political naïveté in the next great crisis confronting them. In the winter of 1937-8 Hitler managed to rid himself of his Minister of War, von Blomberg, and of the Commander-in-Chief of the army, von Fritsch. Von Blomberg was accused—rightly—of marrying a woman who had once been a prostitute or had posed for pornographic photographs. Von Fritsch was accused—falsely—on a charge of homosexuality, and in March 1938 a Court of Honour exculpated him completely. In the meantime, Hitler had accomplished the *Anschluss* with Austria, and the hysterical cheers of the public drowned the protests of the generals. The generals should have stood firm and demanded an immediate investigation, and Himmler would have been exposed and Hitler would have suffered a setback. Nevertheless, something can be said in defence of the hesitation of the generals. First, they were understandably confused. The charge against von Blomberg was correct; might not the charge against von Fritsch also be true? When confronted with the accusation and evidence, von Fritsch had not denied it but disdainfully turned away in silence in accordance with his reserved and somewhat haughty character. Second, few people realized that the Nazis were deliberately striking to eliminate the independence of the army, or that Hitler would not reinstate von Fritsch if and when he was proved innocent. The generals did not understand that the von Fritsch case was a matter not of personal injustice easily cleared up, but one of power politics. Third, the army was flabbergasted by the allegations, and found it impossible to credit that a Head of State could have invented such a story out of thin air. Like others before and after them, they had not taken note of Hitler's own advice in *Mein Kampf* about the efficacy of the Big Lie.

Wonder is often expressed why the army did not revolt at the time of the Fritsch–Blomberg crisis, or later when the atrocious nature of Hitler's policies and actions became obvious. In 1938 and after, revolt would have been a foolhardy venture. At that time the mass of Germans was wholeheartedly behind Hitler on account of the restoration of the economy and German prestige. Many junior officers in the greatly expanded army were from the *Mittelstand* and were much attracted to Nazism; very likely they would have refused to follow their seniors in revolt. It would have been all too simple for Hitler and Goebbels to have represented any *putsch* by army generals as an attempt by a small group of reactionaries to seize power for their own purposes. The various army plots against Hitler evoke admiration for the courage of the conspirators. The intensity of admiration has, however, blinded people to their very poor chance of success. For instance, the failure of General Beck's plot to overthrow Hitler in the autumn of 1938 has been attributed to Chamberlain's weakness at the time of the Munich crisis. But even had Chamberlain stood firm and Hitler suffered a setback, Beck would have gained small support among the German public, and the armed forces would have been divided. The best realism could justifiably envisage was civil war. The thought of an easy overthrow of Hitler was fathered by excessive wishing.

Similarly, the failure of the July Plot in 1944 is often attributed to a series of unfortunate and unforeseeable accidents. Bungling also contributed to failure. The most notable example of inefficiency is the failure to ensure that the switchboard at the Bendlerstrasse was manned by reliable people. Instead, Nazi sympathizers stayed at the switchboard, successfully delaying messages. That experienced staff officers should not realize that this switchboard was the heart of their operations almost defeats comprehension. Nevertheless, had the plotters attended properly to the switchboard, the plot had little chance of success. The mass of ordinary civilians and soldiers had little option but to continue supporting Hitler: the Gestapo had lost none of its ruthless efficiency; Allied bombings of cities and the Allies' insistence on unconditional surrender welded together instead of snapping apart German people and Nazi rulers. Then, too, although the July plot is usually called 'the Generals' Plot', it is forgotten that the German armed forces had hundreds of generals—the Luftwaffe alone had over 400—but only a handful participated in the plot, and only a few score promised or hinted at support if Hitler were killed. There is no guarantee that the army as a whole, or even the greater part of it, would have ceased fighting if the plot had succeeded. What choice was there even for those generals sure of the allegiance of the troops they commanded? To allow Germany to be torn by civil war? To commit treason and stab Germany in the back? To open the floodgates to Stalin's troops? On 20 July 1944 the Western Allies had not yet broken out from Normandy; the Red Army was on the brink of the Vistula. In addition, the SS numbers in 1944 were approaching a million, and German generals had wives and children in Germany who presented easy hostages to the SS and Gestapo. It is all too possible for foreigners to be unaware of any of these practical considerations minimizing the chances of successful revolt; it was completely impossible for German generals to be unaware of them.

Many German officers followed Hitler's lure of promotion and financial rewards; no army lacks that kind of officer. The ravenous demand for officers promoted men to whom the traditional officer's code of honour meant nothing. Conscience was not king to every German officer. Living in a moral void, deprived of a sense of stable values, atomized by mass society, by total war, and by totalitarian rule, many men who became officers had deposed conscience as king, or had never enthroned it.

Yet, many officers were secured to Hitler by their conviction that it was deeply dishonourable to break their oath of allegiance. Condemnation of German officers for refusing to break their oath

138

is perhaps the saddest part of the attacks of historians on the German army under the Nazi régime. Refusal to break their oath, surely, brings nothing but credit on German officers—except in the eyes of those who take vows lightly. Officers like Beck and von Stauffenberg, who chose to dishonour their oath, win unstinted justifiable admiration; but the painfulness of their dilemma must be obvious. Brought up in a military code that stressed honour and in a Christian faith that many still held staunchly, the honourable old-fashioned German officer had no other choice except between what had become two evils. Anyone with a respect for honour can surely have nothing but sympathy and compassion for him in his dilemma, or in his final choice.

On the death of Hindenburg on 2 August 1934 the army had to swear a new oath of allegiance: 'I swear by God this sacred oath that I will render unconditional obedience to Adolf Hitler, the Führer of the German Reich and nation, the Supreme Commander of the Armed Forces, and that I shall be ready as a brave soldier to lay down my life at any time for this oath.' Historians have pointed derisive and accusing fingers at the military leaders for allowing themselves to be swayed into swearing an oath of allegiance to Hitler personally, instead of to the German constitution. But it was simply a return to the form of oath of allegiance to the person of the ruler that prevailed in Germany and elsewhere before 1918, and still prevails in many countries, including Britain. A soldier usually prefers to swear a personal oath of allegiance rather than the impersonal one a civil servant swears.

The problem of whether a soldier should keep a sacred oath merges into the problem of whether he should obey an immoral order. The question of a soldier's duty to obey superior orders is an extremely tangled one. Almost all the accused at war crimes trials excused themselves by pleading obedience to orders. Some —no one can say how many—pleaded falsely. Perhaps not even the Russian army had as large a share of brutal, abominable soldiers as the German army. Not enough whitewash exists to cover over the blood colour of the atrocities committed voluntarily by members of the German army. Too many photographs survive of German soldiers grinning at the side of dangling corpses of civilians or shooting women and children in mass graves. Too much incontrovertible evidence exists of German soldiers beating or kicking to death prisoners of wars. Too many German soldiers acted as

139

guards at concentration camps. No honest German soldier can fail to know that his uniform is stained beyond cleansing because of the deeds he and his comrades committed or helped commit.

Yet, German soldiers ought to be dealt with fairly. Their atrocities ought not to be exaggerated or regarded as unique among soldiers. Also, understanding and compassion ought to be held out to the German soldier, where he acted atrociously not because he was a sadistic brute but because he acted as a fallible and somewhat weak man under terrible stress. Any war brings out the atrocious in men trained to kill or be killed; total war nurses this propensity. The official encouragement or ordering of atrocious behaviour overwhelms what humaneness survives in a soldier.

It is immensely difficult for any soldier to view an enemy soldier as an individual human being. In modern war it is often literally impossible to *see* him as an individual human being; the airman bombs invisible people; the soldier on the ground sees only a tiny uniformed object in the sights of his gun; the tankman sees only a hostile mass of metal. The distance at which modern battles are fought easily banishes humane thoughts of the enemy in all but those with a very large fund of compassion, charity and a sensitivity towards all mankind. At least one Allied soldier never once felt that the enemy blob he had in his sights was a human being like himself, and never once in the sleeping nightmares that followed battle did he feel pity for the enemy he had killed a few hours before he slept; he felt pity only for himself.

No army is composed entirely of honourable, decent men. Willing atrocities were not committed only by German or Russian soldiers. Few Allied soldiers, if honest, could deny witnessing atrocities committed by their own side. Even in the Desert War, which was gentlemanly compared to any other campaign in World War Two, our side shot enemy soldiers who surrendered; bloodlust, sadism, or unwillingness to encumber an operation with prisoners drove out humaneness along with the Geneva Convention. The finger of more than one Italian prisoner caught in a lonely spot was hacked off with a knife to loot a ring which could not be slipped off because, as often happens, the finger had grown too fat; and when two or three privates intervened to stop this barbarity they were driven off by menacing tommy-guns and rifles. Prisoners were beaten-up, kicked to death, tortured. Women

140

were mass-raped. Allied atrocities occurred less frequently than German and Russian atrocities because the Allied authorities draconically punished such behaviour when they knew of it, and because Allied soldiers came from a relatively stable society.

Not all Germans accused of atrocities pleaded obedience to orders falsely. Some obeyed because they thought they had no alternative but their own death, or because they considered it to be their duty. A soldier is thoroughly conditioned by his training to obey orders without question. Few rank-and-file soldiers can discriminate between a moral and immoral order, or even know whether they are expected to use their discrimination. In a front-line operation a soldier can be shot for refusing to obey an order; in fact, sometimes he has to be shot to save the lives of his comrades. What if a soldier knows an order is morally wrong and is threatened with death for disobedience? Gudrun Tempel is a German, but her post-war book *Speaking Frankly about the Germans* is so removed from being an attempt to whitewash Germans that it provoked outrage in her native country. She tells of a friend of her parents who, on leave from the Polish front, related that he had been ordered to kill small Polish children by taking them by the legs and crushing out their brains against a brick wall. Disobedience meant his own death. He obeyed. The day before his leave ended, he hanged himself. Others under similar orders obeyed without pangs of conscience, or drowned their conscience in sophistry, drink, or brothels. They were able to become hardened and think nothing of obeying more atrocious orders. Others who did not become hardened were likely to lose their reason, if they were not put to death. Some who refused the first atrocious order were not shot but sent to penal or suicide battalions, institutions in the German or Russian armies from which it was extremely rare to emerge alive. Dicey put the position well when he wrote that a soldier may 'be liable to be shot by a court-martial if he disobeys an order, and to be hanged by a judge and jury if he obeys it'.

Such situations are more likely to be the lot of the lower ranks. What is a senior officer to do when given an immoral order by his superior acting as a messenger boy for his Führer who is the Head of State and fount of law? The various War Crimes Tribunals decided—not quite unanimously, it is worth noting—that superior orders was no defence. Yet, paragraph 347 of the United States

Field Manual, published by the U.S. War Department in 1940 and entitled Rules of Land War (FM 27–10) reads: 'Individuals of the armed forces will not be punished for those offences in case they are committed under the orders of their government or commanders.' The British Manual of Military Law in its Amendment of January 1936 under paragraph 443 reads: 'It is important, however to note that members of the armed forces who commit such violations of the recognized rules of warfare as are ordered by their government, or by their commander, are not war criminals and cannot therefore be punished by the enemy.' The second edition of W. Winthrop's *Military Law*, published in 1920 and generally regarded as authoritative until the Nuremberg Trials, states that 'as a rule it is not up to the subordinate to determine whether an order issued to him is legal; in practice, this would destroy military discipline'. Was it mere coincidence that both the American and British military manuals were altered so as to make superior orders no defence, in 1944 when the war was seen to be won and trials of German war crimes were put on the Allied postwar agenda?

Until 1945 it was generally recognized that a person could not be charged with criminal actions against international law. His only obligation was to obey the law of his own country. The law of Nazi Germany *was* what Hitler decreed.

Some of Hitler's orders, which were undoubted law to Germans, were not as immoral as tribunals at War Crimes Trials judged. The Commissar Order of 18 October 1942 was one of the Nuremberg crimes for which Hitler's senior generals at his headquarters, Keitel and Jodl, were hung despite the fact that the Order was decreed by Hitler. The Order commanded the immediate execution of all Russian Communist Party Commissars caught in a battle-area or behind the German lines. Yet, the conventional military law of nations held that those caught helping the enemy are liable for execution unless they wear military uniform and are subject to military orders. Russian Commissars did not wear a military uniform, but a party uniform; and they were not subject at all to any military commander but only to their political commander.

German commanders were sentenced to execution or imprisonment by War Crimes Tribunals for exacting reprisals against civilians. Yet, the army of every country involved in guerrilla war or resistance movements behind the lines, has taken hostages and carried out reprisals against civilians. An army has no alternative, unless it is to allow the guerrilla and resistance fighters free play. The right to take reprisals against civilians has never been questioned until the Nuremberg Trials. The only problem concerning reprisals was: how severe should they be?

A human enough hunger for revenge can lead to atrocities. Russians earned counter-atrocities on their soldiers by the atrocities they committed on German soldiers, as well as *vice versa*. German soldiers were convicted of war crimes because they stood by, or assisted, whilst German civilians lynched Allied airmen who had parachuted from shot-down bombers. Yet, can men, who have seen women and children—perhaps their own families—killed and mutilated by bombing raids, be altogether blamed for killing in revenge the airmen who dropped the bombs? In any case, is bombing women and children civilized behaviour? Or is it atrocious?

Those who sat in judgment on War Crimes Tribunals might have had more troubled consciences concerning their decisions had they known of some of the actions of their own side in the war. For instance, the Western Allies compelled thousands of German prisoners to clear minefields, even after the war, despite the express prohibition by the rules of war of this use of prisoners. Again, the list of capital offences for which civilians were executed by the Germans in Russia included being found in a marked prohibited area without a valid pass; the misuse and forgery of proper passes; possession of German weapons or uniforms; destruction of German military equipment or installations; refusal to work for the Germans; hiding or supplying guerrilla fighters; ignoring curfew regulations; deliberately directing German troops into ambushes; being in a guerrilla area without adequate explanation. As soon as the Allied armies reached the Rhine and occupied German territory, General Eisenhower, as Supreme Allied Commander, issued an order making every single one of these offences, including German refusal to work for the Allies, punishable by death.

Finally, some German commanders justified their remaining at a post, which inevitably involved some obedience to the immoral orders of Hitler, not simply by stating that a soldier is not permitted to resign in war, but by claiming that they were able to

143

mitigate somewhat the atrocities. Some, without doubt, made the claim without foundation. But others, men of unquestionable honour, could prove that they were able to lessen the atrocities. It is true that some German soldiers in certain areas assisted the SS in their work of extermination; but the army had strict orders from Hitler not to interfere with the SS who were made the responsible authorities for the administration of conquered territory. The army's duty was solely to supply the SS with food and transport facilities. Even so, some army commanders managed to hamper the SS, and save lives. If they had been removed from their posts, men of less honour and more compliance would have replaced them, and the scale and enormity of atrocities would have been even worse than it was. A similar consideration actuated some senior generals to obey Hitler's order to sit on the Court of Honour, presided over by Field-Marshal von Rundstedt, which had to decide whether officers accused of complicity in the July 1944 plot to assassinate Hitler should be drummed out of the army and therefore be liable to the ministrations of the Gestapo. Von Rundstedt has been excoriated for accepting the post of president of such a court. Yet, with the help of Guderian and a few other army members of the court, he did succeed in saving the lives of a few officers. Were he and those who thought like him to copy Pilate?

It needs repeating that none of what has been said here in defence of German soldiers in the war is intended to absolve them completely, or to mist over the reality of the atrocities committed by German soldiers. Such a task is impossible. The intention is, rather, to avoid a too sweeping, glib, uncritical, uncomprehending, and uncompassionate condemnation by urging a balanced view and humane understanding of the dilemmas in which soldiers are placed by the intensity of total war, the totalitarian rule of the Nazis, the loss of meaning in a mass society, the official encouragement and ordering of barbarism, and the weaknesses that were common to all human beings of every country. An old proverb says that 'it is an ill army where the devil carries the colours'. It needs to be remembered that, many times, a German soldier's only alternatives to obedience were madness or his own death by execution or by his own hand. Who of us could guarantee that, placed in the circumstances of so many German soldiers, we should not choose sanity or life?

The Blomberg–Fritsch crisis in the winter of 1937–8 gave Hitler the opportunity to tighten his control of the army. General von Brauchitsch, a weak and easily swayed man, was appointed Commander-in-Chief in place of von Fritsch; the Ministry of War was abolished and a new organization set up, the OKW (*Oberkommandowehrmacht*, or High Command of the Armed Forces) with Hitler himself in command. Sixteen politically unreliable high-ranking generals were relieved of their commands, and 44 other generals and several other doubtful senior officers were transferred to other duties. In December 1941 Hitler retired von Brauchitsch after the failure to capture Moscow, and himself took over command of the army in the field. Holding all the top posts, he was the only person able to possess a complete strategic view of the whole war; so, in a dispute, he could always trump any of his commanders because their view was necessarily limited to their own restricted spheres. The failure of the plot of 20 July 1944 put the army under his total control. All soldiers had to adopt the Nazi salute and insignia. Immunity from Gestapo investigation ceased. Hundreds of officers—especially those from the aristocracy that Hitler detested—were arrested and executed.

The noose was finally drawn tight around the neck of the once proud German High Command. Symbolizing this was the execution of a German Field-Marshal. Von Witzleben was strung up on a butcher's hook and strangulated by piano-wire. His pirouetting body, which took many minutes to die, was photographed by movie-cameras for the delectation of Hitler and his entourage in the sitting room of the Führer's Berchtesgarten mountain retreat. Power did not bring Nemesis to the German High Command; they never really had power.

8

Control of the economy—the sixth totalitarian trait—was slowly won; once again, only total war permitted total control. Nevertheless, although peacetime control and direction of the economy was partial, the careful studies of Arthur Schweitzer in *Big Business in the Third Reich*, of David Schoenbaum in *Hitler's Social Revolution*, and of others demonstrate that Nazi control and direction was considerably more extensive than in any other country in the 1930s except Stalin's Russia. On the other hand, Burton H. Klein's *Germany's Economic Preparations for War* and

Alan S. Milward's *The German Economy at War* reveal that, para-doxically, in the first half of the war Nazi control was much less than that exercised in wartime England. The powerful rebound of the Allies in 1943 dissipated Hitler's hope of quick victory and dragooned him into total mobilization of the slack German economy.

After 30 January 1933, economic life in the Third Reich was subject to a growing regiment of laws and regulations. A horde of licences controlled prices, and the supply and movement of labour and materials; dividends were limited to 6 per cent and further profits had to be invested in non-negotiable government bonds; thousands of export and import controls regulated foreign trade; rearmament determined increasingly what was manufactured; a Hereditary Law tied the peasant to his land, forbidding him to mortgage it or mortgagees to distrain upon it, and ordering that the land could not be sold, and could be inherited only by either the eldest or youngest son, whichever the local law ordained.

Big business was not unduly bothered by such measures before 1937. Revitalized machinery and profits made the price of control worth while. The big businessman's position was similar in many ways to the army commander's; he was a partner of the Party, and, whilst Schacht controlled the economy from 1933 to 1937, the big businessman did not have to consider himself the junior partner.

The Blood Purge of June 1934 consolidated the partnership. Big business gained from the Purge as did the army—although the gain no more convicts it of being an accomplice in the crime than their gain does the army. Röhm's SA wanted not only a 'people's army' but also an economy of the kind dear to the *Mittelstand*. They wanted protection of small businesses, artisans and peasants, and a decentralized and deurbanized economy free of materialistic capitalism. Hitler had encouraged the SA in their revolutionary conservatism. In *Mein Kampf* he had expressed his own dislike of the cruel city and evil industrialism: he had lauded the virtues of peasant-life and time and again spoken contemptuously of the *bourgeoisie*. Whilst praising the industrial worker at the annual Nuremberg rallies, significantly he had them parade with spades instead of modern machinery. Between January 1933 and June 1934 he was torn as much by the need to choose between small and big business, as by the need to choose between SA and *Reichswehr*.

The victory of big business soon proved pyrrhic. Hitler had

chosen the nationalist revolution, and rearmament bred further controls over the economy. Worse, it split big business into competing groups, so that fifth-columnist business combines, which rearmament favoured, prevented big business presenting a monolithic front to the party and the Führer. At the end of 1937 Schacht's replacement as Minister of Economics by real Nazis deprived big business of an essential shield. From 1937 to 1939 the slipping leaders of big business struggled to salvage what they could. War, however, put paid to any remaining hopes of their real economic freedom. Total war brought them under a subjection to Hitler very similar to that perfected before 1939 by Stalin over the managers of the Russian economy. German big businessmen, like the Russian managers, had their consolation prizes: executive suites, big houses, hunting lodges, champagne dinners, and fur-coated wives. Any economic liberty left to them, however, consisted of what Wittfogel called 'irrelevant freedoms'. Like the German High Command, they had not heeded the wise saying that 'he who sups with the devil needs to take a very long spoon'.

Workers and peasants provided little trouble for Hitler. A few Social Democrats and Communists tried to build up underground opposition. The Gestapo was too strong in a very unequal struggle. Goebbels' propaganda and Ley's Labour Front fought alongside Himmler's Gestapo. So did the material benefits that Hitler's rule brought to workers and peasants. In September 1936 Hitler could announce that the number of unemployed had dropped to a million. By 1939, a labour shortage, especially in rearmament industries, induced employers to offer free bicycles and other bribes to persuade key workers to evade the restrictions on the mobility of labour. The workers' share of the national wealth did fall a little compared with 1928; most workers, however, remembered, not the prosperity of 1928, but the chillness of the Depression. Food in the pantry, clothes in the wardrobe, and a paid-up rent book more than compensated for the constitutional disgrace of the Nazi régime. The price of the basic foods workers ate rose very little, if at all. In the late 1930s, moreover, Hitler's foreign-policy triumphs spread psychological jam on their bread and margarine, and the early years of victorious war increased the helpings. When victory ebbed, patriotism, fear of Russian occupation, skilful propaganda and the Gestapo kept even the workers in bombed cities docile enough.

147

Many peasants were at first happy to be freed of the mortgages that depression had fastened on them. Although a peasant might later have regretted being tied to his land, his allegiance—or passivity—was ensured by steady prices and by cheap labour from occupied countries. When the victory fanfares sounded thin on the radio and the bombs fell thick on the cities, many peasants at least profited, and profiteered, from food prices rocketing on the black market. The dissatisfied had their fear muffled by awareness that the reach of the Gestapo was not limited to the city.

German workers and peasants were as much politically apathetic as Gestapo-cowed. No more than workers in any other country were German workers the noble, romanticized gods which left-wing historians are inclined to worship from afar. German workers were probably as human as workers elsewhere.

9

Terror alone does not explain the poverty of opposition to Hitler's régime. Opposition is regarded as part of human nature by most Englishmen brought up under democracy and mindful of rebellions against the Stuarts and a 400-year-long tradition of nonconformism. Americans, members of a nation sired by opposition, and Frenchmen, viewing politics through a kaleidoscope of changes of governments and régimes too numerous to count since 1789, are of much the same mind as Englishmen. Germans have no such traditions; the 1848 revolutions were failures, and the Reformation, which is the nearest German approach to successful revolution, brought terrible slaughter, suffering, economic backwardness, and a cleavage which still existed in German society. President Ebert's opinion that revolution is worse than sin came even more easily to a German than to those foreigners who realize that revolutions always bring death as well as life.

In a Parliamentary democracy it is not merely the official opposition—Her Majesty's Opposition in Parliament—that symbolizes the necessity for the to-and-fro of discussion, argument and criticism. The idea permeates the whole body of democracy. It is to be discovered in every one of the associations which compose the larger association known as the State. Political parties, local municipalities, trade unions, employers' federations, Churches, universities, societies for the prevention or encouragement of this, that, or the other, even theatre guilds, musical societies, and sporting clubs, all are as much the sinews of Parliamentary democracy as are a Cabinet, civil service, law courts, and police force. They—and more—all make up that 'association of associations' (to use Sir Ernest Barker's illuminating phrase) which constitutes a democracy. Such associations enable individuals with energy, ideas and pet hobby-horses to win friends and influence people. They thereby allow the vitalizing blood of critical appraisal of policies, ideas and actions to flow through the body of state and society. Without this flow, the democratic body politic would die of anaemia.

Dictators are well aware of the vital importance of these associations as citadels of individual liberties. As soon as they win power, their first aim is to wipe them out. It was so in Communist Russia after 1917, Italy after 1922, Communist China after 1949. It was so, too, in Hitler's Germany. Every association, however unpolitical or trivial, was adequately merged into the Nazi Party and government, and so was prevented from opposition or even criticism. The various political parties were co-ordinated out of existence. It took more time to assimilate some associations, the army being one; and the Churches were never completely assimilated.

Associations fell more easily in Germany than they would have fallen in England or the U.S.A. because they were relatively much weaker. Germans had little experience of other than autocratic rule, and the shadow of autocracy stunts the growth of voluntary organizations. Another important cause of weakness was that Germans were separated by rifts too deep for enough interconnections to be established between associations for one to be sufficiently willing to help another. Successful democracy needs in its citizens a sense of basic homogeneity as well as opportunities for heterogeneous behaviour. In Germany, nationhood was too young to bridge particularism; perhaps the vociferousness and aggressiveness of German nationalism were signs of the adolescence of German unity. Enmity between northern and southern Germans was still strong in the 1930s: memories of Prussian conquest and Bismarck's persecution of the Catholics were kept obsessively green by the south's belief that it was exploited by the industrial north. At the local level, especially in rural areas, parish-pump politics, called by Germans *Kirchturmspolitik*, accentuated the want of homogeneity.

Kirchturmspolitik was a main reason for the multiplicity of parties

L

that flawed German politics as much under the Empire as under the Weimar Republic. No dramatic increase in the number of parties marked the charge from autocracy to democracy. A decrease in the number of parties might have occurred after 1919 had it not been for the particular system of voting introduced by the Weimar Constitution. The substitution in 1919 of large election districts for small ones, together with the procedure by which any 60,000 votes elected one Reichstag representative, guaranteed seats to party leaders and so helped divorce them from close contact with constituents. Worse, too many politicians were tempted by the opportunities offered by the new voting system and by the prevalence of *Kirchturmspolitik* to jump off the normal slow promotion escalator of a large party, and form a splinter party thereby mounting swiftly to the top of the ladder, however rickety and lightweight that splintered ladder was.

In a democracy, a political party is not to be likened to a vast public hall where a speaker sways a mass of upturned faces by impassioned appeals to one or more agreed, or imposed, principles. This is the totalitarian style of political architecture. The democratic style is that of a house of many rooms. In each room are gathered various groups of various persons conversing, discussing, coming to agreements on various issues. There is communication between the groups, and the rooms. But it is a communication springing from the interplay of various interests and principles, similar in general, but by no means identical in particulars. Like the democratic state of which it is a vital part, the democratic party is a conglomeration of pressure-groups all trying to influence each other, public opinion, and the government. It, too, is an 'association of associations'. In such a party, there is room for a wide variety of opinions, and rigorous criticism of official lines. Enthusiasts can obtain strategic positions, for example, on local committees from which to bring pressure to bear on the party. In this, by their very zeal and willingness to undertake party hack-work, they have a considerable advantage. Willingness to pick up a passed buck is a method recommended by Dale Carnegie. In the democratic party it is much more efficacious to win friends and influence people from within than from without. Although it does not achieve the same éclat as splintering off from a large party, it does pay higher dividends. We cannot all be generals.

On the German political scene in the 1920s and early 1930s the existence of so many small political armies made up of a super abundance of officers, all with overwhelming confidence in their own ideas of strategy and tactics, militated against successful defence in the face of the Nazi enemy. The sensible general works on the battlefield with the weapons he has to hand, and does not beat the air with theories which have little armour-plating or penetrative value. 'When bad men combine,' said Edmund Burke in his appropriately entitled *Thoughts on the Causes of the Present Discontents*, 'the good must associate, else they will fall, one by one, an unpitied sacrifice in a contemptible struggle.'

The German political parties fell sacrificially one by one in 1933 because *Kirchturmspolitik* afflicted German politics in another damaging way besides unwillingness or inability to form large 'umbrella' parties on the English or American pattern. Parochialism was not the patent of splinter parties in Germany; the large parties were also oddly parochial. Big parties isolated a member from the rest of the community by organizing too much of his life outside as well as inside politics. The Social Democratic and the Catholic Centre parties were prime offenders, although, in mitigation, it needs recalling how persecution under the Empire had forced them in on themselves. The Centre Party regimented its members in religious and trade union matters as well as politics. The Social Democratic Party went much further. It organized its members not only in political and trade union matters, but also in most of their other activities. The party had its own institutions for sports, country-outings, youth activities; it had its own libraries and adult education centres; it ran its own newspapers and magazines; it had its own birth, marriage and burial clubs. The party supervised—and isolated from the rest of the community—the life of a Social Democrat from the womb to the tomb. In a democracy, citizens usually spread their allegiance over a wide range of individual associations. In their trade union branch, or sporting club, or brass band they meet people belonging to yet other independent associations. So, no one single association can dominate their life and isolate them from other citizens of diverse views and concerns. Cross-fertilization of ideas and interests is assisted, and toleration and compromise are nourished. Paradoxically, the heterogeneity of a democrat's allegiancies strengthens the homogeneity of a democracy.

Contrariwise, the homogeneity of a citizen's allegiance weakens

151

his party. The loss of a citizen's sole associative basket containing all his political, economic and social eggs, starves him of support, self-confidence, hope and trust. This malnutrition, in turn, makes him more susceptible to a sense of aloneness and atomization, both of which breed extremism and irresponsibility, and emasculate the opposition of those who manage to stay free from these infections.

Other factors besides its particular brand of *Kirchturmspolitik* weakened the Social Democratic Party. Operating punitively on the party was Michel's 'iron law of oligarchy' by which bureaucrats in any large organization accumulate too much power and lose touch with the rank-and-file. The leadership of the party became autocratic, aged and over-cautious. The party was debilitated by '*Verbonzung, Verkalkung, Verbürgerlichung*', as the current inter-war jibe put it. 'Bossification, ossification, bourgeoisification' made Hitler's job of co-ordinating Social Democrats much easier.

Other large parties were weakened by a somewhat different type of parochialism. The isolation of the Communists is obvious and contributed to their downfall, although their refusal to man the barricades was also due to a dogma and Stalin's orders—in practice the same thing—which can be summed up in the phrase: 'Better Hitler than the Social Democrats', since Hitler was, in Communist eyes, the last ditch stand of capitalism in the face of the inevitably imminent proletarian revolution. 'Better Hitler than any of the Left' was the attitude of many conservatives. Nevertheless, the Conservative Party's downfall was brought about more by the parochialism of caste exclusiveness. Bismarck's constitution safeguarded their privileged position and obviated any need to break through their aristocratic and plutocratic crust to find political allies among the lower orders, in the manner of Tories in England and Republicans in the U.S.A. labouring under a democratic constitution. Exclusiveness was the parochial Achilles heel of the conservatives.

Religion clearly made the Centre Party parochial. Yet, in some ways, it also made them the least parochial of the Weimar parties. The Catholic Party had to take account of many diverse interests, since employers and employees, city and country dwellers were Catholics. This quality could have made them the most viable of all parties in a stable democracy, as it has under the Bonn Republic. The Weimar Republic, however, had none of the stability of the

Bonn Republic, and Weimar Catholics amounted to less than a third of the German population whilst Bonn Catholics number a half. In the crises of the Weimar Republic the many varied interests of the Centre Party inhibited decisive action. In January 1933 the party's only firm conviction was to checkmate Communism, and their dislike of Weimar democracy sprang, as much as from anything else, from a fear that economic and political upheavals would unleash a 1917 Revolution. Their reasons for voting for the Enabling Bill giving Hitler emergency powers were more complex. No one can seriously contend that all, or many, of the Centrists were traitors to the ideals of freedom, or cowards, or turncoats, or bribed. The overriding consideration was their understandable belief that a Hitler denied would plunge ahead on illegal roads running with blood. They trusted Hitler's promises that he would behave moderately. Their political habits inclined them to compromise. They were unable, like others, to foresee the terrifying future. Harsh condemnation of this inability is superficial: they could not be wise before the event as we so easily can be after it.

Hitler's politics in and before 1933 were dirty, if that is not too weak a description. Germans, however, were not unduly surprised. German tradition held that politics were inescapably a dirty business and fit only for the second rate. The tradition was rooted in centuries of autocratic rule where sycophancy and double-dealing were too often the only road to political promotion by an autocratic ruler. It also sprang from the nature of politics under Bismarck and Wilhelm II, and from the unwillingness of able, energetic, decisive men to enter politics under the Empire when industry offered an open frontier where the opportunities, rewards and adventures were much more tempting than the *Reichstag* offered. Probably this tradition largely accounts for the failure of Weimar democracy to produce any great politician, except possibly Stresemann, who, significantly, was confined almost entirely to foreign affairs.

The opinion that politics were a dirty business and not fit for the first-rate was particularly prevalent among German intellectuals. After the fashion of their kind in the Western world, they sneered without pause at the Weimar politicians whose task was rendered all the more difficult by the running fire of these politically dilettante, chair-borne critics. Weimar politics were not edifying and the politicians naturally made grave errors. But at least they put their hand to the plough, and stained their purity with the dust and grime of political agriculture. Not so the intellectuals. All successful political movements and parties need their yeast of intellectuals. Occasionally, they provide leaders; always, a nucleus of back-room boys or brains-trusts. Intellectuals, of course, are seldom as satisfied with the world as they are with themselves. But the more responsible of them have always understood that the way to change things is not to criticize from a brainier-than-thou position. It is not from the academic chair, but in the committee room and party discussion group that changes are hammered out. Among intellectuals in Germany there prevailed too much scorn of the working politician. It was rare, however, to find the intellectuals providing viable alternative policies; and even rarer to find them labouring actively and positively in the political field. Not for them the drudgery of committee work, the leg-weary monotony of door-to-door canvassing, the arduousness of political organization. Instead, for them, the chopping-block was a sufficient plaything, the critical arm-chair a feather-bed for their vanity. This was absentee landlord political agriculture of the worst kind.

The emergency powers granted to Hitler in February and March 1933 put officials at the disposal of whatever the new Chancellor decreed. Officials might have fought loyally against a revolution that did not come in loyalist guise. For instance, the Kapp rightist *putsch* in 1920 had been defeated by the refusal of officials to obey the new illegal régime that held power in Berlin for a few days, as well as by the general strike called by the trade unions. In 1933, however, the respect of officials for the law inhibited resistance. A civil servant in a democracy is closely restricted in his political activities; he must leave his personal political opinions at home, and it is his duty at the office to change his political coat as his political masters change. A judge in a democracy is duty bound to implement the law as he finds it, however politically or morally anathema it may be to him. Earlier than the nineteenth-century judges could infuse morality into their administration of law; but in the nineteenth century a positivist theory of law became prevalent in Western Europe insisting that judges were not concerned with morality but only with the letter of the law. In Germany, the theory was summed up in the legal aphorism *'Gesetz ist Gesetz'*, 'law is law'. Since Hitler came to power legally and governed

154

through legal decrees, civil servants felt obliged to obey. Theirs not to reason the political or moral why.

It is true that the German civil service and the judiciary were two of the last preserves of the conservative, aristocratic caste, and that, in the eyes of many officials, detestation of democracy was sufficient reason to welcome the change in January 1933, and stay in office. Even so, they did not know that the new régime was to become a loathesome Leviathan totally alien to the traditions of the bureaucrat, the judge—and the conservative or aristocrat.

Furthermore, it was not they who had to carry out the loathsome tasks Hitler's rule imposed. Those tasks were entrusted to specially-constituted party bodies and were kept as secret as possible. The Propaganda Ministry, for example, had few regular civil servants; it was staffed by newly recruited young officials. The Ministry of Justice was diluted considerably by new Nazi officials; and the new courts, set up to deal with special 'offences', were rarely manned by members of the regular judiciary. The SS and the Gestapo became completely beyond the control and purview of the judiciary and regular civil service. Of course, some could not avoid suspecting that some of their work assisted the policy of extermination after 1939; those responsible for the railways could not help knowing that trains were being used to deport Jews and Slavs. But Hitler kept the policy and practice of extermination a close secret and cloaked it in a disguise of euphemistic newspeak which became the official Nazi language. Civil servants and judges, moreover, were as prone as anyone else to inability to believe the stories of atrocities. Even if they did penetrate the enveloping cloak of secrecy and newspeak, even if they did believe the stories of extermination, Hitler had made it illegal for them to resign, and fear of the Gestapo stifled protests.

A surprisingly large number did resign in 1933, larger than many allow. Yet, to insist that those who stayed should have followed the example of those who left is a facile judgment revealing ignorance of life under a tyranny and of human nature. Many officials were expert enough at jumping on band-wagons and realized that Nazi promotion-boards had a convenient Nelsonian blind eye for the lukewarm in allegiance. Not all were opportunists with underdeveloped consciences. Many upright men had material and practical reasons for continuing in office. Resistance could too easily mean the concentration camp: even a man courageous enough to risk that fate had to weigh his family's circumstances against his own courageous conscience. Even dismissal without the possibility of finding another job meant ruin for his wife and family as well as for himself. Mere demotion could prevent the children obtaining a proper education. Ironically, such material difficulties and dilemmas afflicted more those in senior positions, and so with more affluence; the petty official was not in a position to achieve worthwhile resistance. It is a dangerous illusion to suppose that the vast majority of men and wives will give up power, privilege and wealth for the sake of the Higher Morality, when it involves the sacrifice, if nothing else, of a substantial part of the family income. Their life may be affluent to a degree that few others in the world are, but this does not mean that their incomes are not fully committed. With the affluent, as J. K. Galbraith suggested, luxuries become necessities. Insurance premiums and mortgages still exercise their stranglehold; and even demotion can throw an affluent budget out of joint. Idealists may point the finger at the rich, and tell them that there is 'naught for your comfort'. But it is precisely the comfort accruing from high office that so often prevents the resistance to tyranny idealists so dearly cherish. Comfort can maim the resistance of the conscientious as well as the conscienceless. The conscientious, too, have given hostages to fortune in the persons of a wife and children, who are 'impediments to great enterprises, either of virtue, or of mischief'.

Small enterprises of virtue were feasible for those who shunned Nazism and yet stayed in office. A judge who remained a judge had to administer laws he abhorred, but until 1943, he was at least able to mitigate sentences. His resignation or dismissal would very likely have replaced him with a savage Nazi. Similar-minded officials could try to moderate Nazi excess and use their position to save lives from the SS and Gestapo. Ernst von Weizsäcker was one of these. A senior member of the Foreign Office, he was condemned after the war to seven years' imprisonment by a war crimes tribunal. Part of his defence was that he stayed in office and accepted promotion in order to act as a brake on Hitler. A further part of his defence was that from his position he could help the resistance movement from within the administration. His success was small but in some measure he encouraged the resistance movement.

In a different sphere, the renowned conductor Wilhelm Furtwängler has incurred contempt and opprobrium because he did not leave Germany in protest, and, instead, in 1933 accepted the position of Vice-President of the *Reichsmusikkammer*, one of the institutions set up to achieve the *Gleichshaltung* of the German arts. After the end of the war, Furtwängler was prohibited by an American general from conducting in West Berlin, and 20 years later some were still refusing to listen to the recordings of 'a collaborator'. Yet, Furtwängler's staying in Germany not only brought comfort of true culture but enabled him also to defy the Nazis in an open article published on 25 November 1934, and make his resignation from his position in the *Reichsmusikkammer* a public protest at the official attempt to gag him. He did not favour Nazism, and his world renown could easily have won him a post in exile as eminent and well-paid as was secured by artists who did go into exile. In the early years of the régime he was able by remaining in Germany to adulterate the barbarism of Nazi culture because Goebbels, conscious of his high international prestige, was willing to concede to him. In later years, still conducting in Germany, he was able to save the lives of Jewish musicians. His humanitarian work cleared him completely in the eyes of the post-war tribunal before which he was brought by his accusers. It is also attested by a host of musicians, many of them Jewish. Similarly, Gustav Gründgens, a leading German actor and producer, was able to use the protection he enjoyed from Goebbels and Göring to help many colleagues escape the Gestapo. Gründgens and Furtwängler did lend some prestige to Nazi Germany. But had they gone into exile there would have been fewer Jews and anti-Nazis alive after 1945.

Men like von Weizsäcker were urged to stay in office by the leaders of the exiguous German resistance to Hitler. Goerdeler, von Hassell, Gisevius, von Schlabrendorff, all prominent in the German resistance, firmly believed that effective resistance was possible only from within the régime, and they desperately urged anti-Nazi officials to retain their strategic positions. Eminent men in occupied Europe recognized the same reality. When Reinhold von Thadden, an anti-Nazi soldier in the war and afterwards a famous Evangelical Church leader, was unwilling to obey an order to arrest the Rector of the University of Louvain, the largest Catholic university in Belgium, the Rector urged him to arrest him. Otherwise, von Thadden would be dismissed and replaced by the

SS who would wreak much worse suffering on Belgians whom von Thadden could protect a little.

It can never be known how many prominent, or lesser, anti-Nazi Germans did what they could to white-ant Hitler's rule from a position within the régime. Resisters and saboteurs, not surprisingly, leave as few documents as possible. Their work cannot draw the cheers from document-dominated historians that have acclaimed those who preferred to leave Germany. Exile, however, has considerable political disadvantages. Exiles are cut off from contact with their homeland. Resisters who stayed in Nazi Germany were angered by the exiles' incomprehension of the difficulties and dilemmas of resistance at home, and were nauseated by the easy righteousness which isolation abroad cultivated. Exile is rarely a political action station.

A few anti-Nazis, like Konrad Adenauer, possessed the financial means to resign their official position as soon as Hitler came to power and to remain passively unsullied until the collapse of Nazi rule. Although Adenauer's decision may have profited post-Nazi Germany, his 12 years of inactivity must have been frustratingly bitter and tragic. Bitterness and tragedy must have been considerably more intensive for those who chose as he did, and yet were unable to make any worthwhile contribution to the reconstruction of Germany after the Nazi devastation. Some of those without the means to go into passive retirement or into exile chose an 'inner emigration' where they strove to afford the minimum of help to Nazi tyranny and to preserve the maximum of personal moral cleanliness. They, too, must often have painfully pondered after 1945 whether their choice was right.

The ordinary German did, or could do, nothing to resist. Even if he was willing to brave the Gestapo, what was the point of an anonymous death? Gestapo executions were carried out in private and were not published in the papers. Resistance was much harder for a German than for those in conquered countries. Resistance movements in occupied Europe could communicate in a language foreign to the Gestapo, were supported by their countrymen's sympathy, and could not be branded traitors.

In peacetime Germany, willingness to resist was greatly diminished by the host of foreign statesmen who paid friendly state visits to Nazi Germany and concluded treaties with Hitler. Goebbels made sure that Germans knew of these friendly treaties and of the statesmen's comments on Hitler's achievements. Even Winston Churchill wrote in 1935 that Hitler might go down in history as the man who restored Germany's 'honour and peace of mind'; it was also Churchill who wrote in an open letter to *The Times* of 7 November 1938: 'I have always said that if Great Britain were defeated in war I hope we should find a Hitler to lead us back to our rightful position among the nations.'

Most foreigners away from the Continent discounted tales of Nazi atrocities. In World War One false stories had been assiduously spread with great success by Lord Rothermere with the aid of Arnold Toynbee and others. In the inter-war years these atrocity stories were disproved so completely that they backfired in World War Two. Jean-Paul Sartre and Simone de Beauvoir were two of many whose ears were still affected by the backfire so they did not believe stories of the Nazi extermination of the Jews.

German inability to resist was further assisted by the way so much of life even under Hitler proceeded normally. English-speaking people, used to the stability and security of democracy, find despotism so strange and alien that they are inclined to think that life under a despotism is always abnormal, always a constant strain, always liable to downfall or overthrow. In fact, the work of the Nazi government was mostly normal. Democrats tend to think of Nazi government exclusively in terms of its dramatic and terrible moments. The duties of the greater part of government servants would be regarded as normal by any democrat. Only a fraction of judicial sittings were devoted to crimes against the State; most concerned breaches of contract, traffic offences, theft, divorce and drunken behaviour. Police occasionally broke down doors at 2 a.m. but mostly they did their mundane routine tasks. Taxation returns, medical health claims and applications for licences more than dwarfed the files on Nuremberg rallies and concentration camps. The basic fabric of German existence was still essentially unchanged, and the Gestapo and its activities were, for most, sinister shadows to be put from mind.

The life of the usual citizen under despotism is not spectacularly different from that of a citizen of a democracy, despite all Technicolor melodramas and history books to the contrary. Even in Nazi Germany in World War Two, with terror all around, the sun still shone. People could still laugh, enjoy parties, go on picnics, play tennis, have fun with their friends and families, make love

159

joyously, listen delightedly to the gurgling of babies. They would not have been human if they could not. The Gestapo and the concentration camp, it is true, were just around the corner. But they were around the corner. Through all the grim greyness, cheerfulness and forgetfulness kept breaking through.

The ordinary humanness of Germans militated against resistance; the power of a totalitarian régime made effective resistance virtually impossible. Opposition was rendered impotent not simply by the omnipotence of a totalitarian rule endowed by modern technology with police and propaganda weapons far surpassing in strength those at the disposal of any former régime. Opposition was rendered impotent also by the deprivation of any associations through which to express opposition. These potential citadels of resistance had been undermined and captured by the insidious gradualness of Hitler's transformation of his dictatorship into a totalitarian despotism, as well as by German lack of awareness of the importance of such citadels and by the inadequacy of German training in manning them. The Nazi *Gleichshaltung* of society furthered an atomization already far advanced by processes starting with the Industrial Revolution. Totalitarianism, with the aid of total war, completed the atomization. In their atomized aloneness, Germans, who might otherwise have resisted, were bribed until 1942 by the restoration of prosperity and prestige; after 1942 they were threatened by the stigma of treason in total war. Any faint chance opposition might have had was further enfeebled after 1943 by Allied unwillingness or inability to discriminate between Germans, and to encourage German opposition by offering terms instead of insisting on unconditional surrender. Probably, total war made the Allied statesmen and people forget that Germans were human beings not entirely unlike themselves.

4   Absolute Corruption*

I

THE LITTLE TOWN OF AUSCHWITZ is situated about 180 miles south-west of Warsaw and 37 miles west of Cracow. In 1939, not far from the town of 12,000 inhabitants, stood some old Polish army barracks together with a derelict factory which had belonged to the Polish Tobacco Monopoly. In May 1940 the area was sealed off from the town, and the buildings were turned by the Germans into a concentration camp. On 1 May 1940 SS Captain Rudolf Höss was transferred from Sachsenhausen concentration camp to be Commandant of Auschwitz. In 1941 the camp was chosen to be the main centre for the extermination of Jews, Poles and other 'inferior' and 'hostile' elements. The nearby town of Birkenau— its Polish name means 'birchgrove'—was evacuated and converted into a sister camp, Auschwitz II. Behind the screen of beautiful birch trees, crematoria were built to burn the bodies of the unwanted.

Höss claimed that from 1941 until January 1945 when rapidly advancing Russian armies forced evacuation of the camp, 2½ million men, women and children were exterminated at Auschwitz. Höss was given to exaggeration; but he ceased to be Commandant in December 1943, 13 months before the camp's evacuation, and it was in 1944 that Auschwitz reached its peak of extermination. So, in fact, he may have underestimated the number killed. The number was certainly not less than one million, and may have been as high as four million. Newer camps—Chelmno, Neuengamme, Belsen—and older ones—Dachau, Buchenwald, Treblinka—as

* This chapter does not attempt to provide a full description and history of the extermination policy and concentration camp system. Its aim is to explain why human beings could be so absolutely corrupted to enable the extermination and degradation of so many. Books containing detailed descriptions and the history of the extermination policy and concentration camps are suggested in the Bibliographical Chapter.

161

well as hundreds of camps with less well-known names, contributed their share to the millions exterminated.

A conservative estimate puts the total number of civilian men, women and children liquidated under the Nazi régime at eight million. The number is probably higher, exceeding ten million. Any accurate estimate is prevented by the destruction of many concentration camp files by the SS, by the lack of need for the SS to record the deaths of those liquidated immediately on arrival at camps, and by the haphazardness of the killing of Jews in ghettoes and Slavs in towns and villages. No one can ever know the precise figure, or even the exact number of millions, of those exterminated.

People were exterminated by gassing and shooting; by garrotting and flaying; by being beaten or kicked to death; by being worked or starved to death; by being tortured or torn to pieces by specially trained dogs; by disease or lack of medical care; by fatal injections or being driven to suicide. Thousands, chiefly babies and small children, were burnt alive. An orchestra, formed by the commandant from inmates who had been musicians, was ordered to play loudly 'The Blue Danube' waltz and Schubert's 'Rosamunde' to drown the screams coming from the blazing pits.

Anyone who has seen a gas chamber filled to a height of six feet with the corpses of those who had fought so terribly against asphyxiation that they were constricted inseparably together and stained horribly with the excrement of terror, will never forget the sight. He will never forget how the victims were driven into the gas chambers by blows, kicks and whips. He will never forget the sound of the victims' shrieks coming from the gas chamber, the sound of their cries, struggles and desperate beating on the walls. He will never forget that obviously some of the stronger victims, before dying, fought and killed their fellow-sufferers ruthlessly and viciously in order to reach up to the rapidly diminishing pure air at the top of the growing pile of corpses.

Nor will he ever forget that other inmates of the camp were compelled to shave the hair from the dead bodies due to be burned to ashes. The hair was packed in 20-kilogramme bags and transported to Germany to stuff mattresses, to make blankets and carpet-felt, and to provide watertight wadding for torpedo warheads. He will not forget that yet other inmates had to extract gold from the teeth of the corpses to help fill the Nazi Treasury; each dead body, before being consigned to burning, needed an official stamp on the chest to indicate that it had been properly examined for dental gold. He will never forget that inmates were glad to perform these tasks, since it kept them from immediate extermination.

Nor will he ever forget how, in the queue to the gas chamber, amidst all this awful degradation and hideous inhumanity of man to man, some fathers and mothers, stripped naked and aware that inevitable death was only minutes away, held their little children in their arms and told them happy and favourite nursery tales and rhymes so that at least some of the children's last moments on earth should be filled, not with terror, but with love.

On 20 December 1963 at Frankfurt began a trial lasting 20 months of 22 men who had been on the staff at Auschwitz. From the witness stand came accounts of atrocities that were literally almost unspeakable. Nearly as horrifying as the accounts of atrocities is the fact that all the accused had settled down into a normal, quiet life after the first chaotic years in Germany after 1945. This fact may reflect on the state and society of Western Germany; but it is much more important—and terrifying—because of the light it throws on men who carried out Hitler's extermination and concentration camp policy. The 22 accused at Frankfurt had discarded their uniforms in 1945, soon found jobs or started a business, and had become—and remained—respectable members of the community. Some were not only respectable but also respected for their law-abiding and irreproachable behaviour. One of them, Oswald Kaduk, became a male nurse in West Berlin, and treated his patients so well that they called him 'Papa Kaduk'. At the end of the trial in 1965 he was found guilty of mass murder at Auschwitz. Yet, after 1945 he, like most of his co-defendants, had worked conscientiously once stability had returned to Western Germany, gone home from work to his family, played with his children, read the paper or watched TV, voted in elections, chatted to neighbours, gone to football matches, visited friends with whom he had a meal, played cards, or drank a glass of beer or schnapps. From Auschwitz, these men had soon returned to normality.

The business of extermination was not confined to concentration camps. Mass executions took place elsewhere. *Einsatzkommandos*, special action groups, conscripted from the SS, were formed to cleanse the East of Jews and other undesirables. Within the first few months of their operations, the *Einsatzkommandos*, numbering in all less than 3,000 men, had killed 350,000 Jews. In 1942 the *Einsatzkommandos* were dispersed among other detachments policing occupied territories and conducting warfare against partisans. By the spring of 1942 the *Einsatzkommandos*, with some aid, had exterminated more than a million Jews. After the disbandment of the *Einsatzkommandos*, liquidation of Jews and Slavs in mass-graves scarring the countryside continued apace.

On 5 October 1943 at Dubno in the Ukraine, a German engineer named Hermann Gräbe was an involuntary witness of a mass execution. Gräbe was the manager and engineer in charge of the branch office in the Ukraine of a German construction firm. He had about 100 Jews working for him, and, when the preparations for the mass execution took place, knowing he could do nothing to prevent it, he had frantically tried to save at least his 100 Jews by arguing that they were essential workers. At the Nuremberg war crimes trials, the prosecution used his testimony, and his account of the mass execution he witnessed is contained in Document Number 2992—PS.

'In the company of Mönnikes I drove to the construction area and saw in its vicinity a heap of earth, about 30 metres long and 2 metres high. Several trucks stood in front of the heap. Armed Ukrainian militia chased people off the trucks under the supervision of an SS man. The militia men were guards on the trucks and drove them to and from the excavation. All the other people had the prescribed yellow badges on the front and back of their clothes, and so were recognizable as Jews.

'Mönnikes and I went directly to the excavation. Nobody bothered us. Now we heard shots in quick succession from behind one of the earth mounds. The people who had got off the trucks—men, women and children of all ages—had to undress under the orders of an SS man who carried a riding or dog whip. They had to put down their clothes in appointed places, so that they were sorted according to shoes, suits and dresses, and underclothes. I saw a pile of shoes of about 800 to 1,000 pairs, and great piles of clothing. Without screaming or crying, these people undressed, stood in family groups, kissed each other, said their farewells, and waited for the nod of another SS man, who stood near the excavation, also with a whip in his hand. During the 15 minutes that I stood near the excavation I heard no complaint and no request for

164

mercy. I watched a family of about 8 persons, a man and a woman, both about 50, with their children of 1, 8 and 10, and two grown-up daughters of about 20 to 24. An old woman with snow-white hair held the one-year-old child in her arms and sang to it and tickled it. The child was squealing with joy. The couple looked on with tears in their eyes. The father held the hand of a boy about 10 years old and spoke to him softly; the boy was fighting back his tears. The father pointed toward the sky, fondled his hand, and seemed to explain something to him. At that moment the SS man at the excavation called out something to his comrades. The latter counted off about 20 persons and told them to walk behind the earth mound. Among them was the family which I have mentioned. I remember very well a girl, blackhaired and slender, passing near me; she pointed at herself and said, "23 years old." I walked around the mound, and stood in front of a tremendous grave. Closely pressed together, executed people were lying on top of each other so that only their heads were visible. Several of the people shot still moved. Some lifted their arms and turned their heads to show that they were still alive. The excavation was already two-thirds full. I estimated that it contained about 1,000 people. I looked for the man who did the shooting. I saw an SS man who sat at the rim of the narrow end of the excavation, his feet dangling into the excavation. On his knees he had a machine pistol, and he was smoking a cigarette. The completely naked people went down a stairway which was dug into the clay of the excavation and stumbled and slipped over the heads of the people lying there already, to the place to which the SS man directed them. They lay down in front of the dead or injured people; some touched tenderly those who were still alive and spoke to them in a low voice. Then I heard a number of shots. I looked into the excavation and saw how the bodies jerked or how the heads rested already motionless on top of the bodies that lay below them. Blood was running from their necks. I was surprised that I was not chased away, but I saw there were two or three postal officers in uniform nearby. Now already the next group approached, went down into the excavation, lay down in a line alongside the previous victims, and were shot. When I walked back around the mound, I noticed another transport which had just arrived. This time it included sick and frail persons. An old, very thin woman with terribly thin legs was undressed by others who were already naked while two persons held her up. Apparently the woman was paralysed. The naked people carried the woman around the mound. I left with Mönnikes and drove with my car back to Dubno.'

An old Jewish story tells of a rabbi who had lost his way in a lonely countryside as darkness began to fall. He sought shelter for the night in an isolated barn. Inside the barn he dimly discerned a figure slumped in a corner. He went over to the figure, struck a light, and saw it was God. Astonished he asked God, 'What are you doing here?' And God replied, 'I am weary, rabbi, weary unto death.'

2

'How can you find any pleasure, Herr Kersten, in shooting from behind cover at poor creatures [like deer], browsing on the edge of a wood, innocent, defenceless and unsuspecting? Properly considered, it's pure murder. I've often bagged a deer but I must tell you I've had a bad conscience each time I've looked into its dead eyes.' A mild-mannered man speaking, one would think; sensitive, inoffensive, probably undistinguished in appearance. In fact, the speaker did look like that.

On another occasion he said: 'One basic principle must be the absolute rule for SS men. We must be honest, decent, loyal and comradely to members of our own blood and nobody else. What happens to a Russian or a Czech, does not interest me in the least. ... Whether nations live in prosperity or starve to death interests me only in so far as we need them for our own culture. ... We shall never be rough and heartless where it is not necessary, that is clear. We Germans, who are the only people in the world who have a decent attitude towards animals, will also assume a decent attitude towards these human animals. ... Most of you know what it means when a hundred corpses are lying side by side, or five hundred, or a thousand. To have stuck it out, and at the same time —apart from exceptions caused by human enough weakness—to have remained decent fellows, that is what has made us strong. This is a page of glory in our history. ... We had the moral right. We had the duty to our people, to destroy these people who wanted to destroy us ... our spirit, our soul, our character has not been injured by it.' These words come from a secret speech delivered in 1943 at Posen to SS leaders, whose task it was to liquidate undesirable races, by SS *Reichsführer* Heinrich Himmler, that mild-mannered man who expressed to Felix Kersten his distress about deer-shooting, who looked like an ordinary school-teacher or junior civil servant, and whose name is indelibly associated with the murder of at least eight million human beings and the sufferings of countless others.

Neither of Himmler's statements is tinged with the least trace of brutal humour or rough cynicism. Both are the expression of what Himmler really thought. At first sight, this seems incredible. How can a man feel pity for slaughtered animals and none for slaughtered human beings? How can a man exemplify, as Himmler did, virtues like thrift, lack of ostentation, financial honesty, a great capacity for hard work, impeccable politeness, reverence of women, and a deep disgust for all sexual perversion and for all obscenity, and yet be so appallingly obscene himself? How can a man sincerely use words like 'honest, decent, loyal and comradely', 'a decent attitude', 'decent fellows', 'a page of glory in our history', 'moral right', in the hideous context of a policy of terror and death for millions?

How could Höss continue to act as commandant of Auschwitz, and yet go home in the evening to a quiet, cosy, normal domesticity where he drank only moderately and behaved peaceably and calmly? How could he superintend the gassing of millions of human beings, and yet, as a youth, want to be a missionary; become during World War One the youngest non-commissioned officer in the German army, winning the Iron Cross, both First and Second Class; and sincerely believe in the dignity of labour so that, without intending any mockery, he had the motto *'Arbeit macht frei'*, 'work makes free', inscribed over the main gate at Auschwitz where Dante's words 'Abandon hope, all you who enter here' would have been so much more apt?

How could Adolf Eichmann be responsible for the administration of the Final Solution, and work calmly and busily at his desk on files and correspondence dispatching millions of Jews from all over occupied Europe to a terrible death, and yet pride himself on only doing his duty and on only once inflicting personal violence on anyone, that exception being slapping the face of a Jew for which he expressed sincere shame? How could Otto Ohlendorff command an *Einsatzkommando*, which he admitted had exterminated 90,000 human beings, and yet, as was testified by his adjutant

Heinz Schubert, a descendant of the great composer and a serious and earnest young man, be sincerely worried that those to be exterminated should be shot in the most humane and military manner possible so that 'the emotional or psychical strain (*seelische Belastung*)' should be bearable for the execution squad? How could Ludwig Ramdohr be an SS man at Ravensbrück concentration camp for women and torture inmates in the cruellest manner, and yet love the creations of nature so much that he would take care to avoid stepping on a snail, and buried his mother-in-law's dead canary tenderly in a box covered with a rose? How could another SS camp official, taking his little daughter for a walk near the camp, seize a Jewish baby, throw it in the air, and shoot it like a clay pigeon, and yet listen good-humouredly to his small daughter call out 'More, Daddy! More, Daddy!', refuse her request gently, take her home, and lovingly watch her playing with her dolls?

Obviously, it is completely inadequate to call these men, and the thousands like them, 'madmen', 'brutes', or 'thugs'. Conventional labels convey no understanding of them. Understanding needs resort elsewhere. The human mind has two sides, the rational and the idealistic, and to live morally and humanely, it is imperative to bridge the gap between the two sides by what can be called 'the exercise of sympathy'. Briefly, this means a sense, a realization, an appreciation of the reality of other people as human beings like oneself—in one Christian word, 'neighbourliness'. It is the exact opposite of the phrasaic assumption that 'I am not as other men'. Where Jews, Slavs, Gipsies and other enemies of Nazism were concerned, Himmler, Höss, Eichmann, and the rest suffered from a grave disjunction of the two sides of the mind, the rational and the idealistic, and they could not bridge the gap. They had no sense, no realization, no appreciation that those who they were convinced were enemies of Nazism were human beings at all like themselves. They were poisoned by a moral disease which—to use the South African term for 'separation' or 'segregation'—can be aptly called 'apartheid of the mind'.

There can be no doubt that Himmler's mind had its idealistic side. His speech at Posen in 1943 to SS leaders is one of many pieces of evidence of his idealism. He tried hard to form his SS in an idealistic mould. He chose the SS motto, '*Meine Ehre heisst Treue*', or 'Loyalty is my honour'. He believed utterly that the SS were the élite of the Nazi party, which was the élite of the German

168

Volk, which, in turn, was the élite of the world. He modelled the SS on the medieval Order of Knights, and was convinced that the greatest distinction a German could achieve was membership of the SS Order. He established Castles of the Order, schools to indoctrinate SS members in his ideals. He hoped to breed a new type of ideal human being, 'far finer and more valuable than the world had yet seen', by careful selection and training of SS men and their wives. He insisted that every SS man must give himself wholly to the SS ideals of bravery, loyalty, self-sacrifice and obedience. He himself held obedience to Hitler so dear, until he cracked under the strain of the last days of the régime, that he said with complete sincerity that, if Hitler ordered it, he would hang himself. His SS men were to be shot immediately for disobeying an order, and any SS man violating the laws or principles of Nazi Germany was to receive double the punishment meted out to the normal citizen. In 1937 he told SS men that they were working for ideological principles conceived only once in 2,000 years. He insisted on honesty and incorruptibility in SS men, and in his secret speech at Posen in 1943 he promised that 'any man who steals so much as a mark is a dead man. A certain number of members of the SS— they are not many—have infringed my order. They will die without mercy. . . . I will not tolerate the slightest stain of corruption among us.' It is irrelevant that, without Himmler's knowledge, many SS men did steal; what is relevant is Himmler's idealistic obsession with incorruptibility. Himmler had Karl Koch, SS Commandant at Buchenwald, executed for corruption.

Blood and soil, especially German blood and soil, were mystically sacred to Himmler. In the 1920s he had joined a 'back-to-the soil' movement. He was hostile to capitalism and urbanism rather in the manner of the revolutionary conservatism of many of the *Mittelstand*. Evidence exists that the SS had post-war plans to destroy capitalism in Germany; and many of Himmler's plans for a regenerated Europe proposed a multitude of settlements of *Bauern*, or peasants, who would live healthily bound to the soil. He, himself, was an ardent believer in nature healing and the medicinal value of herbs. Blood was, to Himmler, the true bond of the German people, and his ultimate aim was to create an order of good blood to serve Germany. Each member of the SS had to be able to trace pure ancestry as far back as 1750, and could marry only women of complete racial purity. Himmler established

169

centres where unmarried women were brought so that SS men could sow the seed of a racially superior generation. Blood was so mystical to Himmler that he confessed that he could never believe a person with the Aryan traits of blond hair and blue eyes could commit as heinous crimes as a person without them. Aryan-looking children were kidnapped from Slav parents, on his orders, to improve the purity of German blood.

Although Himmler believed in God, he was hostile to Churches, and would not permit any SS member to belong to a Church. He intended eventually to restore the old Germanic gods, and considered that Hitler might be included among them after he died.

The cult of the German past was very dear to Himmler's heart. He made a special study of Henry the Fowler, Heinrich I, the king reputed to have founded the German Reich a thousand years before Hitler founded the Third Reich. Himmler's interest in German history was not that of a historian, but of a mystical idealist, and he collected old German relics, not as a museum keeper, but as a believer in a mystical religion. His mysticism ranged widely from an interest in Mohammedanism to some very odd by-ways. He kept assistants busy at the most critical times of the war investigating the symbolism of the suppression of the harp in Ulster, the Rosicrucian brotherhood, and the occult meaning of Gothic towers and Eton top hats. On the day following the surrender at Stalingrad, the worst defeat Nazi Germany had suffered, he gave orders for the tracing of an old Danish woman reputed to be the only person acquainted with the knitting methods of the Vikings. Such interests would be pathetic or comic were they not part of a cast of mind engraving tragedy for millions.

His idealism found expression in his personal manner of life. He lived in a very simple style on a salary very small for a person in such a position of power. He despised the taking of perquisites and was furious at anyone offering him a bribe. He was always respectful to women, and, although he kept a mistress, he could not stand the use of obscene language or innuendo. His health had never been strong, and he regularly did strenuous exercises to improve his physique. He was moderate over food, and an abstemious drinker. He did not look at all like a fanatic or crank. Stephen Roberts, the Australian historian who met him before the war, described him as exquisitely courteous, interested in the simple things of life, and as normal as anyone he had encountered in

Germany. Many other sensible foreigners who met Himmler echoed Roberts' judgment of his appearance. He was neither pretentious nor pompous; he had a quiet modest sense of humour, and he took pains to help others relax. As his personal aide, he chose Colonel Brandt, an idealist similar to his master. Himmler's hatred of Goebbels sprang as much from detestation of his rival's cynicism, as from the struggle between them for influence over Hitler. Himmler's close associates liked, respected and admired him for his capacity for hard work, his consideration for them, and for his unselfishness.

Himmler claimed that unselfishness was his personal ideal. He told Kersten in all seriousness, 'I try to help people and do good, to relieve the oppressed and remove injustice wherever I can.' He hoped to cease being a policeman after the war and—incredible as it may seem—become Minister for Religious Affairs. In the Götterdämmerung days of April 1945 when his dreams, which were nightmares for others, were dissolving before the final Allied thrusts, he told Kersten with tears in his eyes, 'Petty minds, bent on revenge, will hand down to posterity, a false account of the great and good things which I, looking further ahead, have accomplished for Germany. . . . The finest elements perish with the National Socialists: that is the real tragedy.' He saw himself as the pure force of order and the fount of honour and he could never understand that others could see him only as the atrocious force of destruction and the fount of degradation. It is impossible to deny Himmler's idealism; but his was—to use Edward Crankshaw's illuminating phrase—an 'idealism gone rotten'.

Himmler was also rational, if rationality consists in the capacity to order information efficiently in pursuit of aims and so to plan carefully. In their biography of Himmler, Roger Manvell and Heinrich Fraenkel scornfully belittle Himmler's intelligence and efficiency as much as they belittle everything about him except his dreadfulness. Yet, the untold number of mass graves and burnt human ashes, the life-long physical and mental scars of concentration camp inmates, give the lie to the denial by Manvell and Fraenkel of Himmler's efficiency and ability to plan and administrate rationally. If those graves, ashes and scars are not enough evidence that Himmler had these qualities, there are the long-term plans of the Nazis for the tomorrow when the world would be theirs. Himmler had ready careful and detailed plans to move millions

171

of people hither and thither; towns and villages were specified in the plans. A belt around Berlin, 100 kilometres wide, was to be depopulated and reafforested; in the woods villas were to be built and in them were to live a German élite cleansed of the taint of urbanism, and purified by contact with soil and nature. Even the furniture of the villas had been thought out. Detailed plans to colonize the East when it was finally conquered were ready. Himmler had in mind moving five million Dutch to replace Slavs. Germans were to be established in the East in *Wehrbauern* settlements, soldier-peasant settlements, to cultivate the soil, hold down the local Slav serfs, and act as a defensive shield for Western civilization against the inroads of Slav barbarism. Each settlement was thoroughly planned in advance to comprise 40 farms, each of 300 acres; a party headquarters; a manor-house for the SS or party teacher; an agricultural instruction centre; a house for a community nurse; and a cinema. The proposed site of each settlement was marked on the map, and the site of each building in the settlement was allotted. The exact amount of military equipment had been calculated, as well as precisely what weapons each soldier-peasant would need.

Himmler demonstrated his capacity for rational and efficient administration by his control of the SS and Gestapo. These special forces had immensely great power but surprisingly few members. The concentration camp system was run by an SS force no larger than 70,000. The *Einsatzkommandos* never comprised in all more than 3,000 men. The Gestapo, the terror of occupied Europe as well as Germany, never numbered more than 40,000, including women and clerks. The amount of degradation and death which little more than 100,000 people could inflict on little short of 200 million people was, certainly, abominable; and, equally certainly, evil is always easier to do than good. But that so much evil could be done by so few, witnesses the efficiency and rationality of both Himmler and the people he led. After 1945 there would have been more people alive and unscarred mentally or physically, had Himmler not been efficient and rational.

It is a mistake of considerable consequence to suppose that evil can be neither efficient nor rational; or that rationality is not a neutral capacity to be used for evil as well as good. True, Himmler and his servants did not work alone; they were aided by Hitler's régime, German armed might, accomplices in occupied territories, modern technology, and the atomization of mass society. Nevertheless to deny rationality to Himmler is as obtuse as to deny intelligence to Hitler. Worse, it is to turn the tragedy that befell so many in Himmler's power into a melodrama with a villain to be hissed or laughed at. There can be no doubt that Himmler was rational. But his was a rationalism, like his idealism, gone rotten. Both the rationalism and idealism of Himmler and his like had been turned rotten by apartheid of the mind.

Pharisaism is the rotten fruit of apartheid of the mind. The Pharisees of whom St Matthew wrote were not its first cultivators, and there can have been few, if any, human beings who have not, at some time or in some way, been lineal descendants of the Pharisees and have not feasted in the same orchard. Himmler and the Nazis were similar in kind to the Pharisees and their imitators, but they were, it hardly needs saying, far worse in degree. Pharisaism always leads to some form of crucifixion of others, but it is not usually lethal. The unrivalled power possessed by Himmler and Nazis enabled their pharisaism to crucify millions mortally.

A human tendency to pharisaism was encouraged and greatly intensified by constant Nazi indoctrination. Hitler's example, Goebbels' propaganda, Himmler's exhortations could hardly fail to move the idealistic. In his *Diary of a German Soldier*, Wilhelm Prüller shows himself a simple, but proud, idealist. He seems to have been a decent young man, and his diary is not at all an account of atrocities committed in the name of idealism. The information that he was a member of the SS is revealed only in the book's closing pages; and the crumbling of his personality after the war, when he became a habitual drunkard, may be testimony to the depth of an idealism shattered by the failure of Nazism.

Some were warped in youth into an idealism gone rotten. One was Irma Grese. To those who knew the utter degradation and death of Belsen in its final months, her name spells nightmare. It means once again feeling her lash on your back or face; it means again seeing her kill a friend whom you had spoken to or touched a minute before; it means staring petrified at her finger as it moved slowly past you pointing out those to be exterminated. Irma Grese; not the person in Belsen most hated by inmates, but the most feared; so feared that hatred of her had been driven out by fear of her.

On 10 December 1945 at Hamelin, where once, legend tells, the

Pied Piper performed his feat with rats, Irma Grese was hung by the neck until she died, in accordance with the sentence of a war crimes tribunal. She was barely 22 years old.

She was born in October 1923, the year of the great inflation, one of post-war Germany's worst economic panics, the child of ordinary, respectable, peasant parents. She was not yet 10 when Hitler came to power, still in primary school. From that age, she was subject to indoctrination in obedience to the Führer and in loyalty to *Volk* and *Reich*. She was a timid, susceptible child, not independent-minded or intelligent, not given to questioning what she was told. Like many others, she joined the Nazi League of Young Girls, where her indoctrination continued. She was not yet 16 when war began in 1939; she had left school at 14, worked on a farm, and then in a shop. When she was 15, she became an assistant nurse at the hospital at Hohenlychen. Nursing is not a profession attractive to the naturally brutal or sadistic. Hohenlychen Hospital specialized in plastic surgery, and, when war started, officers came to have burned and wounded faces treated. Some officers were air aces, the equivalent then for idolizing teenage girls of film stars or pop singers in peacetime Western society. In the hospital Irma was noticed by one of Germany's leading surgeons, who was an ardent Nazi. He carried forward her indoctrination. Later this doctor, with the aid of Himmler, turned the hospital into a centre for the vivisection of inmates of concentration camps. Wounds were cut without anaesthetics in their bodies and artificially infected to simulate battle-wounds, so that new drugs could be tested. Some died in agony; many were maimed for life.

Irma Grese took no part in these experiments. They were not begun until 1942, and she had already left the hospital to work in a dairy in Fürstenberg. In 1942, when she was not yet 19, she was persuaded to join the SS and was ordered on to the staff of the concentration camp at Ravensbrück. Here she received her initial training in brutality. Trainee guards showing mercy to inmates were liable to liquidation or to become inmates themselves. From Ravensbrück she went to Auschwitz and then to Belsen.

Edmund Burke rightly said that 'to speak mildly of vice is treason to virtue'. Yet, surely, it is not treason to virtue to ask what chance of avoiding apartheid of the mind had a young girl like Irma Grese brought up in Nazi Germany and force-trained in brutality. When she was executed in December 1945 I applauded

174

wholeheartedly; I exulted in vengeance for the terrors and horrors of Belsen. I have since changed my mind and feelings. A civilized person would have regarded Irma Grese as a psychological casualty of the war, one of the lost generation of the 1930s. Who of us can be sure that we would have behaved differently in her circumstances? It is perhaps irrelevant to add that my opinion now is that it was useless to hang Irma Grese as a deterrent; the example of her execution has not prevented others since 1945 committing atrocities, the equal of hers. Moreover, her execution was barbaric. Revenge, however sweet, always is barbaric; and the vengefulness of the trial and hanging of Irma Grese proves the point that, in some measure, we on the Allied side—and I include myself—were not entirely different from the Nazis, however holier-than-them we thought ourselves.

Unlike Irma Grese and Wilhelm Prüller, others joined the SS for more mundane reasons. The lure of adventure or of an élite uniform attractive to girls, monotonous work or a nagging wife, unemployment or a low status, have always been good recruiting sergeants. Special bait to join the SS was dangled: exemption from the labour service which was compulsory for all Germans between the ages of 18 and 20; freedom from military service, and the status and pension, although not the work, of a civil servant, for those enlisting for a 12-year period; the prospect of quick promotion in a rapidly expanding force. Especially during the war, foreigners were accepted into the SS, and Aryan-enough Dutchmen, Rumanians and others had, as added inducements to join, the need to obtain better food and some power as well as to escape forced labour and prosecution for crimes. In the last years of the war, some Germans were conscripted into the SS, especially *Volksdeutsche*, Germans who had lived outside Germany until their country was occupied. Worldly-wise volunteers and forced conscripts were not, however, exempt from indoctrination; and some of the SS idealism gone rotten and apartheid of the mind rubbed off into their consciousness. Wherever two or three were gathered together, the Führer was always also present.

Very few SS men volunteered for duty in concentration camps; and those that did had little or no idea of what awful duties were expected of them. Mostly, they volunteered to escape front-line service in the army, especially on the Russian front. The halcyon days of the German army in Russia were soon over. Although advances continued in 1942, the frightfulness of the front line was already common knowledge in Germany. The terrible winter of 1941–2 had decimated German ranks. Generals January and February, whom Tsar Nicholas I had dubbed Russia's best generals, had received invaluable assistance from Hitler's certainty that Russia would be his in a few swift weeks or months, and by his consequent failure to make any provision for winter clothing or equipment for his troops. Vicious war was waged behind the lines between Russian partisans and German soldiers. Front-line fighting was the most deadly, atrocious, and frightful of all the German army's campaigns.

Nearly all the extermination and concentration camp SS staff were conscripted into their death-head duties. None of the *Einsatz-kommandos* men were real volunteers. They either received orders to join these special units or were tricked into them. Those who picked the leaders showed a surprising predeliction for academics. Of the 23 *Einsatzkommando* men tried at Nuremberg in 1947 and 1948, 17 were university graduates, and one was a dentist, another an engineer, and a third an opera singer. One had been a professor at the university in Königsberg, and seven had obtained Ph.D.s either in law or economics. None were volunteers. No more were their subordinates, volunteers. Some had been hoodwinked into the special force. An offence, sometimes as trivial as being late or falling asleep on duty, had earned them a court-martial sentence and the offer to avoid imprisonment, or worse, by volunteering for unspecified 'special duties'. When, too late, they realized what was expected of them and refused to share in mass-murder, they were told that either they obeyed orders to shoot or were themselves shot. Some chose their own death; but most, out of human necessity, went where the devil drove.

In the camps, not many of the SS were simple sadists, thugs, or paranoiacs. These had abounded in the early days of the Nazi régimes when SA men controlled the camps. But Himmler soon made determined and successful efforts to weed them out. Bruno Bettelheim, who was an inmate in 1938 and 1939, and Eugen Kogon, who was an inmate at Auschwitz, have each written psychological studies of the concentration camp system, and both insist that, after the early days, perversion, sadism and individual bestiality were conspicuously absent in SS personnel. Instead, brutality was coldly and systematically efficient. Inmates were no longer viewed as vents for sadistic pleasure, but were seen as stereotypes. SS staff were indoctrinated to regard the Jews as diabolically dangerous plotters of the destruction of Germany. The Slavs were stamped as an inferior barbaric race of huge numbers constituting a perilous threat to German—and Western—civilization. German political prisoners and foreign members of resistance groups were regarded as treacherous enemies willing to stop at nothing to overthrow 'the New Order'.

No doubt, some SS men did discover enjoyment in brutality. What started as duty, became habit, and then pleasure. Also, SS men were at times encouraged to haphazardly shoot inmates, 'attempting to escape', by rewards of extra pay, cigarettes, rations, or a few days' leave. Yet, administrators had a cold-blooded, utilitarian reason for encouraging haphazard brutality. It furthered the creation of an atmosphere of unpredictability in the minds of inmates who could never be sure of staying alive however strictly they obeyed rules and regulations, and this atmosphere of unpredictability increased the feeling of impotence in the inmates. This feeling was a vital safeguard to the SS; the guards were few, the inmates many. For instance at Treblinka, an extermination centre where at least 800,000 Jews were gassed, there were only 40 SS staff, assisted by about 200 Ukrainians. Again, one SS man was set to guard nearly 1,000 people awaiting deportation in a railway yard. He made them all squat for several hours on their heels with their hands on their heads. He probably did not care that he was inflicting terrible torture. What mattered to him was that he knew that keeping them in that position prevented their attacking and killing him; their being allowed to stand up and mill around not only would help them retain courage but would also give them a stance for attack. His automatic weapon could account for 30 or 40, but, even so, he was no match for a swarm of several hundreds determined to risk their lives for a chance to escape or exact revenge in a mob attack.

Höss estimated that the total SS staff at all the extermination and concentration camps combined was about 30,000, assisted by some 10,000 men detailed from the army, navy and air force. Himmler employed no more than 70,000 SS in running the whole camp system, and this figure included 7,000 at desks in the offices of the central administration, and a considerable proportion of the remainder working outside camps.

One reason for keeping the SS staff small was the wish or need to maintain maximum secrecy about the atrocious system. When the Nazi euthanasia programme in 1939 and 1940 was exterminating those Germans regarded as physically or mentally incurable, every person on the staff of the extermination centres had to swear not to reveal what was happening, and some, imprudent enough to tattle, were sent to concentration camps as inmates. SS members at extermination and concentration camps had to swear a similar oath. Himmler and his subordinates stressed constantly that no information about the exterminations in camps should be allowed to reach the public, and that talkative staff must be severely punished. Himmler had his own nephew, SS First Lieutenant Hans Himmler, sentenced to death for careless talk while drunk; he was reprieved, but later he was executed at Dachau for again being unable to control his tongue.

The enveloping cloak of secrecy was thickened by isolating camps in out-of-way places. Treblinka was camouflaged by a screen of branches, cut periodically by groups of inmates sent under guard into the woods more than a mile away. Outside camps an area several miles wide was marked off, cleared of trees and bushes, and prominent notices warned that any unauthorized person found in this area would be shot on sight. All the talk about German women coming several miles to Buchenwald from Weimar to jeer and flaunt their figures from outside the wire at inmates inside is mere myth. Secrecy, added to the need for the security of the few guards, was an important—though, of course, unjustifiable —reason for transporting deportees to camps in sealed wagons which were not opened on the journey to give the victims additional food or water, or even to relieve nature once the completely inadequate bucket provided overflowed. Brutality, for its own sake, no doubt, often played its part; but it did not act alone.

The secrecy enshrouding the atrocious extermination had the added advantage that it shielded SS men from ostracism by the ordinary German unaware of the unmentionable horrors perpetrated. True, Germans knew that there were camps and that Jews were being maltreated. The Gestapo and Goebbels made sure that opposition from Germans was reduced by knowledge that concentration camps existed and that their purpose was not to provide a rest-cure; but they did not reveal the actual horror of the camps. Also, no German could fail to notice Jews wearing the

Yellow Star or to be aware of the gradual disappearance of Jews from the streets. Yet, there appears to be no reason—except unthinking blanket condemnation or hatred of all Germans—to doubt the plentiful evidence that few Germans knew of the atrocious camp conditions or that a policy of extermination was being practised. The cloud of secrecy was dense enough to prevent the outrage from the German public that Hitler and Himmler expressly said they feared. Secrecy was also aided by special language rules, officially known as *Sprachregulung*. The use of words like 'extermination', 'killing', 'liquidation' was forbidden and they were replaced by euphemisms: 'final solution', 'evacuation', 'special treatment', 'resettlement', 'labour in the East'. *Sprachregulung* helped deceive victims; but it also assisted SS officials to avoid having to face squarely the reality of the whole horror.

Other methods were effective in encouraging inhumanity and discouraging humanity. When a new member joined the SS concentration camp staff, he was put through an intensive period of gruelling, humiliating and savage parade-ground discipline until, as soldiers say, 'the juice boiled in his tail'. Then, he was let loose on inmates to blow off steam. Those who demonstrated that they had been adequately toughened were quickly promoted. Those who showed any distaste for their appointed tasks were as quickly and as appropriately dealt with. It is true that some SS members who were too squeamish managed a transfer to a less painful position. But significantly, all the examples that are quoted by those who contend that SS camp personnel did not have to carry on with their gruesome work unless they wished, are of SS men in leading positions, and even they more often than not found it hard to obtain a transfer. Those in the lower ranks who showed any sympathy or softness to inmates were lucky if they were expelled from the SS and sent to the Russian front to join a penal 'suicide' battalion, where discipline was murderous and from which it was rare to emerge alive. Also lucky were those who only received 25 lashes for squeamishness. Some were shot. Perhaps the most unlucky were those who were sent to join the inmates on the other side of the wire, where they stood little chance of survival. Either they died at the hands of former SS colleagues, offended by their 'treason', or by the way they had shamed them by showing up their own lack of human sympathy or of courage to disobey orders; or they died at the hands of inmates who found in them an easy surrogate for their hatred of the SS: 'once an SS man, always an SS man' was part of most inmates' stereotyped philosophy. Transfer from one side of the wire to the other occurred often enough to induce SS men to repress human sympathy; they, too, suffered from the usual human fear of pain and death. They were not the supermen that they liked to think themselves and that many camp inmates came to imagine them.

No record exists of how many SS tender consciences were severely punished. But the statement that it was easy to 'resign' from extermination or concentration camp duties is completely false. Many former inmates know of examples to the contrary. For instance, SS Sergeant Saubier, who prevented colleagues from beating inmates in a sub-camp at Buchenwald, was made an inmate of the main camp by the camp commandant, SS Lieutenant Kenn. A few former inmates record similar examples in their accounts of their own experiences. Others, who have written accounts, perhaps have omitted them because a memory, seared by SS inhumanity, not unnaturally, conflates all SS members into a stereotype and is unable to recall exceptions to the stereotype. Another possible reason for failure to mention SS personnel who kept their conscience alive, or revived it, is that most accounts have been written by inmates who held privileged positions in the camp. These privileged positions whilst preserving their own life, helped destroy the lives of others. The natural need to obliterate their shame, or to forget that they allowed themselves to become part of the machinery of extermination in order to win for themselves a better chance of survival, more food, and less discomfort and fear, would make most people wish to obscure the fact that there were members of even the hated SS who provided a shining example to show that it was not necessary to become part of the holocaust machinery if one was prepared to risk death. It is much easier for an inmate who never held a privileged position to remember and acknowledge the example of those few SS men.

Most SS members were too frightened of death to fail in their duty. Many were automatons who reacted unthinkingly to the flicking on and off of switches by superiors or to ideological Pavlovian reflexes. Refuges could be found from the uncomfortable prickings of conscience. Himmler gave comfort by the assurance that members of the SS had no personal responsibility for the atrocities they committed; it was their duty to obey the orders of the Head of the State who, as is generally believed on the European continent, could not commit a crime or give a criminal order. Insanity was another refuge, although it, at times, led to death: at Auschwitz one SS man, who went out of his mind, was immediately gassed. More usual refuges were drink, or wild orgies. Sexual intercourse with inmates was a common refuge; it was, without doubt, in most cases no more than a simple lust conveniently easy to satisfy. Yet, in some cases, it may have been an unconscious desire to show sympathy for inmates—to, as it were, straddle the barbed wire.

Indoctrination, or fear, or obedience, or pleasure were not the only parents of atrocities. Loss of self-respect also fathered a willingness to break bread with the beast. Benno Zieser, a German writer who was on the Russian front in its worst days, relates in his documentary novel, *In Their Shallow Graves*, a revealing story. Some raw recruits, ordinary, decent young Germans, are being transported along Russian roads in lorries. They pass corpses heaped by the roadside. Since the recruits are too many to sit in the back of the lorry, they have to duck their heads to avoid being brushed by dangling corpses of executed civilians strung up on trees overhanging the narrow roads. They pass long columns of Russian scarecrow prisoners who have been ill-treated, force-marched and starved to the point of exhaustion, and who are not allowed to fall out from the column even to relieve nature. Those who can go no further are simply shot. The young recruits are deeply shocked. But what can they do, mere privates under army discipline? Then, three of them are detailed to guard a depot where starved and brutally treated Russians are used as forced labour until they die of exhaustion. The Russian prisoners are so hungry that they eat rotting scraps from dustbins. The three young recruits charitably give them some of their own food; but there are so many prisoners with such ravenous hunger that, even if the recruits gave them all their food, it would be only a drop in an ocean of starvation. The result is that the recruits develop a corrosive feeling of frustration and shame at being part of the cause of this degradation. One day, some Russian prisoners start fighting among themselves for scraps of food. One of the three recruits suddenly rushes at the Russians, hitting them with his rifle and kicking them. He yells that they are no more than mangy

N

animals and deserve to be killed for behaving like animals. His two friends manage to pull him away from the Russians and quieten him down. He breaks down weeping. Then, he says he is sorry, he cannot stand the sight of such misery any longer; he is being driven mad by being a cause of the misery and by not being able to do anything about it. He volunteers to give up what is regarded generally as a soft billet, and to go to the front line.

Release from this kind of frustration and from the damage done to self-respect by being an accomplice in brutality was one drive pushing concentration camps to further and further brutality. Most, perhaps all, always retained some shreds of decency and humaneness. Tragically, it was these very shreds that helped them to increasing indecent brutality. Winston Churchill once said that we must never forget that there is a treasure—if it can be found—in the heart of every man. It is precisely this treasure that helps make a man come to hate those he maltreats long enough.

David Rousset, a French inmate of Buchenwald and other camps, records in *Les Jours de notre Mort* ('The Days of Our Death') the case of an SS man who was ordered to flog prisoners. The SS man found that flogging gave him a sexual orgasm. He used to be perfectly normal. He grew so ashamed of his sexual pleasure in flogging that he could not face his wife and three children in Breslau, and, so he ceased going home on leave. That SS man obviously retained some shreds of decency; and, almost certainly, it was the war those shreds waged with his knowledge of his betrayal of his own decency and humanity, that helped him to behave brutally at the flogging-block and at his other camp duties.

A man named Roque was guarding some starving prisoners. He regarded them with contempt and hostility, but he was not a murderous person. The prisoners constantly begged him for bread. Constantly he told them he had none. He pointed his gun at them to stop their cries for bread. One prisoner continued imploring. Roque fired into the mass of prisoners, killing one. This episode did not happen in Germany, nor even in the twentieth century. It comes from Flaubert's *A Sentimental Education*, which contains an account of what Flaubert witnessed during the 1848 Revolution in Paris and its savage suppression in the bloody days of June 1848.

An SS man told me of the incident that had started him on a career of brutality. I had been ordered to drag a cart-load of equipment back to the store at the end of a long exhausting work kommando. For some reason which I do not know, this SS man had chosen to guard me and the cart's contents himself, something which made me very afraid since he was by no means the least brutal of the SS men. It was snowing, the last winter of the war. The cart and its load were heavy enough to need a horse, and, at intervals, the SS man gave me a helping hand. I feared he was playing with me before turning on me. When we neared a hut, he allowed me to go inside with him to rest and find a few moments of warmth. Probably he helped me a little, allowed me some rest and warmth, did not curse and beat me as usually happened, and told me his story, because he knew that Germany had already lost the war and he was worried what would happen to him when final defeat came.

When he started as a young conscript, he had been an ordinary man who had never done anything exceptionally wrong. He had been neither for nor against Nazism, and, in fact, had had little interest in politics, like so many others of his age and comparatively low status. He had volunteered for the SS because he considered them a crack corps. After his initial training, he was sent to Czechoslovakia as part of the occupation forces. Late one night, he and some others were ordered out of barracks, put in lorries, and driven to a disused factory on the outskirts of the city. In the yard a number of naked Czech women were lined up against the wall; they were to be shot as a reprisal for the killing of a German by Czech resistance fighters. But the SS officer in charge, presumably concerned to further the training of his men in brutality, ordered that the men were to rape the Czech women before executing them. When he gave the order to rape the women, none of the men moved. The officer said that when he gave the order again he would shoot anyone who disobeyed. He gave the order a second time, but still no one moved. So, he shot the man nearest him. When he gave the order a third time, every man obeyed and raped the women. Then, the women were shot. My guard then said that he had never since been able to regard himself as a decent, ordinary human being. He ended up by asking me, forgetting to use the contemptuous '*du*': 'what would you have done?' I had to admit that I, too, had a great love for my own life. At the time I persuaded myself that I was humouring him because disagreeing with him would have meant a beating or worse. But since then, I

183

have come to realize that I can have no confidence at all that I would not have behaved as he did.

The best-intentioned character can be quickly marred by the general atmosphere of SS work; by the feeling that inmates bitterly hated the SS; by the dangers of walking alone in the camp or overseeing a work kommando, where it was always best tactics to shoot first and ask questions afterwards. Pressure operated strongly, impelling down the Gadarene slope. Abundant evidence makes it all too tragically evident that this 'staining' of men of ordinary honour and this destruction of habits of decency can occur. A new SS recruit goes out on a night action in a ghetto. In conformity with, and under pressure from, his colleagues he takes the easy and brutal way out with a Jew. This scars his self-respect so that it is hard for him to maintain his image of himself as honourable and decent. Soon his self-respect is irretrievably damaged; what he did from fear in a dark ghetto street, he can soon do on principle or for pleasure in a well-lit concentration camp block. Of all the power tending to corruption, violent and terrorist power corrupts most. Virgil was right when he said that 'the way down to hell is easy. The grim devil's gates stand open night and day. But to retrace one's steps and escape upwards into the light, that is really hard, that is real labour.'

It was somewhat different for those German doctors who murdered and maimed concentration camp inmates in experiments in conditions contrary to the medical code. Yet, it is pertinent to question why those doctors should have incurred a very special opprobrium, much worse than that of university graduates with Ph.D.s like Otto Ohlendorff, simply because they were medical doctors who had sworn a Hippocratic oath. The very special opprobrium in which they have been held is a mark of the extraordinary mystical aura in which the medical profession is held, an aura not all that dissimilar to that surrounding witch doctors in primitive societies. A medical degree does not confer perpetual, or even temporary, purity on its holder. The medical profession does not lack its share of inefficient, immoral, uncaring men and women. Doctors hold no peculiar lien on pity, compassion, soft-heartedness. In fact, the exact opposite is the case: by the very nature of his occupation a doctor becomes inured, even indifferent, to sufferings, and he needs to learn to suppress any soft-heartedness in order to be a good doctor. A doctor, because he is human and not superhuman or magical, is as capable as others of becoming a Nazi, and of viewing some human beings as less than human.

Nazi indoctrination, assisted by other factors, built on the common-place human tendency to pharisaism and on the widespread human habit of refusing, or not caring enough, to make the effort to perceive and appreciate the reality of every person as a human being not unlike oneself. A Jew, a Slav, a concentration camp inmate, became no more than a thing. Primo Levi, an Italian Jew, relates in his appropriately entitled *If This is a Man* how he heard an SS officer ask, at a roll-call of Jews awaiting deportation to Auschwitz in 1943, *'Wieviel Stücke?'*, or, 'How many pieces?'; Aaron Walter Lindenstrauss, a Jewish lawyer, recalled that in 1939 SS men called him and his three companions *'vier Stücke'*; and a priest imprisoned at Deschenschule, a punishment camp for foreign slave labour, said that the SS always spoke of inmates as *Stücke* and, when referring to inmates' meals, invariably used the German *fressen*, the word for animals eating, instead of *essen*, the word for human beings eating. Those SS men suffered from the same disease of apartheid of the mind as Himmler, Höss and Eichmann. The gulf between the two unbridged sides of their minds gaped so capaciously that it created a Hell into which camp inmates were cast. Tragically the gulf was immeasurably widened by the capacity of SS camp personnel to view inmates as subhuman. The view of the SS was not incorrect. That is what inmates were—or, rather, what they became.

3

Camp inmates were degraded and debased to a subhuman level by omnipresent death and disease, starvation and beating, torture and terror, impermanence and impotence, atomization and loss of individuality. They were scarecrows with match-stick thin limbs. Their shaven heads were hangdog and dirty, their skins scaly and scabby with sores and starvation. They were filthy with ingrained dirt for lack of adequate water or washing facilities, or for lack of any personal care for their appearance. Lice or fleas covered their bodies. Inmates were reduced to relieving themselves or defecating in their clothes wherever they stood especially during punishment parades lasting for hours, sometimes all night. Punishments—cruel beatings and torture which often killed weakened, emaciated bodies—made inmates fawn on guards, whine and beg abjectly for mercy, scream in agony when the blows fell again and again and again. And no fellow inmate dared show a gesture of sympathy or move to help even a friend. Extreme hunger dragged inmates down so that they betrayed each other, stole from each other, and fought each other desperately and ruthlessly for any scrap of food however filthy or rotten. It was all too tempting for the SS to look on inmates as inherently subhuman, unworthy of any respect or pity, fit only for extermination. Inmates appeared an offence against the human race. It is a terrible perversion of the just and proper way of regarding anybody; but, equally terrible, it easily happens.

Pre-war camps were terrifying enough to drag down all but the strongest, mentally, morally and physically. The ubiquity of cruel killings and savage brutality, and exhausting work on inadequate food, weakened inmates excessively. A cold and efficient system of haphazard murder, beatings, and constant, devastating harassment was deliberately designed to make life unpredictable and, so, reduce inmates to impotence. Camps during the war, especially in the last three years, were many times worse. Conditions before 1939 were further apart from conditions in 1944 and 1945 than purgatory is from hell.

By 1944, camps generally, and the particular blocks where unprivileged prisoners ate and slept, were hopelessly overcrowded. Where one lived in 1938 and 1939 ten existed in 1944 and 1945. There were no beds for inmates holding no privileged position. They slept in long tiers holding 40 or 50, crammed on wooden slats so tightly that when one turned over, the others all had to turn over with him. The weak had to conform to the sleeping habits of the stronger. There were no mattresses or palliasses or straw. A single blanket was the only covering, and it was thin, threadbare, and too small to provide any real warmth. Blocks in winter were often unheated and never properly heated. An inmate's uniform was thin and his underclothing scarce or non-existent. Warmth on a winter night came only from two bodies pressed hard into the middle one, and from the fug of great overcrowding. Sleep was disturbed by the nightmares of others as well as the inmate's own, by the groans of those sick or suffering from wounds received in beatings or from sores due to bad and niggardly food. The ration of bread was tiny; the rest of the food was such watery 'soup' that inmates needed to urinate many times in the night. Use

186

of the latrines outside was prohibited and a bucket was provided for night use. It soon overflowed, dripping on to the floor. It took only a few days to become used to the stench and to paddling through urine and excrement. Those with dysentery or other stomach ailments defecated in bed. The weak in health or in consideration for others urinated in bed. It was difficult to disentangle yourself from your neighbours, climb out, stumble over to the bucket, find your sleeping place again, crawl back over cursing awakened bodies. The mess leaked down on to those lying in the tier below. Those on the top tier were not immune. The strongest inmates took planks and climbed on to the cross-beams to sleep undirtied. Once up, they would not come down to use the bucket. Inmates had to learn to disregard urine or faeces dripping on their faces. In any case, most were too exhausted to care.

The day began before dawn. About 15 to 20 minutes were allowed for personal hygiene. Inmates slept in their uniforms and kept their footwear under their heads to prevent its being stolen. Inadequate footwear invited frostbite; too small a shoe or clog caused chaffing sores; both frostbite and sores could become lethally gangrenous. Adequate footwear was absolutely essential to stay alive. Washing facilities and latrines were few. A constant, bitter struggle for them took place as soon as inmates were beaten out of sleep. Valuable nervous energy and moral self-respect was consumed in daily anxiety to secure water to wash and a place at the latrines. Fellow-inmates showered curses and obscenities on those using the latrines; they always seemed to take much longer than necessary. Opportunity to open one's bowels on a work kommando was rare, and it always required permission from the SS person in charge or from the Kapo—the privileged inmate heading a work kommando—and either might answer a request for permission to fall out with blows or kicks. An old inmate told me when I arrived: 'Keep your bowels open regularly.' I soon discovered that the psychological advantage of following his wise advice was greater than the physical need. Opening bowels daily was the only regular action possible to an unprivileged inmate. It was the only way to feel that he retained some control over his own person— and personality. No lavatory paper was provided; and paper was extremely hard to come by. Every scrap lying about was picked up, even though an inmate could be shot for picking up paper. Fingers were used to clean oneself after using the latrine; if they

187

were not used, sores chaffed the crutch and could be lethal. Some inmates tore pieces from their own clothes, or from those of weak inmates or corpses. But, obviously, pieces of clothing were in limited and uncertain supply; and, in any case, tearing clothes was an offence severely punished: clothes were the property of the Reich. Women inmates were far worse off. They menstruated. It must have been some small compensation and relief to them when starvation or constant fear ended their menstruating. Most did soon cease menstruation, if they did not die first. Things that are trivial in an ordinary citizen's life—lack of paper, size of shoes, dragging oneself out of the stupor of sleep, the effort to keep bowels open regularly—could wear an inmate down and be as murderous as an SS revolver or a Kapo's iron bar.

'Coffee', made from acorns or worse, was not doled out until after roll-call. Wise and resolute inmates hoarded a part of their famine-sized bread ration to help keep out winter cold on the roll-call square or during exhausting day-time forced labour; it was, however, hazardous to keep bread overnight, even when clutched in the hand. I have seen bread stolen from the hand of an exhausted sleeper, and thefts were common from under heads or from inside clothes of a sleeper. At night the safest place to hide bread was between the thighs. Roll-call on the square was a drawn-out ordeal while inmates were counted, work kommandos assigned, and SS orders announced. Morning roll-call, however, was not as awful as evening roll-call; in the morning, the need to start work early made the SS avoid delay. In the evening, it was only inmates' time that was wasted. At roll-calls, inmates struggled for a place in the centre of their group. Those on the outside drew notice for any infringements of rules, and received most of the indiscriminate blows and kicks of SS men and Kapos dissatisfied with a group's behaviour. Those on the inside could, with care and practice, talk unnoticed.

The best work kommando assignments were inside where there was some warmth and comparative seclusion from SS personnel moving about the camp and labour sites. Work as a tailor, machine-worker, or cobbler, or in the 'hospital', laundry, or offices, was eagerly sought. Inmates bribed, fawned, connived, fought to be chosen for these duties. Cleaning up the filth in the block was privileged work. Even cleaning latrines was regarded as a good kommando, although no implements were provided and hands had to be used to scoop up the contents and scrape off the poles or planks over the pits which constituted latrines. The worst kommandos were quarry work, ditch-digging, or railway construction. Working in these kommandos, inmates in their thin striped uniforms were at the mercy of winter weather, and of brutal Kapos and any passing SS. Work was performed at the double. It often lasted 12 or 14 hours. No mechanical aid was provided; two or three inmates had to lift and carry heavy rails or similar loads. Each inmate at the quarry had to carry large rocks up steep slopes; if he selected a small rock and was noticed, he was beaten, sometimes to death, or pushed over the edge to crash down to the bottom. Kapos of kommandos moved about beating and kicking on workers to greater effort. Kapos were chosen from the inmates and were privileged. Their kommando had an unbearably high quota to fill, and terror was the means used to fulfil it. Only terror could. If a Kapo was lenient, or if his kommando did not achieve its quota, he would likely lose his position and, with it, his privileges of better food, comfortable sleeping accommodation, and freedom from gruelling work. Once removed from his position, he was usually assigned to the worst kommando. If he did not die there from exhaustion, unprivileged inmates would do their best to exact revenge and see that he did not live long. Only one or two short breaks from work were allowed. The arrival of 'soup' was one break anxiously awaited. The 'soup' was mainly water, sometimes with only nettles in the bottom. Inmates bribed and toadied to Kapos to be given full or extra scoops, or to obtain their share from the bottom of the bucket where the mess was thicker. Lack of watches made it impossible to keep track of time and know when the moment approached for 'soup' or return to roll-call. It was another apparently trivial thing wearing down resistance. Considerable ingenuity was needed to go slow at work or find a secure place for a few minutes' rest. It also brought considerable risk; if discovered, savage punishment followed. Kapos found that a quick and easy method of killing was to force a person to lie down on his back; the Kapo placed the iron bar which he usually carried for beating, over the throat of his victim, stood on the iron bar, a foot on each side of the body, and rocked to and fro until the victim was suffocated or had his neck broken.

When the work period was over, the inmates marched back as nearly at the double as could be managed by exhausted bodies urged on by blows and kicks. Stronger inmates helped the weaker or those maimed by blows and kicks, not from charity, but because lateness at roll-call meant punishment for the whole kommando. Those who had been killed or died from exhaustion during the day, had to be also carried back to be placed in the roll-call ranks. Dead or alive, the number of inmates had to tally at morning and evening roll-call. Only after roll-call were dead bodies of workers consigned to the crematoria or burning-pits. The job of carrying back the dead was one to be avoided; it put an extra strain on already failing strength.

Evening roll-calls sometimes took hours. At times, they lasted long into the night; occasionally inmates were forced to stand on roll-call all through the night. In winter, there would always be some who died from the bitter cold, or from the exhaustion of continuous standing at long roll-calls. Roll-calls could be unbearably long because the SS had difficulty in counting correctly or because it was a simple method of punishment. Sometimes it would be the whole unprivileged part of the camp which had to stand for hours awaiting release, and, with it, food and a hot drink. Sometimes it would be a group picked out for 'shirking work', or for some infringement of rules, or simply at the whim of one of the SS.

Inmates witnessed punishments at roll-calls. The usual punishment was flogging. An inmate was trussed to a slatted bench with his hands tied to the bench and his legs pulled apart under the bench and tied near his hands. So, the skin to be flogged was stretched tight. Twenty-five lashes were the standard number, never less. Lashes were usually laid on by a fellow inmate who might receive a reward for a flogging well done, or would be flogged in his turn for half-heartedness. The most competent floggers aimed at exposed genitals. The inmate being flogged had to count aloud each lash as it landed. Failure to count properly was punished by a further 25 lashes. Some died on the bench. Many died later from the deep gashes inflicted, for which no medical attention was permitted or possible.

A worse punishment, much favoured by the SS in some camps, was to knot an inmate's hands behind his back, attach a piece of rope to the knot, and then string him up to a tree or beam, so that his shoulders were dislocated and every struggling movement brought agonizing pain. He was left for hours, sometimes for more than a day, sometimes to die. If he was unlucky, he was shot after he had been punished enough; if he was less unlucky, he was cut down to crash to the ground and sometimes break a bone or two. If he could not stagger away, he was killed. If he did manage to stagger away, he needed a sympathetic, skilful, and strong fellow-inmate—and a sufficient reserve of courage of his own—to force his dislocated shoulders back into place. He was permitted no period for recuperation; he was due back in his work kommando the next day. Work with shoulders dislocated is, of course, impossible; and inability to work to standard spelt death. So, having dislocated shoulders forced back into place was a necessity for continued life. Even so, the pain in, and weakness of, the tortured shoulders often reduced the ability to work properly to a level meriting execution. Perhaps, after all, those who died on their tree or were shot when cut down were the least unlucky since the interval between the start of the punishment and the end of life was less long.

More serious offenders were hung. Inmates acted as executioners for the reward of a few cigarettes, which were good currency with which to buy food. The person to be executed was stood on a stool under the gibbet—a permanent fixture—with a rope around his neck. The stool was pushed away. He did not find a mercifully quick release from a broken neck; instead he swung, slowly strangling to a garrotted death. In some camps, the other inmates had to file by the dead body, look into its eyes, and each touch the corpse with his hand. Worse punishments occurred. Perhaps the SS was feeling especially ferocious; he might have received a reprimand from a superior, or he might be feeling the cold, or his wife might have been nagging him. Some inmates were tortured before execution, or tortured to death. Inmates were forced to drink bucketfuls of water until they suffocated; others in winter were soaked with water and left staked out all night in the snow or frost to freeze to death. I saw an inmate slowly chopped to pieces by a steel spade. More than once, the wrong number of an inmate was taken for punishment, or the man, scheduled for punishment in a few days, died and his number was allotted to a new inmate. It made no difference; it was a number not a man who was punished.

Inmates were punished by imprisonment in the bunker for days, weeks, or even months. The bunker was too small to lie down. It had no windows. There was little air; no beds or blankets. No food or water was provided for days. Those imprisoned licked the moisture from the walls to quench thirst. There were no lavatory facilities and a bunker inmate was not allowed to the latrines. When the bunker was crowded—and it usually was—its occupants fought each other for space to sit down or for a place near the moist walls. I was in the bunker when a strong inmate killed another occupant so that he could sit on his corpse. The other occupants and myself were not strong enough—physically or morally—to do anything about this murder. The only extenuating circumstance for our failure was that, in a crammed bunker, lack of room made it impossible for the four or five others to attack the murderer all together, because he would inevitably be able to throttle to death the one nearest to him before weight of numbers told.

Inmates learned to suppress human sympathy for those punished. What could they do to prevent it? Even if they chose to protest and to be inevitably killed themselves, the punishment would not be stopped or prevented. Mass attack was theoretically feasible; but inmates were too broken and atomized to risk their own death from the heavy machine guns trained on them, or from SS revolvers, Kapo iron bars, and the tearing teeth of ferocious watch-dogs, all at the ready. Inmates became inured to, and uncaring of, the agonizing screams of those being flogged or tortured. I recall ceasing to hear the shrieks of one person being flogged; I thought only of the food to come afterwards. Another time, I hoped the person being flogged would count the lashes correctly, not because I felt any pity for him having to endure another 25 lashes, but simply because I did not want the procedure to be dragged out and delay my release to my block, and food and rest. I was far from being the only one who felt like that. Self came first with practically all inmates; and sympathy for others simply exhausted, wrecked, and broke an inmate's hold on himself, and so reduced his chance of survival. It might have been different if sympathy could have prevented suffering. But it could not. That was one of the very few things we knew for certain.

Elie Wiesel, a Hungarian Jew at Auschwitz and Buchenwald, relates in his book *Night*, that he saw his father being beaten with an iron bar by a Kapo. Elie Wiesel confesses that he not only kept quiet and still, but thought how he could move away from his father without being noticed, to avoid the possibility of the Kapo's violence being turned on him. He does not remember feeling sympathy for his father; instead, he felt angry, not at the Kapo, but at his father because he had not been clever enough to avoid the Kapo's attack. I can sympathize with Elie Wiesel since I felt anger at a fellow-inmate being beaten next to me because he had drawn the Kapo's brutality in my direction. At the time I felt no sympathy at all for the victim.

I never stole anything from a fellow-inmate. Nor did I trade for food; being unprivileged, I had nothing with which to trade. Sometimes, I gave away some of my food to those weaker than myself. Yet, more than once when I had done so, I later felt resentment at the recipient of my gift because I considered he had lowered my chance of survival. For a time, I slept next to a man who had developed a large suppurating sore on his leg. His shoes had been stolen, and the pair he had acquired had been the wrong size, and rubbed a sore on his heel which had spread up his leg. I used to clean the pus from his stinking sore for him; he was too weak to do it himself; so weak in fact, that he had almost become a 'Mussulman', an inmate who had resigned himself to death and lost the will to do anything to help himself survive. I shall always remember, on one occasion while I was wiping away the pus, thinking to myself, 'Die quickly, you bastard; then I shan't have to do this filthy job any more.' He did die a few weeks later. One day, his sore had a sweet smell, and I knew gangrene had set in. He had to go to the 'hospital', and, although I implored a hospital attendant to spare him, he was selected for extermination and given a lethal injection. Afterwards, a moment came when I thought what a fool I had been in drawing attention to myself by imploring so loud and long for his life. That way, lay my own possible extermination. An unprivileged inmate should never draw attention to himself; remaining inconspicuous was the best way to survive.

The necessity to block human sympathy for others made friendships difficult. Once you had seen your friend beaten, or killed, or die before your eyes, you realized how greatly sorrow could impair your will to survive. Worse, your failure to do something to prevent his death cut a deep wound in your self-respect. True, you could not have prevented his suffering; but at least you could have shown your love for him by dying with him. Perhaps, seeing that sympathy might have made his own death easier for him.

193

So, some cultivated loneliness. There, at least, you could preserve unmaimed some little part of good in yourself. There, you could isolate yourself from the constant talk of food which, for so many, was a form of gastronomic masturbation. There, you could wage a war to conquer the temptations to throw away what shreds of self-respect were left to you.

But, although an unprivileged inmate could be lonely, he could never be alone. He was always part of a crowd. There was no solitary physical place to act as a refuge to recover inner composure. Bodies were always rubbing you; eyes were always prying at you; no physical privacy was possible. An unprivileged inmate was beaten down on the concentration camp anvil into a unit in a mass. His individuality was denied by what he was compelled to do—or not do. His individuality was denied by his having no name; he was only a number. When addressing an SS man an inmate had to state only his number and group—Jew, political prisoner, and so on. SS personnel always used the contemptuous 'du' form of address to inmates. Always they added obscenities, the most common being 'shit'. That term had a certain aptness, since camps were a Nazi means of eliminating waste products.

If an SS man called an inmate over to him, it was death to approach nearer than a certain number of paces. If he called you closer, it was wise to respectfully beg to say that his rules did not permit you to approach nearer than the limit he had prescribed. If he was going to kill you in any case, he would repeat his order, or he might set his dog on you; these dogs were specially trained to attack the genitals. Alternatively, he might relent because you were such a nicely perfected automaton. But the SS were unpredictable, and nurtured unpredictability. Unpredictability was the sole predictable thing in camp life.

Unpredictability was a major factor turning an inmate into the ultimate atomized mass man. Some were so atomized that they became 'Mussulmen', living corpses. Mussulmen did not walk, but shuffled; they did not watch people or things but kept their eyes unturned and on the ground; they did not react to any kindness but accepted it without acknowledgment. Inevitably, Mussulmen dropped dead or were selected for extermination. Occasionally, a Mussulman walked into the electrified wire surrounding the camp; a small but sufficient spark of life and personality may have flickered to enable him to choose his own moment and way

194

of death. Or, perhaps, he simply did not realize where he was going.

When, for some reason or other, there was no work, inmates were not left to their own resources. They were compelled to do 'sport'. 'Sport' took various forms: 40 or 50 push-ups; hundreds of somersaults; frog-jumps squatting on the heels with hands over the head; time and again throwing oneself down in the dirt or mud and jumping up; pushing one's prone body like a snake for hundreds of yards. Anyone reacting slowly was whipped. Those who fell exhausted and could not rise despite kicks were despatched with a shot, or by a stick thrust down their throat. In pre-war camps, 'sport' was an initiation to break morale. Later, work kommandos and the camp atmosphere served that purpose.

Starvation disintegrates character even more than fear of violent death. The effects of starvation can never be wholly understood by someone who has not starved. Elie Wiesel saw a son kill his own father for a small piece of bread; he saw another father steal food from his own son who was too weak to move from his bunk to line up for his rations; and he saw yet another son leave his emaciated father to die alone on a forced march so that he need not encumber himself with his father's weight and imperil his own chance of survival.

Starvation reduced others to cannibalism. At Wöbbelin, a sub-camp of Buchenwald, inmates killed each other for food, and tried to eat the flesh of corpses thrown outside the huts. At more than one camp some inmates spoke with relish of the nutritive value and the delicious flavour of human liver which they had eaten. More than once, when a man was executed on the spot by a bullet in the back of the neck, his near-by fellow-inmates threw themselves on the ground and fought each other to claw up the scattered brains and stuff them into their mouths. They continued until no more brains were left, ignoring the SS man shooting at, and killing, some of them, and when his revolver was empty, kicking and beating them. After a time, an inmate became hardened to blows and kicks; and, in any case, pain of starvation easily took precedence over pain of blows and kicks. In the last days, I saw a woman inmate cut some flesh from a corpse lying in the compound—how newly dead, I do not know—and put it in her small cooking-pot and eat it. I also saw others hack slices from corpses and eat them raw. I thought of trying to stop these cases of cannibalism; but then decided it did not matter. The cannibalized corpses were, after all, the bodies of those very few inmates who had died that others might live. Although I was nauseated at the sight, I wondered how long it would be before I was acting similarly, if the rumours that the war was almost won were incorrect. I still am in doubt whether it was solely belief in the nearness of liberation that kept me from being a cannibal. I was hungry enough and physically weak enough. I might have been morally weak enough, except for that hope.

The hope that the war would be over soon, and the certainty that the Allies would win, played some part in stopping my trying to obtain a privileged position and so move out of the perilous ranks of the unprivileged, where death was always near, hunger always gnawed viciously, and complete degradation into a mere atom in a mass was always a threat. There were, however, other obstacles. A practical one was that I had no possessions and no connections with the privileged. Also, I was moved between three main camps. Then, too, I had learnt a lot in several years of POW camps before being sent to a concentration camp. A further obstacle was that I retained enough of the romantic idealism that had, from the 1930s, made me want to fight tyranny and be no part of it by assisting the enemy in any way whatever; I despised POWs who volunteered for work to obtain more food, or who, by trading with the enemy, enabled Germans to enjoy, and sustain their morale on, real coffee, proper soup, and other articles from Red Cross parcels unobtainable in the Axis countries. Finally, perhaps the most important obstacle was that, although I never deliberately sought death during the war, I was completely convinced, from September 1939 until the end, that I would sooner or later be killed. Paradoxically, this gave me a strength not available to others. Of course, I did not have this conviction every moment of the six years, but I could always fall back on it in the worst moments. It can hardly, however, be called a moral strength; and it certainly did not belong even to the same species as the strength of those—and there were some, even if they were not many—who, hoping to retain life, nevertheless made sacrifices for others that endangered or killed themselves.

Inmates could occupy privileged positions because the concentration camps—and the extermination of the Jews—were run on a system of indirect rule, not dissimilar from that developed by the

British in their Indian Empire and by Lugard in Nigeria. The SS were managers or supervisors. They appointed inmates or Jews to administer the camps or ghettoes. These administrative positions carried important privileges: much more food; much better clothes; much easier work; much more comfortable living quarters, sometimes a cubicle or small room to oneself; the chance to grow rich; and the opportunity to save the lives of friends and favourites. They also meant the privilege to enjoy women; in both Auschwitz and Buchenwald there were brothels, in which women were glad to prostitute themselves for food and a better chance of survival. Privileged inmates were permitted use of these facilities; and could, in any case, always buy women inmates outside the brothels. The unprivileged soon lost any desire for sex; starvation and sexual desire do not dwell together.

Bitter conflict resulted from efforts to obtain and retain privileged positions. In some camps conflict was a war literally to the death. The privileged had to band together if they were not individuals protected by the SS. The privileged formed factions which tried to win total power by ousting members of other factions. The most obvious way to eliminate a rival faction was to arrange for its members to be transferred to the worst kommandos or put on a list of those selected for extermination, or to arrange their death when they had the misfortune to have to go to the 'hospital'. So, clerkships in the office assigning work duties and drawing up extermination lists, and posts in the 'hospital' were the most important positions for factions. But it was important also for a faction to ensure that its men and women were Kapos of work kommandos or block officials, both of whom could attend to the liquidation of rivals or undesirables. At Buchenwald a deadly struggle continued between Communists and German 'politicals'. In many camps, superior organization, greater ruthlessness, tighter loyalty and ideological fervour gave the Communists the edge over opponents. Once in power, they saw to the liquidation of those they knew had rightist political principles, even those who were ordinary inmates.

A similar condition prevailed in Jewish ghettoes. The SS appointed a Jewish Council, and this *Judenrat* in turn appointed subordinates to carry out necessary duties. The SS ordered the *Judenrat* to supply a certain number of Jews for deportation to extermination. The *Judenrat* chose the individuals who made up

o

the transport. Jewish police were used to collect them and bring them to the *Umschlagplatz*, or place of assembly. Some Jewish police were more brutal and assiduous in catching other Jews than SS men were. In *Scroll of Agony* Chaim A. Kaplan states that Jewish police readily accepted bribes. One instance he relates is of some Jewish policemen who arrested 800 Jews, ostensibly on SS orders, instead of only 400 as, in fact, ordered. The 400 wealthiest had been released by the police after payment of large bribes. In the extermination camps, Jews fought for privileged positions —even stoking the crematoria and feeding them with corpses. Hannah Arendt is absolutely correct in her judgment in *Eichmann in Jerusalem* that the SS would not have been able to carry out the extermination policy as they did had it not been for Jewish help.

Yet the Jews who assisted did not always act for entirely selfish motives. Even Jewish policemen accepted bribes to buy food at hugely inflated prices for their family and friends who were starving on the rations allowed by the SS. Others obtained administrative posts to try to save the lives of their family and friends as well as their own life. The father of Janina David became a Jewish policeman in the Warsaw ghetto, and so was able to smuggle her out to live first with a non-Jewish Polish family and then in Catholic convents. He and the rest of his family were exterminated. She survived to tell the tale in *A Square of Sky* and *A Touch of Earth*. The terrible dilemma in which her father was caught by having to force others to their death in order to try to save his own family must have been agonizing. Probably, when he finally was exterminated, he welcomed death as a release from the memory of the terrible deeds he had been compelled to do.

In concentration camps some of the worst floggings were inflicted by inmates on inmates. Some of the worst brutalities and murders were the work of Kapos. Some had little or no alternative if they wanted to stay alive. They, too, were human beings corruptible by pressures similar to those operating on SS personnel. Perhaps the only difference between them and the SS was that they were not motivated by ideology; but the urgent need for self-preservation more than filled that gap. Some Kapos tried to grow rich, and a few did so. At the camp at Neuengamme the kitchen Kapo and the crematorium Kapo connived together and sold to civilians the meat provided for camp inmates. They replaced it with human corpses smuggled out of the crematorium. The

198

practice was revealed, after about a month, by the discovery of a human jaw bone in the soup. Both Kapos were executed. How many inmates of Neuengamme have been unwilling cannibals cannot be known. Probably only a few of the unprivileged have been, since they rarely saw meat. Similar schemes to grow rich remained undiscovered. The capital founding post-war businesses for some inmates came from corpses.

Some of the non-Jewish privileged must have suffered agonies similar to those of the father of Janina David. Many people owe to them their emergence alive from the camps in 1945. But at how high a price in the death of other human beings? How many were sent to their death for each one preserved? Even those brave enough to risk death by refusing to carry out an atrocity ordered by an SS man or woman, did in some part assist in other atrocities and in extermination. Like the German judge or civil servant, they could always plead in extenuation that somebody else would immediately take their place if they 'resigned'. An unprivileged ex-inmate who survived can have understanding and compassion for the privileged. Yet, he can have no more than a limited respect for any of them, however brave they were and however many they saved. The price in helping to cause too many deaths is too high for respect to be any more than limited.

Nevertheless, we of the unprivileged are not in any impregnable position from which to be able to throw stones. Whilst in the camps most of us envied the privileged. Since release, if and when we search our heart and conscience, we know that we could have volunteered to die, and so allowed someone else, selected for extermination, to live to be free. The number of dead was, after all, finite; and hearts and consciences demand, and can do, a little simple arithmetic. Because of what we did not do when we could have done it, we, too, are not stainless. We never will be. That is a part of the tragedy of Nazi Germany. A small part, perhaps; but, nevertheless, a part.

We can have little, or no, respect for those who escaped. Understanding and compassion, yes; but respect, never. Those who escaped knew that others would die simply because they had escaped. For every escapee, the SS executed five or more inmates. If such reprisals did nothing else, they encouraged informing to the SS of proposed escapes. On occasions, retribution was visited on the family of the escapee, and they were lucky if they were allowed to stay alive as inmates. For every escape, in addition to executions, rations were cut and many more hours had to be stood on roll-call squares. Both punishments added more corpses to the pile of those already executed in reprisal. Even those who escaped to warn their fellow-Jews outside, or to inform the world of the atrocities being committed behind the SS cloak of secrecy, can find little comforting palliative for the deaths their action caused, since Jews remained disbelieving and the Allies did next to nothing to help halt or slow down the atrocities except carry on their military measures to overthrow Nazism. They would, in any event, have done that. So, in any event, would the Papacy and the Catholic Church have performed its work of mercy. Since almost all escapees were privileged persons—they were the only inmates able to acquire facilities and opportunities for escape—their consciences must be doubly troubled. It is certain that, had inmates not escaped, more people would have been alive on the day of liberation.

Jews have often been blamed for the passivity with which they went to gas chambers or mass graves. The blame is so wantonly misplaced that the sole charitable excuses for it are gross lack of thoughtful imagination or a plenitude of ignorance. The passivity of Jews is easily explicable. From centuries of pogroms Jews learned the value of passive resistance long before Gandhi brought it to the world's attention. Jewish religion emphasizes that God visits his wrath on his chosen people for their sins—and for the rest of the world's sins—and that God's wrath must be passively borne. It is not only Gentiles who have made Jews scapegoats. So has their religion; and any Christian who mocks at those Jews who believe in a Jew's self-appointed role as scapegoat, has forgotten —or never learned—the lesson Christ tried to teach on his cross. It may not be a lesson a non-Christian finds valuable, but at least he should not deny it admiration. Many religious Jews also believed that God would not allow his chosen people to be completely exterminated. Although they may have been wrong in believing it God's work, they were right in believing that all Jews would not be exterminated. Moreover, those exterminated did not die entirely in vain. Because of what Jews suffered under Hitler, there is less anti-Semitism in the world today; and almost certainly the British would not have surrendered Palestine as they did, and the oil-hungry Western powers would not have held their hand as they did when the Arab states were at war with Israel, if Hitler had not won, by his terrible deeds, a sympathy for Jews which they had never before enjoyed. Ironically, Hitler may aptly be numbered among the founders and preservers of Israel.

Jews under Hitler were as incredulous as most other people at the thought of their extermination. The Big Truth is as unbelievable as the Big Lie is believable. The thick curtain of secrecy with which the SS obscured the horrible truth of the Final Solution aided incredulity. The gradualness of increasing severity against Jews helped deceive them into believing that each downward step was the bottom step, instead of a death-ridden escalator to eternity.

Once in the train carrying them to extermination, they were packed so tight, given so little air and food and water, shot at so often for screaming or beating on the sides of wagons, compelled to stay for so many days in an atmosphere of sealed wagons so fetid with urine and excrement on the floor, saw so many of their companions, or loved ones, die of exhaustion or be killed by stronger and pitiless Jews wanting food or air, or room to sit down, that the shock was too traumatic for survival of the capacity for resistance. When the wagon doors were opened at their final destination, all they could think of was gulping down lungfuls of fresh air and thankfulness that the journey's hell was over. If they were received by kicks, blows and shots, the trauma continued and they were easily herded into gas chambers. If they were received kindly by SS, anxious to have as little fuss as possible, they were all too willing to believe assurances that they were only going to take a shower-bath in what was really a gas chamber. Who could retain initiative in such circumstances? The queue went that way; and how many people in peaceful democracies do not live a queue-like life? Even at the worst times, it was only too human not to *want* to believe in their own extinction. Who would?

There were very few examples of Jews resisting. Those that did resist met a terrible fate. Some Dutch Jews, who resisted and killed SS men, died a thousand deaths a thousand times over under slow, cruel torture inflicted during a period of weeks. The single death of a gas chamber would have been infinitely preferable.

How were Jews to resist? They had no weapons, and no means of obtaining weapons anywhere near the equal of the enemy's. When a man knows he is going to die and that he is impotent to prevent his execution, the only worthwhile behaviour seems to him to try to die with the maximum of dignity and the minimum of satisfaction to executioners enjoying the abasement of his humanity. It is a pertinent question how what goes on in a man's mind in the moments before his execution can be known. I know because, in prison in Italy, I was told I was going to be shot. With some others, I was tied to a stake, and compulsorily blindfolded despite my protests. I heard orders given and rifle-bolts rattle. I was certain I was about to die. My sole obsessive thought was the preservation of my dignity. In fact, although the others were shot, I was not. The sham was part of the torture used to try to extract information from me. The same cat-and-mouse technique was used on several successive days; and, although it became harder each time to maintain any dignity I had, it was still the thought of my dignity that completely filled my mind. That particular torture was discontinued perhaps because the law of diminishing returns applies to such torture techniques, or, more probably, because it was slow. Although different, quicker methods were used, I still stuck to my cover-story; and I was eventually transported to Germany without having been broken. If such a lack of initiative and of resistance in the face of execution could be shown by someone not yet starved and demoralized, how much initiative and resistance can be expected of Jews who had been subjected to long starvation and appalling demoralization?

At Treblinka extermination camp some Jews set up an escape committee, and on 2 August 1943 revolted and killed a number of guards—there were 240 guards in all, 40 SS and 200 Ukrainians. About 600 Jews escaped of the 1,000 who revolted. Only 40 were still alive at the end of the war; the others had died of wounds, or been killed by Germans, Poles, or partisans. Jean-François Steiner wrote *Treblinka* to commemorate this revolt. In the preface to the book, Simone de Beauvoir says that those who revolted—and Steiner's book—demonstrate that 'the Jewish people had not allowed themselves to be led to the slaughter-house like a flock of sheep'. She adds that 'it seems monstrous that fatalistic resignation could have been imputed to the Jews'. She could hardly be more wide of the mark. Her egregious error originates in a cast of mind that thinks and speaks in categories: 'the Jewish people', 'the Jews'. At Treblinka, and elsewhere—notably in the Warsaw ghetto in 1943—*some* few thousand Jews revolted. Millions more, however, *were* led to the slaughter-house like sheep. Simone de

Beauvoir argues that 'the circumstances' explain the helplessness of 'the Jews'. But it is also 'the circumstances' that allow sheep to be led to the slaughter-house as many Jews were led to the gas chambers at Treblinka and elsewhere. Her worst error—if that is not too charitable a word—is that her obsessive categorizing deprives Jews of their humanity, in the same way as categorizing workers as 'the working class' or black people as 'the negroes' deprives them of their humanity. There is no such person as 'the Jew', 'the worker', 'the negro'; there are, instead, Jewish persons, working persons, negro persons. Simone de Beauvoir's categorizing also makes her miss most of the meaning the revolt and Steiner's book holds: that, out of over 800,000 Jews who came to Treblinka between 1942 and 1943, only 1,000 revolted. Also, she does not seem to realize that those 1,000 men and women who revolted all held privileged positions. Their revolt was built on, and only made possible by, the ashes of 800,000 fellow-Jews whom they had helped to kill in the Treblinka gas chambers.

The survival of only 40 of the 600 who revolted and escaped points to another reason why Jews were passive in the face of extermination. Where could they find refuge? In the countries where Jews were, many Gentiles were anti-Semitic. Of those who were not, few were willing to risk their whole family's execution for concealing a Jew. Those brave and charitable enough to run the risk, faced formidable and perplexing problems. How were rationed food, soap and other necessities to be obtained for a Jew without a ration-card? How was a Jew who fell ill to be cared for? A doctor could not be called; a prescription for necessary medicine could not be had. What if the illness was infectious? How could a Jew be effectively concealed when people, other than the family, came to the house, or if an electrician or plumber had to be summoned for repairs? What if the house or flat was bomb-damaged? The Jew would almost certainly be discovered, and the family concealing him executed. Bruno Bettelheim overlooks, or is ignorant of, these and other similar difficulties when, in his *The Informed Heart*, he blames Anne Frank's family for staying together instead of splitting up and seeking refuge in Gentile homes. He forgets also that a Jew has only his synagogue and his family as 'associations' to which he can belong; and a person can only be the 'autonomous individual', which Bettelheim so ardently believes a person should be, if he can belong to associations. Without 'associations', a person is not an individual, nor even a person; he is an atom. It was a right instinct, though, as it transpired a fatal one, which made the Frank family stay together. It is curious that someone who is himself Jewish, should fail to see why the family is, perforce, all-important to Jews. It is significant that the Jews most willing to revolt were either Zionists or Communists; they had another 'association' to sustain them.

It is a popular belief that adversity inevitably nurtures virtue. Adversity may do so in some cases. In the case of Jews and camp inmates under Hitler's régime, adversity came in a too terrifying shape and quantity for there to be more than a handful of Jobs. Omnipresent death, terror, torture, starvation, and equal tribulations helped break and degrade Jews and other camp inmates. They—and the subhuman condition to which they brought their victims—fertilized the absolute corruption of victims and of the SS. They helped, or rather enabled, the concentration camp and extermination system to work. Like the SS, but for different reasons and with much greater excuse, inmates fell victim to the disease of apartheid of the mind. Most forgot, if they had ever known, that each of their fellow-inmates was also a fellow-human being. Only the saintlike remembered that SS men and women were not devils, but fellow-human beings. In such circumstances it was immeasurably hard—probably impossible—to bridge the gap with the necessary sense of sympathy for others whoever they were. So, inmates confirmed and aggravated by their behaviour the apartheid of the mind from which all human beings suffer in some measure. Inmates can scarcely be blamed; they were human beings subject to human failings and fears. Their terror, greed, uncaringness were so much greater than those shown by the ordinary citizen in normal circumstances, because they existed—to say 'lived' would be cruel mockery—in conditions of extreme stress. But it would be wrong to think that any more than a difference of degree separated camp inmate from normal citizen. However degraded, inmates were still human, until they were dead; and even the dead remain human to those who remember and understand them.

In regard to inmates, this view is easy to accept. In regard to the members of the SS and the *Einsatzkommandos*, however, it is extremely and painfully hard to accept. Yet, it must be accepted; whoever degraded and degrading they, too, were human to those who do not gaze through spectacles which can only be focused on stereotypes or categories. They still are human to those who can bear to bring themselves to remember and understand what they did and why they did it. But their existence and behaviour will be always incomprehensible to those who themselves suffer over-much from apartheid of the mind, and will always inspire hate, and therefore, sterility in them.

On both sides of the barbed wire—though more on the inside than the outside—one essentially human and common, and ordinarily often beneficial, emotion moved people to the absolute corruption which comes from too great a loss of respect for almost, if not all, others, but which probably comes most from too great a loss of self-respect. That emotion was hope. With a terribly tragic irony, hope destroyed on both sides of the wire, humaneness, sense of others, sympathy for others. For SS men and women, hope for a millennium. For inmates, hope that we would stay alive. And hope that there was beyond the barbed wire a world where prevailed love, kindness, tenderness, gentleness, beauty, truth, freedom, peacefulness.

Is there such a world? Can there ever be?

5   There but for the Grace of God . . .

HITLER WAS A PIONEER. He blazed a trail into new territories of evil and despotism. Whereas Alan Bullock's influential biography of Hitler emphasized in its epilogue that Hitler was the last figure in the history of the old Europe, it would seem that Hitler was rather an early figure in the history of a new Europe. The significance of Hitler for our generation is not so much that he destroyed the old world but that he pointed the way to a new world of totalitarian tendencies. The diverse sources of totalitarianism, in the past and in the present, deserve closer analysis; and such an analysis suggests that totalitarian autocracy will become, not rare, but prevalent.

Inhumanity is the natural inhabitant of a moral void. Any forces which deeply undermine morality—the variegated links between human beings—prepare the way for totalitarianism. Was it surprising that the succession of hammer blows from the industrial revolution, the first world war, and the accompanying depressions should have dissolved German morality, civilization and culture? So many Germans were cast into a moral void that the beast which is so near the surface in all of us was able to emerge in all its ferocity. In a real sense it was not German culture that nurtured Nazism but the breakdown of German culture. The old Germany would never have tolerated what the Nazis did; the Nazis could act as they did only because the old Germany had been broken into helpless fragments. The Nazi totalitarianism was not an expression of German national character or of powerful strands in German morality but rather an expression of the collapse of character and morality.

What happened in Germany during Hitler's rule has often been seen as a sign of traditional characteristics which Germany, alone of the countries of Western Europe, reputedly had in strong measure. In fact it was a sign of material and social conditions which appeared in modern Germany. No other country in Western

Europe had in modern times suffered so many swift and successive seismic disturbances. It is true that England lost the depression of the 1930s but it had won the war of 1914–18, and, in the 1930s had a well-functioning, firmly established democratic system to uphold state and society. England after 1918 had, like other countries, her hollow men, but there were not enough of them for Fascism or Communism to be more than a political lunatic fringe. She had had a political revolution in the seventeenth century, and an industrial one starting in the eighteenth, but she was lucky since both happened before the age of the mass franchise, and her Industrial Revolution was slow compared to Germany's. The English are much given to appeals to tradition and precedents, and like to underplay the revolutionary nature of English changes; but their society, especially in the nineteenth century, has undergone changes in many ways more radical than those accomplished by peoples like the French, who are conventionally thought to be more revolutionary. England, however, has a much larger and stronger sense of unity and community than Germany. In England, tradition and change are reconciled as new classes, new persons, new forces take over traditional appearances, often for protection against attacks on their newness. When the new middle classes in the nineteenth century, in their progress from the counting-house to the country-house, occupied the shells of the public-school system, of the civil service, of the representative institutions, they were not unduly hampered by the kind of caste system that prevailed in France and Germany, and they were able to make life very different inside those old habitations. The same kind of phenomenon can be seen in the new 'new classes' in post-1945 Britain. In this sense, the English are a nation of hermit-crabs.

At the end of the eighteenth century, France underwent a devastating revolution and a series of wars. In the next 150 years Frenchmen periodically had bouts of revolutionary fervour, brought on partly by the wines bottled in '93 or in the years of Marengo, Austerlitz or Jena, although, as the years wore on, more bottles bore red labels and the insignia of the hammer and sickle. But France never had an industrial revolution as extensive as Britain's or as breakneck as Germany's, and her stolid, conservative peasant substructure saved her in the depression of the 1930s from effects as economically, politically, and socially destructive as afflicted Germany. And although World War One brought more sorrow to France than to England, she did at least emerge among the victors.

Small industrialized countries like Sweden, Switzerland, Belgium and small agricultural countries like Denmark and Holland have been cushioned by continuing prosperity, by the solidarity that comes from smallness, and usually by freedom from the worst rigours of war. Their very smallness has saved them from damaging pretensions. Backward, agrarian countries like Spain, Portugal, the Balkans, even Italy did not achieve enough industrialization to shake traditional society to the foundations. Even Italy did not become truly totalitarian under Mussolini and so never deteriorated into anything like Nazi inhumanity.

In Eastern Europe there was one country which suffered the kind of seismic shocks which had hit Germany; significantly those shocks led ultimately to totalitarianism. Since the mid-nineteenth century a series of hammer-blows had smashed Russian society and opened up a moral vacuum. In 1861 the emancipation of the serfs had eroded essential pillars of the aristocratic, Tsarist régime. Towards the end of the nineteenth century, industrialization began to have radical effects in the main cities. World War One brought extensive disorder and dislocation, and then revolution. In October 1917, after a period of chaos, the Communists seized power in some areas, but they took three years of bitter, bloody civil war to gain real and complete power. By 1921 Russia was exhausted. Lenin allowed economic relaxation, but tightened the political reins, unwittingly preparing the way for Stalin. Lenin's death in 1924 led to an acrid power-struggle from which Stalin emerged victorious by 1928; and that year can be seen as Russia's equivalent of Germany's 1933. Many traditional values in Russia had already been destroyed when Stalin started a second revolution, forced collectivization and industrialism, and completely uprooted the remnants of the old society. Political measures, and the liquidation of millions in the Great Purges of 1936-8, assisted the erection of a Communist totalitarian despotism; and war furthered this despotism. Changing the things that have to be changed, this case history was similar to that of modern Germany's. Is it, then, mere coincidence that much the same terrible inhumanity and totalitarianism marked Stalin's régime as Hitler's, and that the Communists liquidated at least as many millions of human beings as the Nazis?

Some political scientists and historians object to Communist Russia being put in the same totalitarian company as Nazi Germany. One of their contentions is that Communist Russia belongs to the left and Nazi Germany to the right of the political spectrum. Application, however, of the metaphor of a spectrum to the position of political parties is out of date. The terms 'left' and 'right' were coined for parties in nineteenth-century France, when progressives sat on the left and conservatives on the right in the Chamber of Deputies; but it is a very misleading metaphor in modern times. A more suitable metaphor is that of a horse-shoe, with democratic parties at the curved base and despotic parties at the converging ends. Communism and Nazism are much nearer to each other than Communism is to democratic Socialism or Nazism is to democratic Conservatism.

Most people, though not those wearing red spectacles, would agree that Communist Russia, like Nazi Germany, has only one party, a total ideology, a terroristic police, and a monopoly of communications and armed forces. It is spurious to claim that the Communist economy is socialist whereas the Nazi economy was capitalist; the German economy under Hitler was as much under the control of the Nazis and as little under the control of capitalists as the Communist economy. The Communist economy, like Nazi Germany's, is manipulated by a few in the interests of the few whether those interests are ideological or selfish. In fact, although Communist theory says that the Russian people own the economy, the real owners are the new class of managers, who derive disproportionate incomes and other lucrative rewards which would make greedy capitalists envious and all true Socialists angry. It is economic control that is important in twentieth-century economies with their large-scale enterprises, vertical and horizontal combines, and gigantic trusts; ownership was more important in nineteenth-century economies composed of small enterprises. In the twentieth century how much control of the best part of the economy is possessed by shareholders, who are legal owners? Control is exercised by a few men in executive suites and government offices. Communist control of the Russian economy is not only similar to Nazi control of the German economy, but for all the superficial differences it bears surprising resemblance to that exercised in the U.S.A.

The claim that the Communist party is élitist whilst the Nazi party was a mass movement is also spurious. The Nazi régime became a régime dominated by an élite, mainly SS. In any case, neither in Communist Russia nor Nazi Germany did the party hold power after the initial stages, for the dictator and a small group of his immediate associates soon dominated the régime, using the party as office-boy. Equally spurious is the claim that Nazi support was middle class and Communist support lower class; this may have been so initially, but very many bourgeoisified 'proletarians' in Russia have come to have as great a vested interest in the Communist régime, as very many workers had in the Nazi régime. Ironically, there is considerable cause to suppose that most opposition to the Russian Communist régime comes from workers in field or factory, as most opposition to Hitler came from what Communists would call 'the upper classes'.

The Nazi and Russian Communist ideologies are not essentially different. Both ideologies are incoherent extensions of a single concept; both are self-righteous, dogmatic, and quasi-religious; both are chiliastic, looking forward to the shaping of the world in a millenarian mould; both divide humankind into higher and lower forms of life; both believe that ends justify means and so people must be forced to be free; both justify huge-scale extermination of the unrighteous and unfit, all in the name of 'the good life'; both accept the necessity of revolution and corrosive conflict until Elysium is attained. Nazi ideology was imperialist in a more obvious and apparently traditional way; but Communist ideology, also, aims at conquest of the world and imposing a new order on it. 'Today Russia, tomorrow the world' has been the Communist clarion-call, however muted at times it has been by the expediency of co-existence. The main difference between the imperialism of Communism and that of Nazism has been that Stalin succeeded in winning his *Lebensraum* in the West whilst Hitler failed to win his in the East.

Communist Russia, since Stalin's death in 1953, has certainly become less totalitarian; and it may be that time and increasing prosperity will improve the ruling régime into an ordinary despotism. But prosperity does not inevitably bring freedom; and time is no longer on the side of increasing freedom in Russia, now that Communist China strides swiftly to the status of a super-power. Communist Russia today may be significantly dissimilar in some ways to Nazi Germany, but under Stalin it was basically similar. Stalin, like Hitler, was a pioneer on the totalitarian frontier.

Mussolini was not such a ruthless pioneer although he had several years' start. His Fascist régime was never as totalitarian as Hitler's or Stalin's. The Fascist party did become the sole party, and Mussolini its single leader. Fascist ideology was basically similar to Nazi or Communist ideology; but it was imposed with little of the ruthlessness and fervency that prevailed in Hitler's Germany or Stalin's Russia. The Catholic Church was effective in preventing a Goebbels-like monopoly of communications; the OVRA secret police never achieved a Beria-like police terror. The Italian armed forces always retained a fraction of loyalty to the king; and it was no accident that the army, supported by the king, played a major role in the overthrow of Mussolini in 1943. Mussolini exercised control of the economy only by fits and starts. That Mussolini fell short of Hitler or Stalin in totalitarianism may have been due partly to his different personality and temperament; he seems to have been much less inhumane, single-minded, intelligent, and hardworking. However, it was much more the result of less atomization of Italian society than occurred in Hitler's Germany or Stalin's Russia. Mussolini, moreover, never attempted to aggravate atomization by a Stalinist industrial and agricultural revolution. When he paid Hitler the sincerest form of flattery by going to war, it was to pick up the crumbs of Nazi victory in 1940; and, when he was compelled to continue the meal, he did not engage in total war. Only in 1943-5 did full-scale totalitarianism emerge in Italy; and even then it prevailed only in North Italy, and only as an outpost of Nazi totalitarianism which employed a worn-out and emasculated Mussolini as a figure-head.

Similarly, state and society in Japan were not atomized enough for full-scale, or even true, totalitarianism to prevail there in 1941-5. Enough of Japanese traditional society was symbolized in, and protected by, the person of the Emperor. It is true that the Bushido Code filled a moral void for many Japanese, and that the Kempetai secret police would not have been complete misfits in Gestapo or N.K.V.D. offices. It is also true that the atrocities perpetrated on European 'outsiders' would have won the admiration of Himmler or Beria. Nevertheless, the despotism that ruled Japan at the height of the war was never as totalitarian as that in Hitler's Germany or Stalin's Russia.

The three twentieth-century examples of Russia, Italy and Japan indicate that Hitler's régime was not unique. His régime was not the whim of an aberrant moment; it was not out of phase with the times. Hitler's régime was not trying to swim against the ebb-race of modern realities, however much it may have been against the tide in Western democracies. It was not the régime of a few knaves or fools who happened accidentally to come to power. The fact that one of these powerful totalitarian régimes, Soviet Russia, continued unchecked after 1945 makes one hesitate to accept Alan Bullock's dictum that 1945 was the end of an era and that Hitler was henceforth a symbol of the past. An examination of the modern world makes his dictum even more untenable.

2

The open season for conceiving Utopias is when state and society are in flux. It was no coincidence that Christianity was born when the Roman Empire was fumbling its way to security and stability. It was no coincidence that the waning of the Middle Ages bred so much mysticism and millenarianism. It is no coincidence that Communism, Fascism and Nazism were sired when new political, social, intellectual and technological developments were rendering completely obsolete the dating of the beginning of modern times at 1500 or thereabouts. Plato dreamed his ideal republic when Athens was teetering towards decline and fall. Augustine saw his vision of the city of God when the barbarians were battering at Roman gates. Thomas More published his *Utopia*, and Bacon published his imaginative account of a new scientific world, *The New Atlantis*, when the Middle Ages were waning and a new age waxing. Samuel Butler, William Morris, Edward Bellamy wrote their Utopias whilst Victorian industrialization was revolutionizing England and the world. Aldous Huxley wrote his *Brave New World* in 1932 after World War One had dissolved the last of Victorian England and it is not surprising that Orwell's *1984* followed World War Two.

This is a time for new ideologies and a time for new weapons with which to enforce these ideologies. Hitler's totalitarian weapons were primitive compared to those available today. Computers, and ever improving punch-card and electrical filing systems, ease the task of secret police. Modern microphones smaller than a watch need not be planted in a spied-on room; they are so sensitive that they can pick up talk through walls at a distance of several hundreds of yards. Helicopters simplify aerial suppression of revolt in the countryside or town in a manner not possible for old-fashioned bombers and fighter planes. Huge jet planes, each capable of carrying hundreds of troops, or several jeeps, or heavy artillery, or tanks, can rush military might to a disaffected area more than a thousand miles distant in two or three hours. The armoury of propaganda has acquired a new weapon in television. New drugs have transformed brainwashing into a scientific art, and have enabled secret police to dispense with some of their brutal torturing. A totalitarian régime in the second half of the twentieth century need have considerably less fear of opposition and revolution than did Hitler and Stalin.

Totalitarian régimes, however, cannot be built solely on ideology and technology. The totalitarian dictator needs subjects who have already fallen into a moral void, and he enlarges the void by the encouragement of, or compulsion to, apartheid of the mind. This is what Hitler perceived, perhaps from an intelligent and acute appreciation of twentieth-century mass society, perhaps by intuition. One of the lessons from the history of Nazi Germany is the danger of the moral void; and in the world as a whole that danger was not suddenly averted by the death of Hitler and the collapse of the Third Reich.

3

The great majority of Western democrats do not fear a trend to totalitarianism in their own countries. Prosperity has brought a stability and security, pitted only rarely and to a shallow depth by race riots and sit-ins. Governments, instructed by economists, have broken the constant cycle of booms and slumps that characterized industrial society before 1939. Credit cards keep the wheels of affluence turning even if some 10 per cent of the inhabitants of Western democracies live below a standard nowadays regarded as acceptable. Affluence does exact the price J. K. Galbraith tagged in his *The Affluent Society*: for instance, uglification of city and country, and failure to spend sufficient on public amenities. Yet, affluence has bought a previously unparalleled number of hospitals, old people's homes and civic amenities.

The tendency to conformism and the cult of togetherness which have worried—and made the literary fortunes of—the Reismans and the Whytes seem to be counteracted by improving education and increasing leisure in which to develop individual personality, and no past society has not had its share of Joneses and neighbours who envied them. A twentieth-century democracy can comfort itself that its lack of a Leonardo, a Shakespeare, a Beethoven is more than counterbalanced by its lack of illiterate and leisureless citizens.

Television, films, and a Press—cheap in both senses of the word —may be further vulgarizing common taste; but it is tranquillizing to remember that never before has so much good literature been read, and so much good music heard, by so many. Not all paperbacks and long-playing records pander to the lowest common multiple; more than a million copies of each of E. V. Rieu's translations of *The Iliad* and *The Odyssey* have found buyers—amongst about 300 million Western English-speaking citizens.

Individual liberties, enjoyed in past societies by those with enough wealth, are ravenously wolfed by gluttonous governments and gargantuan business corporations; but J. K. Galbraith's theory of countervailing power has brought up to date, for liberal Micawbers, nineteenth-century *laisser-faire* optimism; the power of even political and economic mammoths can countervail each other.

An ordinary citizen in a Western democracy in the 1960s has no reason to doubt that he lives immeasurably better and longer and with less pain than his counterpart in the 1860s—or even in the 1930s. He has more legal justice, more economic justice, more social comfort. A jittery queue may knock on every psychologist's door; but at least most neurotics come to the psychologist's couch voluntarily instead of being locked up in what, not long ago, passed for asylums.

Political stability, legal and economic justice, material plenty are considerable accomplishments, but, by themselves, they are not enough for a civilized person. They are only the clothes of a civilization, and clothes do not make a civilized man. A generation or two ago, an age of hope believed that Western civilization would automatically improve, would automatically gain increasing control over nature, would automatically go on becoming more

214

humane. Then Western civilization was regarded as springing from the Middle East, swelling to a river in the age of the Greek city state, flowing into the Tiber at Rome, irrigating the Middle Ages with Christianity, and reaching the open sea of modern times by way of science, industrialization, and liberal democracy. The ports of call where the most valuable cargo was taken aboard were Athens for rational thought, Rome for law and order, and Jerusalem for religion. This optimistic view was one more product of the habit of intellectuals of confining their attention to society's top crust, and for ranking civilization according to their own suppositions and interests.

Today, definition of Western civilization is much less easy. Is it Plato or James Watt? Philosophy or penicillin? Caesar or God? The rule of law or the rule of the Gestapo? The Louvre or Auschwitz? The Acropolis or the Empire State Building? The Houses of Parliament in London or the Lubianka Prison in Moscow? Nuclear missiles or television? Beethoven or the Beatles? Hamlet or James Bond? The Venus de Milo or the latest sex-symbol? Sport on the baseball and football field or 'sport' in the concentration camp? Hiroshima or the public hospital?

Two world wars, atomic bombs, and Nazi and Communist death camps have brutally slain the cosy view of Western civilization as surely as they slew millions in the trenches, bombed cities and concentration camps. No longer is it sensible to claim that it is obvious that man is improving morally, if it ever was for the open-eyed and open-minded.

Humaneness is not the abundant commodity in Western democracies that their citizens like to think it is, when they make self-congratulatory comparisons with Nazi Germany and other totalitarian countries. The reasons for lack of humaneness in democracies are diverse. One is that training in humaneness is being prevented in educational institutions by training in specialisms. The expulsion is not restricted to the scientific disciplines despite all the hypocritical cries of those who look down on 'technicians' from the height of a degree in Arts. The expulsion is also occurring in what are, by now, misnamed 'the humanities'. The pressures pushing people, who are charitably called educated, towards specialism are powerful. The technological needs of society demand an abundance of specialists; disproportionate rewards assure an eager supply of them. Educational systems, parental ambitions for the young, and the myth-like hold science has over the modern mind, all press society in the direction of a specialist meritocracy.

Not only are experts in different disciplines usually unable to converse profitably, but real communication is impossible between experts in different fields of the same discipline. The time and energy consumed in training as an expert, and in remaining one, is so great that little is left for training in humaneness—for the study of mankind. The study of literature becomes increasingly immersed in specialist technicalia. Very few historians study man; instead they study bits of him, and rarely bits of *her*; certainly not the bits likely to cultivate humaneness. Alternatively, they study an abstract or collectivized 'man' which is far from reality—or humanity. They may know their way around their specialism blindfold; but, outside their own intensively cultivated field, they are too often babes in an inhumane wood.

For instance, they may favour toleration; but too often theirs is an unthinking toleration that springs not from humaneness but from a weak refusal to take a firm stand that might offend someone, from a steady leaking away of the sense of responsibility without which humaneness, and democracy, is impossible. It is popular among intellectuals, claiming to be democrats, to repeat the rote lesson that everyone is entitled to his own opinion. But everyone is emphatically not entitled to his own opinion: Hitler and Stalin were not entitled to theirs. Anyone who has studied individual man properly cannot fail to understand that opinions and actions are inseparable; there is no clean-cutting line dividing them. Their indivisibility is especially dangerous when the opinion-holder has great power; but all of us have power in some degree. Similarly, scholars, especially in the 'humanities', are fond of supporting 'good causes'; but the simple-minded and boringly repetitive habit the campaigns have of being directed against the powers-that-be, instead of being good causes to bring comfort to, say, the aged or spastics, invites quite uncynical speculation whether the real motives of some supporting 'good causes' are, not humaneness, but a desire to make a show of courage and independence of mind, which are, in fact, false, or a liking for hearing their medals, self-awarded in previous campaigns, tinkle as they march in yet another protest parade. Humaneness cannot burgeon and ripen in a mind which obsessively divides society into 'them' and 'us'. Robert

Burns concisely summed up humaneness in his *Address to the Unco' Guid* when he said:

> 'Then gently scan your brother man,
> Still gentler sister woman;
> Tho' they may gang a Kennin wrong,
> To step aside is human.'

If our educators lack gentle humaneness and a proper understanding of man, how are those to be educated to acquire it? Who is to educate our educators?

One not insignificant signpost of, and towards, insufficient humaneness—especially towards 'still gentler sister woman'—is the popularity with inadequately educated people, with both high and low I.Q.s, of sex-and-sadism thrillers in paperbacks and on TV and cinema screens, of 'girlie' magazines, of 'bare-top' nightspots, nude shows, strippers and pornography. The inadequately educated who enjoy and succumb to sex-and-sadism thrillers and 41-inch pin-ups and pornography do not come exclusively from the ranks of the young and the lower social strata. They are not hard to find among those with university degrees. The brainy are not born with a humane spoon in their mouths; and an inhumane mind can as easily be found beneath a bowler-hat or a homburg as beneath a cloth-cap or a school-cap.

The plots and style of sex-and-sadism thrillers are drenched with the dead clichéness of daydreams. An opinion recurring insistently in sex-and-sadism novels is that all women want to be swept off their feet and dream of being slung over a man's shoulder, taken into a cave and raped. Possibly, some women feel this want and dream this dream; but certainly, nearly all women would regard such treatment as a nightmare. The dream is in the mind of men who would like women to have such dreams.

Sex-and-sadism 'entertainment' is a form of drug-taking. These drugs offer an entrance-ticket to a degraded and degrading nirvana where the drug-taker can vicariously knuckle-dust the teeth of whoever stands in his way, kick his opponent in the groin and, with satisfying sadism, watch his victim writhe on the floor—and, all the time, he need feel no pricks of conscience: he is, after all, on the side of the 'goodies'. Sex-and-sadism thrillers are an even more brutalized form of cowboy and Indian films, where the Red Indians fall uncounted and unpitied victims, their humanity conveniently concealed behind their race, their war-paint, and the audience's blood-lust. Sex-and-sadism thrillers give the chance to feel that a way can be carved to wish-fulfilment dreams by violence. The world can be rid by force of what prevents a sense of stability and satisfaction. All those desirable female bodies can be bedded by proxy when they are, in the real world inhabited for most waking and working hours, removed far from reach by one's being married, respectable, low-salaried, bashful, or unprepossessing. When marriage has failed—and many more fail than ever appear in divorce-courts—or when no real love is known, an imaginary recompense is available in daydreaming seduction of the semi-naked sex symbols sold in the slave-markets of advertisements, cheap magazines, strip shows, and on the screens of 23-inch TV sets or Panoramic cinemas.

The pressures pushing people into this spurious nirvana are strong and insidious. Many of the young are disillusioned, not only by the difficulties of adolescence, but also by the dead-end, uninteresting jobs which are their inevitable lot. They are embittered by broken or unsatisfactory parent–child relationships. They are frustrated by society that conventionally frowns on pre-marital relations but makes no attempt to discover an acceptable alternative. Many older people find that ageing domesticity brings shades of the prison-house with mounting bills, and the ulcerous rat-race of promotion and conspicuous consumption. Children grow away from parents ten or so years before they hive off into their own married domesticity, leaving isolated, middle-aged elders bereft of love and of much that had once given purpose and meaning to life; re-education is difficult in middle age. Ambitions are given to most only to be thwarted. There may be room at the top; but most of those who rise to the top are personable, or lucky, or unscrupulous, or prepared to sacrifice their own and other people's humanity—and, by definition, there can only be few at the top. The race is rarely to the deserving, and Christ's parable of the talents has taken on a new meaning in a materialist world where, so often, to him that has shall be given. Frustrations build up and mouths turn down.

The middle-aged mind, more often than not endowed with a legacy of sham education in youth and rusted into rigidity with advancing years, cannot always be reaching for a do-it-yourself hobby kit or be sufficiently occupied with mowing the lawn or

cleaning the car. So, for lack of awareness of anything better to
fill the leisure that is one of the gifts—and curses—of an industrial,
mass age, the middle-aged mind reaches for the vicarious thrill
which provides an easeful death for those who find self-responsibility too difficult, too frustrating, too exacting. Cheap, facile
thrills offer a quick escape from the disappointments, disillusions
and distresses that are meted out by the unimaginative and un-
cultured 'civilization' in which most citizens are imprisoned.

Government even in a democracy seems to be of the many, by
the few, for the few. What satisfaction does having a vote bring in
mass society? The little men and women, who constitute some
90 per cent of mass society, cannot affect the doings of the mighty
or of the grinding mill-stones of mass political party machines.
Politicians on the world stage play at bombmanship which could
cause nuclear destruction or perhaps the extinction of the world;
and the ordinary citizen's finger is as far from the vital—or deadly
—nuclear buttons as he himself is from the moon. The little man
and woman have—perhaps inevitably—no say in their own ultimate fate. On the domestic political stage, small attention is given
to them. Only at election times do they become an object of
professional affection from politicians whose object is to gull them
or cynically bribe them into materialist acquiescence.

In any case, how can politics help solve the little citizen's baffle-
ment at an unlovely life when he is no more than a small cog in a
large machine, and when he finds it hard and uncomfortable to
discover some great new cause or living religion which might take
him out of his puny, worried, shattered shell of self and bring him
into communion with others and with a whole and fulfilling self?
So, if he cannot, or will not, discover love, he can easily find a
substitute in the mental masturbation provided by sex and sadism.

Sociologists and psychologists minimize the effects of sex-and-
sadism 'entertainment'. They pontificate that such 'entertainment'
has not swelled statistics of crime or increased the incidence of
rape or sexual perversion. Some even comfortingly claim that this
'entertainment' provides a harmless release for drives which would
otherwise lead to crime, rape and sexual perversion. That comforting claim throws a garish light on the quality of modern
civilization and on those who make the claim. Yet, even if sociologists and psychologists are right—and it is difficult to know how
they come by the scientific statements—they are aiming at entirely

the wrong target. The real poison in the sex that is peddled in pornography, bare-tops, stripping, 'girlie' magazines, crudely sexual
advertisements and novels, is that it deprives half the human race
—women—of their humanity, as surely as the Nazi anti-semitic
view deprived Jews of their humanity, and as surely as the Communist view deprives capitalists and their 'running-dogs' of their
humanity. These drug-laden crudely sexual 'entertainments' indoctrinate a view of a woman that regards her, not as a person like
oneself, but as no more than a pair of legs, a pair of breasts, a pair
of thighs. She becomes a thing, a *Stück*. In them there is no love
of a woman, no exercise of the sympathy Hume thought necessary
for a moral life, no realization that each woman is a fellow human
being. She becomes simply a thing for man's gratification of himself. Sex without love, sex merely using the sleeping partner for
physical or psychological relief and nothing else, is irresponsible.
More, it is immoral and inhumane, if Kant's categorical imperative, never to use another human being as a means, holds true.
Even though this inhumanity may be rather distantly related to
totalitarian inhumanity, it does hang on the same family tree. The
crude sexual drugs flooding mass minds and mass emotions in-
culcate and reinforce a Himmler-like habit of apartheid of the
mind in the sexual life of ordinary citizens, and perhaps even a
habit that transfers into other sides of life, especially where the
flavour of vicarious sadism and masochism is added.

Sociologists and psychologists, poring over crime-rates to but-
tress their tolerance of sex-and-sadism *ersatz*, can never know how
many rapes have been effected in marriage beds; and yet it is
sound speculation that they certainly are not few. They can never
know how much these drugs strengthen apartheid of the mind;
and yet it is undeniable that it is strengthened in some measure.
Sex-and-sadism 'entertainments' are a strip-tease uncovering inhumane minds and emotions. By coincidence, sex and sadism have
the same initials as the SS; but it is no coincidence that they differ
only in degree, not in kind.

Sex-and-sadism 'entertainment', compared to the SS, may seem
very banal. Nevertheless, banality, that is, commonplaceness and
triteness, is very relevant to the tragedy of Nazi Germany. When
Hannah Arendt published her book *Eichmann in Jerusalem*, she
subtitled this account of Eichmann's trial and execution, 'a report
on the banality of evil'. In her book, she expressed shocked

surprise, emphasized by her own italicizing, at 'the fearsome, word-and-thought defying *banality of evil*', and by her conclusion that the trial of Eichmann and all it revealed had taught the lesson of the banality of evil. Reviewers and readers echoed her shock and amazement, and applauded her discovery of the lesson. It is a sad mark of the stability and security of Western democracies, and of the small interest and thought people in officially Christian countries give to the nature of evil, that the idea that evil is banal should shock and amaze, and should be greeted as a novel discovery.

Evil is, always has been, and always will be banal, whilst human beings are human beings. Evil is banal not simply because it is always with us, and always has been with us since the serpent was so persuasive in the Garden of Eden. Evil is banal not simply because eating the fruit of the tree of knowledge destroys innocence, and gives each person the commonplace ability to tritely commit actions both evil and good. Evil is banal, also, because it is not an abstraction. Evil is not committed by the Devil; evil is individual deeds done by commonplace people and given triteness by a ceaseless repetition that allows only slight variations in the techniques and means by which the evil deeds are committed.

There are, of course, greater evils. Some, at first sight, seem so immense that they cannot be called banal. Hitler's Final Solution exterminating and torturing millions seems to defy description as a banal evil. However, to allow the mind to be overwhelmed by the millionness of the Final Solution is to fall into error. Each 'statistic' murdered was, in fact, an individual. Evil is, and can only be, committed by an individual on an individual. The extermination of millions was not *an* evil deed; it was *millions* of evil deeds. With an awful irony, it is that fact that helped make it commonplace and trite, that is, banal.

Like 'evil', 'genocide' is a portmanteau word, too often mindlessly used so that its true meaning is missed. When the portmanteau's lid is lifted, the contents of the word 'genocide' can be unpacked so that they are revealed as not one event but many events, not one deed but many deeds, not one evil but many evils. A closer examination of the contents shows that the motives, thoughts and emotions of the killers and torturers were commonplace and trite, and that their killings and tortures were, also, commonplace and trite. They were banal because millions of

221

people were involved; but they were also banal because the motives, thoughts and emotions, and killings, all involved, have been commonplace and trite throughout history. It is true that there are superficial differences between, on the one hand, the motivation of an SS killer and the techniques he used to kill, and, on the other hand, those of, say, Crippen or a Roman slave-owner. Basically, however, the act of killing and the motivation for it were similar. Murder has always been all too trite and common-place since Cain killed Abel. So too has been the motivation for it; it springs from banal emotions: hatred, hostility, fear, obedience, contempt and the like. Even Hitler and Himmler were moved by banal considerations. Even Catherine de Medici and the King of France, planning and ordering the Massacre of St Bartholomew in 1572, were moved by banal considerations, for all their sceptred and orbed majesty. They were human beings, extraordinary only in their high and mighty enthroned position. Properly compre-hended, all evil is banal. That is why it is so easy to fall into temptation—and yield to it.

That a visit to the trial of Eichmann was needed to reveal the truth of the truism that evil is banal to a person so obviously intelligent and so concerned with issues of political morality and with the study of totalitarianism as Dr Hannah Arendt is, partly results from the fact that only a tiny fraction of what has been written on Nazi atrocities has attempted any more than a des-cription of *how* the extermination and concentration camp system worked. Details of *how* so many were killed and tortured over-whelm the mind, and sympathy for *how* the victims suffered and hatred for *how* the murderers and torturers caused suffering, over-flows so abundantly that no capacity, no willingness, nor even nervous energy are left for consideration of *why* it was so. The very scarce explanations offered have been either superficial or sweeping. Either a superficial, accusing finger has been pointed at racialism or 'the German national character'; or sweeping labels, mostly psychological, have been pasted on the problem. Neither kind of 'explanation' will do. Explanation from racialism or 'national character' is quite inadequate because of its obvious obtuseness and ignorance. Explanation by labelling is inadequate because it takes a view from on high, which inevitably reduces human beings to the size of ants and cannot help but merge them into an ant-hill society. Psychological 'explanations' too are characterized by the skyscraper view. The social psychologist has a distinct liking for sweeping explanations and pasting labels; and even the psychologist, whose interest is the individual, seems unable to avoid putting patients into pigeonholes with labels like 'paranoia', 'schizophrenia', 'aggression'. Explanation of this aspect of the tragedy of Nazi Germany cannot be had from the top of a skyscraper.

One instance of its inadequacy was when Dr Arendt gave an ant-hill talk on the BBC in August 1964 entitled 'Personal Responsibility under Dictatorship'. In her talk she discussed the excuse of superior orders so often advanced by those accused of Nazi atrocities. She argued that this excuse is invalid, because, despite a millennium-old misconception, it is not obedience, but support, which cements a society together. Obedience, she stated, belongs only in the nursery or the slave compound; an adult puts away obedience as a childish thing. Therefore, her argument continued, in a dictatorial régime those who are not reduced to slave-like obedience at pistol-point ought to refuse the régime support; they are adults and cannot justify or excuse their behaviour by a nursery plea. The gaping flaw in her argument, which displays her inadequate appreciation of the human condition, is that we all, willy-nilly, carry a certain amount of our childhood, and of our childishness, into adulthood, and all through our grown-up lives into the grave. It is precisely because we all do remain, to some degree, childish that obedience is needed to cement together any society, even a democracy. It is precisely because we all do remain, to some degree, childish that dictators, and especially totalitarian régimes, can come into existence, extend their power, and persuade subjects to commit atrocities—and other evils. Only a view from a skyscraping ivory tower could fail to see that all but, possibly, saints continue to be human and therefore cannot put away all childish things. So, the world does need a considerable measure of obedience to rulers, simply because human beings, partly childish, are not ruled by virtue alone.

A flourishing democracy is always capable of inhumanity. The prevalence of sex-and-sadism 'entertainment' proves that. There is ample other evidence. During the war, when Britain was fighting in a 'righteous cause', against Nazism, Winston Churchill stated in the House of Commons on 27 February 1940 that he was tired of considering the rights of neutrals, and on 30 March 1940 he broadcast over the BBC his view that it 'would not be right if the Western Powers in the life and death battle hold fast to legal provisions'. On 6 April 1940 the British Minister of Labour, Ernest Brown, said that neither Germany nor the neutral countries could rely on the 'Western powers keeping to the letter of international law'. Similar statements from German mouths were brought as evidence against Nazi leaders in the war crimes trials when the 'righteous cause' had triumphed.

On 14 February 1945 Allied air forces raided Dresden and, in 14 hours and 10 minutes, killed uncountable tens of thousands of men, women and children, possibly more than the whole number of British men, women and children killed by all the German air raids on Britain during the whole war. The raid on Dresden was intended by the British government to impress Stalin at the Yalta Conference. Bad weather, however, postponed the raid until after the conclusion of the conference. Nobody, however, thought to cancel it. There was no valid military reason for raiding Dresden. The British government was aware that the war was, to all intents and purposes, won, and the destruction of Dresden would not hasten the approach of Nazi surrender. The government knew that Dresden was not a military target; too many refugees from the advancing Russian armies in the East were flooding into the city for it to be used by the German army as a military centre of communications. The government knew that Dresden held no industrial plants assisting the German war effort. Dresden was chosen as a target, because there the maximum destruction of property and life could be effected. It was effected—with an inhumanity of means and purpose.

Phosphorus bombs were used in air raids on Germany. Phosphorus burns through human skin, spreading to vital regions of the body and burning so long as the phosphorus is in contact with air. In the air raid on Hamburg in July–August 1943, a much more destructive raid than any earlier one, most victims of phosphorus bombs could obtain no medical assistance. Many went to the river and stood in it to prevent the phosphorus burning their body to death. Some stood in the river for several days—the raid lasted several days—until constant immersion in water caused their skin to slip from their body. Those with phosphorus burns on the head had to keep ducking their head in the river to minimize the lethal effects of the phosphorus, but they had to bring their

224

head up every few minutes to breathe. Eventually, the Hamburg authorities ordered police to go to the river and shoot those of the phosphorus-burned who still clung to life, to put them out of their agony. Who was the more inhumane—the Hamburg police or the Allies?

Soon after the first batch of Nazis had been tried for war crimes, the American government appointed a commission of enquiry, consisting of Judge Van Roden, Judge Simpson and Colonel Laurenzen, to investigate allegations of maltreatment of SS men and other Germans in order to obtain confessions of crimes. The Commission reported that 137 of the 139 German prisoners, whose cases they had investigated, had had their testicles destroyed by kicks from members of the American war crimes investigation team.

These examples, and the multitude of other atrocities committed by Allied forces, do not prove—and are not intended to prove—that Western democrats committed as many evils as Nazis did. That would be an impossible and stupid task. Worse, it would be one that insulted those who suffered in Auschwitz, Belsen, Buchenwald, and similar places; it would be a task that would sully, not the memory of their suffering, but the person who attempted the task. They do prove, however, as the example of sex-and-sadism entertainments proves in its way, that apartheid of the mind is not a monopoly of those indoctrinated in, or given to, totalitarianism.

It would be silly to suggest that Western democracies are well on the way to totalitarianism because they suffer from certain domestic ills, including apartheid of the mind. One lesson taught by Nazi Germany, Communist Russia and Communist China is that totalitarianism only gains a stronghold when a sense of community and a realization of the humanity of others has been effectively destroyed by seismic shocks atomizing society. There remains in Western democracies in very many citizens sufficient sense of community and sufficient sense of realization of the humanity of fellow-citizens for Western democrats not to fear that their societies will become totalitarian because of what their rulers and fellow-citizens do.

4

The threat of totalitarianism comes from what democratic citizens and rulers do *not* do, and comes also from beyond their borders. The world is now divided into 'two nations'—to use Disraeli's words describing the condition of mid-nineteenth-century England. 'Two nations between whom there is no intercourse and no sympathy; who are so ignorant of each other's habits, thoughts and feelings, as if they were dwellers in different zones, or inhabitants of different planets, who are formed by a different breeding, are fed by different foods, are ordered by different manners, and are not governed by the same laws.' Disraeli warned that violent and bloody revolution would occur unless the gulf between the two nations was bridged. For him, the two nations were the rich and poor in England. More than a hundred years later, they are the rich and poor in the world. If the world avoids destruction in a thermo-nuclear apocalypse—a bold assumption to make—the existence of the two nations of the rich Western countries and the poor underdeveloped countries is more than likely to extend totalitarianism so that its spread will not be halted by an English Channel, or a Pacific or Atlantic Ocean.

Over-population is manacled to underdevelopedness. On the first Christmas morning the world's population was probably about 250 million. It took 1,600 years for that figure to double. In 1800, the world's population was still only about 800 million. In 1930 it had more than doubled to 2,000 million. Within 35 years more it had crescendoed to 3,500 million. In another 35 years it will be near 7,000 million. Only total war, total famine, or some other cataclysm can considerably cut down that figure; even widespread birth control would work too slowly to be able to do more than whittle down population increase a little, in only a generation. The dramatic nature of modern population increase is best illustrated by the astounding fact that of all the people who have ever lived in the world, 1 in 4 is alive today.

The population grows fastest in Asia, Africa and Latin America —the underdeveloped parts of the world—and they hold nearly 80 per cent of the human race. By A.D. 2000, India will probably have 1,000 million inhabitants. China's population will have reached that figure more than a decade earlier.

Poverty is the shadow of over-population. In A.D. 1600 the

average income in the West was probably little more than it is in Asia today. In 350 years, the Westerner's annual average income has multiplied many times. This concomitant rise in Western population and prosperity was both cause and effect largely of industrialization. In the West, the rising population went to the cities; in Asia, Africa and South America they went to the cemeteries—until twentieth-century medical science and other developments kept them from the cemeteries long enough to produce large families. But rocketing population growth has pressed increasingly on scarce food resources so that only a small fraction of the inhabitants of underdeveloped countries is properly nourished, and a considerable proportion live on a bare subsistence level, and sooner or later die below it. These conditions do not nurture a democracy, which will not arise or survive on an empty rice-bowl.

To the educated in the underdeveloped countries, industrialization and technological growth seems the only way out of the dead-end of over-population and poverty. They have the example of the Western world and Japan to teach them that. Yet, they cannot afford the comparative slowness of Western industrial revolution. Population growth makes it imperative to press hard on the accelerator; and the example of Stalin's Russia and, now, Mao's China, invites them to steer a despotic way. A further signpost beckoning down the despotic road is the exiguousness of the educated élite in underdeveloped countries. Even if members of that élite wanted to choose the democratic way to modernization, how are they to peaceably persuade uneducated, illiterate masses of peasants to adopt modern methods of agriculture or move from field to factory? It does not seem selfish to idealistic members of the educated élite to want to drag their backward people kicking and screaming into twentieth-century modernization; and, if they are selfish, they know that it is themselves who will be the new rulers with all the satisfying power and privilege.

Modernization will, by definition, dislocate traditional societies in Asia, Africa and South America. Atomization, alienation, a *Meinungschaos*, will follow, reminiscent of the condition of Germany and of Russia which held the stirrup for Hitler and Stalin. Modernization in the new non-European countries will occur even more swiftly than it did in Germany or even in Russia; its speed will be boosted by political, economic and technological developments since the first half of the twentieth century, as well as by the example of Hitler and Stalin; and so traditional societies in the non-European world will be ravaged even more rapidly. Hot-houses ripening atomization in the second half of the twentieth century are equipped with much more effective machinery, and potting-sheds contain many more new and double-strength fertil-izers, than were available to pioneering totalitarians in the first half of the twentieth century. Totalitarian horticulture is easily learned—and improved—by Asians, Africans and South Ameri-cans. Europeans are not the only ones gifted with totalitarian green fingers.

As underdeveloped countries become despotic and acquire technology, how are they to avoid a transformation of old-fashioned despotism into new model totalitarian despotism? How will the West save what democracy remains? Who, with Stalin's lesson of rapid modernization before him, can sensibly proclaim that Com-munist China will need generations to equal or surpass the industrial and military might of the U.S.A., when a huge popula-tion is an advantage to a country that has taken off into industrial-ization? Only those with a plentiful supply of cotton-wool to pull over their minds can afford such whistling in the dark. When countries, which are now underdeveloped, become shortly super-powers with modern armaments and a thousand million subjects, how are we in the West with only a few hundred million citizens to defend ourselves? What alternatives will we have but, on the one hand, resort to nuclear bombs or, on the other hand, resigna-tion to being red rather than dead?

Hitler and Stalin showed the power of ideology in modern mass society. They showed what could be done with an atomized society. They showed to what profit inhumanity can be turned. Who can smugly dismiss the possibility—the probability—that black or brown or yellow people will be atomized by modernization and indoctrinated to consider themselves members of a *Herrenvolk*, or master race; and will dogmatically believe that all white people are naturally corrupt, sinful, damned to perdition by their white-ness; and will attribute all that has gone wrong in the past, and all that is wrong in the present, to a conspiracy of white Elders of Zion? Already in the 1960s Radio Peking speaks with a voice which, if the appropriate words are changed, is all too reminis-cent of Goebbels' Nazi anti-Semitic propaganda. Increasingly, we,

228

the whites, are the Jews of today in more than a thousand million black, brown and yellow eyes. Those Europeans who think they have impressed non-whites by catching the anti-imperialist morning tide and rowing as hard as possible, suffer from one more illusion if they imagine that their sympathy for the non-white cause will assuage the bitter anger of non-whites making a world revolution. If and when the days of wrath come, it will not be the possession of a Communist Party card or of a trunkful of anti-imperialist speeches that will separate the goats to be slaughtered from the sheep to be spared. It will be the colour of a person's skin.

Some will take comfort in a nineteenth-century optimism which sees tyranny doomed to failure. Leaning on a Whig interpretation of history they will argue, like Peter Benenson in his introduction to *Persecution 1961*, that 'the history of *homo sapiens* can be explained in terms of continuous endeavour to increase his liberty. No tyrannical government has ever endured. Even if not overthrown by internal unrest, it has gone rotten. Sooner or later, the will of man to govern himself always asserts itself.' But the timeless phrase, 'sooner or later', would be little consolation to those who live under the tyranny in the present, and less to those who die under it. It could be no solace to the Russian peasant in 1600, 1800 or 1900, unaware that in 1917 the Tsarist tyranny would be overthrown and replaced by another which would one day feed his descendants better. Only elderly Englishmen blindfold these forty years, can still explain the past 'in terms of [man's] continuous endeavour to increase his liberty'. Many a man, in the process of increasing his own liberty, has been able, and willing, to diminish that of others. History cannot properly be told as the story of liberty; it is at best the story of liberties in competition, of liberty and tyranny in conflict, or tyranny and tyranny in combat.

Most people have always lived under some form of tyranny; and most people still do. Despotism does not diminish in area, but extends its territory. As Asia's—and particularly China's—exploding populations acquire industry and armaments, how will the West combat its challenge and save the democratic way of life? Especially when their people have lost so much of their democratic faith and hope, and are unwilling to try charity? Protected in suburban smugness by safe jobs, cyclone fences, and wall-to-wall respectability, they pay little or despairing attention to the barbarians at the gates. They are, in their way like the Romans of the fifth century, and it may well be that they have already passed their A.D. 476. It may well be that we have been born into the closing days of the decline and fall of the Western Empire. It may well be that the future lies not with the white race, but with the coloured races. The nineteenth century was the century of Europe. The twenty-first century will almost certainly be that of Asia. With the transition will, almost certainly, come not more democracy, but more totalitarianism. It may not be Hitler and the Nazis who were swimming against the tide of history.

Are all the courageous efforts for freedom wasted, then? Have the valiant actions of the fighters for freedom, the well-meaning, energetic, self-sacrificing work of liberals, the agony of millions tortured and exterminated, all been in vain? For their immediate purposes, for the most part, yes. They may have enabled some to hold their heads high, to keep the flag of freedom flying against the wind; they may have inspired others to look into their own consciences, and see the imperfections there; they may have helped focus attention on the pernicious effects of ideology, racialism, and the like. But this is only small gain. The price exacted in the fight for freedom is seldom, if ever, commensurate with the gains made. There are no amends the world can ever make for the incineration of the Jews, or for the murder of millions in Stalinist purges. Much of the blood that is reputed to water the tree of liberty runs to waste in the sands of human apathy, uncaringness, forgetfulness, apartheid of the mind, and the need to go on living. Part of all tragedy is the waste involved.

This was also true of the tragedy of Nazi Germany. It was a tragedy because German man was caught in a net which was the product partly of his external circumstances and partly of his human passions. Greek tragedy expressed the emotions and reasonings aroused by man's battle with the external forces that appeared to govern his life—in the words of Sophocles, 'the encounters of man with more than man'. The tragedy of Oedipus is that the pattern of his life has been set before he lives it, and that his own passions help to bring it to fulfilment. In Shakespearian tragedy, the passions are more important, the external circumstances less. But still, Shakespeare's tragic hero is caught in a net; and his humanity ensnares him further in it, and brings him to his tragic culmination.

It was similar with Nazi Germany. Nazi Germany was no melodrama, no contest of gratuitous villainy with simple truth. Nazi Germany was a tragedy of humanity ensnared, a tragedy inscrutable to those who cannot understand that all Germans are human beings, whether they were Nazi or non-Nazi, Hitler or Pastor Niemöller, SS or concentration camp inmate.

We cannot change Germany's Nazi past, but there is still point in understanding it, for what it tells us of our own society and ourselves. We cannot resurrect the exterminated, but at least the lesson to be learnt from them may help us to control our own future. From a sensitive appreciation of the tragedy of Nazi Germany, we can understand the extent of human involvement in racialism, prejudice, selfishness, uncaringness, inhumanity, and perhaps be delivered from their undue influence. If we recognize, in part, our own self, when we study other times and other places, we may understand the realities and sadness of German human beings yesterday.

The world will continue to moralize pharisaically about the iniquities of Nazi Germany. Indignant, progressive people will continue to write indignant, progressive books to be read with approval by other indignant, progressive people. But until the world, or some sufficiently powerful part of it, is willing and able to devise methods of feeding and aiding underdeveloped Asians, Africans and South Americans, the hot air will bring no relief to the starving and suffering. Moral indignation by itself is not enough. It needs teeth as well as tongue. The hand of the morally indignant person should be on his wallet as well as his heart.

We all practise apartheid of the mind. We are white members of a *Herrenvolk* in a world where most whites are relatively rich and all the non-white rest are poor. Our incomes compare with theirs, as did Nazi German incomes with those of Slav *Untermenschen*. Our economic policies, our taxes and tariffs and immigration laws, our political absolutes of living standards and full employment, are the deliberate defences of our power and privileges and élitism, and we cling to them with no more intention of ever letting go than did Nazis. We defend them—but for how long?—with effective enough armed force. We have the *Lebensraum*, and what we have, we hold. We make elaborate protestations of respect for our coloured brethren; we say we want them to develop, but we leave them to starve and suffer just as surely as Nazis

231

did subjects in occupied Eastern Europe. We have our equivalent of Nazi ideology. In practice we attend to our master-racism, and leave the poor to struggle unhelped and increasingly bitter for equality. We have our concentration camps beyond our borders where people starve to death, and we too, like the Germans but with less excuse, do not *want* to know of their existence. We write books on the problems of underdeveloped countries, and also on the brotherhood of man. But it only requires a practical suggestion that we spend 1 per cent of national incomes on capital aid to the brotherhood, for our hypocrisy to falter and our master-racism to show. The cost of any real and effective investment in brotherhood would unseat all the vote-wary democratic governments. We are as committed to our comforts, as corrupted by them, and probably as ready to kill for them, as any Nazi German. We play a similar game to him, but without his logical ruthlessness. Unlike him, we have not got rid of the fatal, weakening divisions in white society. We are not making sure we monopolize the weapons. We do not police the world. As *Herrenvolk*, we do not know our business.

It is not beyond the resources of the Western economies to begin the long haul to human equality. It would require massive and continuous economic aid to the non-white races. We know that it could be done. We know that we will not do it. What we would have to give up is not only trivial comfort, and not only for ourselves. Our wealth and privilege and power buy safety and gentleness and beauty for our children, and freedom—for the time being—from bloodshed and disease and oppression. They buy the political environment in which our form of exclusive, racialist democracy can continue without too painful rifts in our own society, without too much harmful mistrust of our own rulers, without our periodic elections bringing more than a ripple on the surface of placid, everyday life. As well as the nastiest human ostentation, our wealth and privilege and power underwrite the finest human achievements: all the paint and music and subtle communication and self-understanding of a high culture. It is a substantial slice of all this, and not just the second car or the third gin, that we would have to sacrifice.

It is too much probably. The same attitude prevailed in Nazi Germany. They were human like us. They succumbed to circumstances, fear, temptation, necessity, just as we are doing, a white *Herrenvolk* in a wider world.

It is just possible that we have a fraction more compassion and misgiving and courage left than they had. And it is just possible that we have perhaps another generation, a last chance to avoid the culmination of our tragedy with the roles reversed so that we play the Jews while coloured people play the SS. It is just possible that we have this last chance, not because of any difference between our humanity and German humanity, but because their tragedy is a lesson we still may learn.

Bibliographical Note

Very much has been published on Nazi Germany: my own bibliographical file has over a thousand titles of books and articles, and several hundreds of them are in English. However, the aim of this chapter is no more than to suggest to the general reader a small selection which may help in further discussion of the tragedy of Nazi Germany. The books mentioned will, in turn, suggest in their bibliographies and footnotes yet other material which may be useful. Scholars should themselves be able to cater for their own bibliographical needs.

I have omitted the titles of books mentioned in earlier chapters to minimize the clogging that is an inevitable characteristic of bibliographical chapters, however short. I have confined myself to works in English since few readers will know German. I have also thought it best to deal separately with each chapter; for obvious reasons, I have included no suggestions for Chapter 5.

Chapter 1
Unfortunately the material is scanty for those who do not read German. Translated German novels, plays and poetry are worth seeking. The best way to find out which are translated is either to consult any handy history of German literature or to ask a librarian in which section of the library are the shelves of German literature.

Indispensable are Robert H. Lowie: *The German People: A Social Portrait to 1914* (New York 1945) and *Towards Understanding Germany* (Chicago 1954). Peter H. Merkl: *Germany, Yesterday and Tomorrow* (New York 1965) is very thoughtful, stimulating and readable. Also useful are Harlan A. Crippen: *Germany, a Self Portrait—a Collection of German Writings from 1914 to 1943* (New York 1944); Hermann Eich: *The Unloved Germans* (London 1965); Hans Kohn: *The Mind of Germany* (London 1961); and Joachim Remak: *The Gentle Critic: Theodor Fontane and German Politics 1848–1898* (Syracuse, U.S.A. 1964).

In English, there is no really good general history of Germany. Most concentrate too much on politics and are superficial on social aspects of German life. Most are marred by obvious bias. On economic history, J. H. Clapham: *Economic Development of France and Germany 1815–1914* (Cambridge 1936) is balanced and informative. Otherwise, general histories are more hindrance than help to those interested in the questions raised in this book.

Chapter 2

Information on the traditional order can be had only by wide historical reading. However, it is worth mentioning Friedrich Heer: *The Intellectual History of Europe* (London 1966) and W. H. Bruford: *Germany in the Eighteenth Century: the Social Background of the Literary Revival* (Cambridge 1965).

The nature of mass society is a subject popular among political scientists and sociologists. William Kornhauser: *The Politics of Mass Society* (Glencoe 1959) provides an excellent introduction and suggestions for further reading.

I know of almost nothing in English on the German *Mittelstand*: this lack indicates the small penetration and insight of studies in English into the nature of modern German society. On German revolutionary conservatism, nevertheless, Fritz Stern: *The Politics of Cultural Despair* (Berkeley and Los Angeles 1961) is brilliant. So far as I know, none of the works of Lagarde, Langbehn and van den Bruck have been translated into English, except van den Bruck's *Germany's Third Empire* (London 1934); this is, unhappily, a very ill-condensed version.

Studies in English of the German Social Democratic Party are too concerned with politics and written from the angle of the 'top-people', and so are studies not of ordinary, but select, workers. Richard N. Hunt: *German Social Democracy* (New Haven and London 1964) and Richard A. Comfort: *Revolutionary Hamburg* (Stanford 1966) are the best. German youth movements are described in Walter Z. Laqueur: *Young Germany* (London 1962) and Howard Becker: *German Youth, Bond or Free* (London 1946).

On artistic developments in Europe two books are invaluable: Nello Ponente: *Structures of the Modern World 1850–1900* (Geneva 1965) and Robert L. Delevoy: *Dimensions of the 20th Century*

1900–1945 (Geneva 1965). The superb, lavish illustrations are alone worth the price of these books.

To understand how Germany was affected by World War One, the following can be read in English: Rudolf Binding: *A Fatalist At War* (Boston and New York 1929); Otto Braun: *The Diary of Otto Braun with Selections from His Letters and Poems* (New York 1924); Karl Bröger: *Pillbox 17* (London 1930); Hanna Hafkes-brink: *Unknown Germany: an Inner Chronicle of the First World War based on Letters and Diaries* (New Haven 1948); Ernst Jünger: *The Storm of Steel* (London 1929); Rainer Maria Rilke: *Wartime Letters . . . 1914–1921* (New York 1940); Fritz von Unruh: *Way of Sacrifice* (New York 1928); Philipp Witkop (ed.): *German Students War Letters* (London 1929). The best German war novelist—far superior to the over-praised Erich Maria Remarque—is Ludwig Renn: his *War* (New York 1929) and *After War* (New York 1931) provide profound insight and aesthetic pleasure. On the *Freikorps*, Robert G. L. Waite's *Vanguard of Nazism* (Harvard 1952), although biased, is useful.

In English there is no very good history of Germany between 1918 and 1933. To consider further the aspects raised by this book, I recommend Andreas Dorpalen: *Hindenburg and the Weimar Republic* (Princeton 1964) which contains a good bibliography. Nothing in English approaches, even nearly, in quality Karl Bracher: *Die Auflösung der Weimärer Republik* (Stuttgart and Düsseldorf 1955) or Karl Dietrich Bracher, Gerhard Schulz, and Wolfgang Sauer: *Die national-sozialistische Machtergreifung* (Cologne and Opladen 1960). I disagree radically with much of the interpretation in these books but judge them among the best historical work on Nazi Germany. Translations of them into English are long overdue.

Chapter 3

There are numerous autobiographies, biographies and memoirs in English of leading figures in Nazi Germany. Their titles are easily found in books with lengthy bibliographies.

The autobiography of a very minor Nazi official—Melita Masch-mann: *Account Rendered* (London 1964)—is essential reading, precisely because she was a minor official, because she is one of the rare minor figures who has recorded her experiences, and because her account is so honest, moving, intelligent, and revealing.

The most useful general accounts are Fritz Ernst: *The Germans and their Modern History* (New York 1966); Herman Mau and Helmut Krasnick: *German History 1933–1945* (London 1959); Friedrich Meinecke: *The German Catastrophe* (Boston 1950); David Schoenbaum: *Hitler's Social Revolution* (New York 1966); and Hannah Vogt: *The Burden of Guilt: a Short History of Germany 1914–1945* (Oxford 1964).

A paperback edition of *Mein Kampf* is that translated by Ralph Manheim (Boston 1962). Hitler's *Secret Conversations 1941–1944* (New York 1961), *The Testament of Adolf Hitler* (London 1961) and Norman H. Baynes: *The Speeches of Adolf Hitler* (2 vols.) (Oxford 1942) obviously need to be read. Franz Jetzinger: *Hitler's Youth* (London 1958) is by far the most reliable on Hitler's early life. J. H. McRandle: *The Track of the Wolf* (Evanston 1965) is very stimulating.

Alexander Dallin: *German Rule in Russia 1941–1945* (London 1957); Ernst K. Bramsted: *Goebbels and National Socialist Propaganda 1925–1945* (London 1965); Peter G. J. Pulzer: *The Rise of Political Anti-Semitism in Germany and Austria* (New York 1964); Christopher Thorpe: *The Approach of War 1938–9* (London and New York 1967); Edward L. Homze: *Foreign Labour in Nazi Germany* (Princeton 1967); Karl Demeter: *The German Officer-Corps in Society and State 1660–1945* (London 1965); Arthur Schweitzer: *Big Business in the Third Reich* (London 1964); Alan S. Milward; *The Germany Economy at War* (London 1965); Hamilton T. Burden: *The Nuremberg Party Rallies: 1923–39* (London 1967) are the leaders in their respective spheres.

On the churches, there is in English no general treatment of the Protestant churches except in J. S. Conway: *The Nazi Persecution of the Churches 1933–45* (London 1968). On the Catholic Church, Gunther Lewy: *The Catholic Church and Nazi Germany* (New York and Toronto 1964) is marred by facile and biased interpretation. Gordon C. Zahn: *German Catholics and Hitler's Wars* (London 1963) and *In Solitary Witness* (London 1966) are limited in scope but are very compelling.

Next to the concentration camps, more has been published in English on the resistance than on any other aspect of Nazi Germany. Easily the best book is Mother Mary Alice Gallin: *German Resistance to Hitler* (Washington, D.C. 1961). Gerhard Ritter: *The German Resistance* (London 1958) is very balanced and intelligent.

THE TRAGEDY OF NAZI GERMANY

H. D. Leuner: *When Compassion was a Crime* (London 1966) is moving and revealing.

The many volumes of the proceedings of the various war crimes trials (mentioned under Chapter 4) are invaluable for all aspects of Nazi Germany.

There is no balanced or reliable book on Himmler, the SS, or the Gestapo.

Chapter 4

More books have been published on the camps than on any other aspect of Nazi Germany. Unfortunately, some of the best have not been translated from German or French. Other than those already mentioned in Chapter 4, I suggest here only those in English which seem to me to convey best the atmosphere of absolute corruption. These are:

Alexander Donat: *The Holocaust Kingdom* (London 1965); Viktor E. Frankl: *Man's Search for Meaning* (London 1964); Pierre d'Harcourt: *The Real Enemy* (London 1967); Raul Hilberg: *The Destruction of the European Jews* (Chicago 1961); Eugen Kogon: *The Theory and Practice of Hell* (London 1958); O. Lengyel: *Five Chimneys* (Chicago and New York 1947); Jacques Lusseyran: *And There Was Light* (London 1964); David Rousset: *The Other Kingdom* (New York 1947); Leon Weliczer Wells: *The Janowska Road* (London 1966); Arthur D. Morse: *While Six Million Died* (London 1968).

As well, the volumes on war crimes trials are very useful. There are 42 volumes of *The Trial of the Major War Criminals* (Nuremberg 1947–1948). Most of the evidence is in German, but the volumes contain enough material in English to be of use to those interested but unable to read German. *Nazi Conspiracy and Aggression* (Washington 1946) is not entirely adequate condensation in 8 volumes of these 42 volumes. There are also 15 volumes of the proceedings of other accused Germans by the Americans, *Trials of War Criminals before the Nuernberg Military Tribunals* (Washington 1950 to 1953, and some volumes not dated). There are, finally, nine volumes of trials by the British, Sir David Maxwell Fyfe (general editor): *War Crimes Trials* (London 1948 to 1952). Volume 2 includes the trial of Irma Grese.

Index

Apartheid of the mind: definition of, 168; chapter 4 *passim*
Arendt, Hannah: 182, 198, 223
Aristocracy: and industrialization, 47–51; and political control before 1914, 48–9; and cultural control before 1914, 49–51; and Nazism, 64
Army: pre-1933, 13–18; and January 30, 1933, 69–74, 129–30; and totalitarianism, 86–7; importance of, 126–7; control of by Hitler, 126–45; and World War II, 127; scorn for soldiers from historians, 128–9; and politics, 130–1; and rearmament, 131–4; and June 30, 1934 Purge, 134–6; and Blomberg–Fritsch crisis, 136–7; and July 1944 Plot, 137–8; and oath 138–9; and obedience to orders 139–45
Atomization: and industrialization, chapter 2 *passim*; and World War I, 58–60; and Weimar, 61–5; and Nazi totalitarianism, chapter 3 *passim*; and concentration camps, chapter 4 *passim*; and future, chapter 5 *passim*
Atrocities: compared with past, 3–4; compared with Stalin's, 3; twentieth-century shock at, 4–6; need to remember, 6–8, on Eastern front, 110; and Army, 139–45; Allied, 140, 224–5; chapter 4 *passim*

Bullock, Alan: 28, 136, 206, 212

Centre party: liquidation of, 92; and Enabling Act, 153; lack of resistance, 152–3; *see also* Churches
Churches: and resistance, 115–24; *see also* Pius XII
Communism: fear of in 1933, 70–1; and totalitarianism, 80–9; compared with Nazism, 102–4, 208–211
Concentration camps: chapter 4 *passim*; 1–3; pre-war number of, 77–8; Auschwitz, 161–3; unpredictability in, 177; secrecy of, 178–9; conditions in, 185–205; punishments in, 190; cannibalism in, 195–6; privileged inmates, 196–9; escapees from, 199–200; lack of Jewish resistance in, 200–4; *see also* SS
Culture: and industrialization, 49–51

Deutschland über alles: 20–1

Economy: and totalitarianism, 87–88; gradual control of, 145–8; big business, 146–7
Eichmann: 167; trial of, 222
Einsatzkommandos: 163–6
Emergency Decree, February 1933; 90–2
Enabling Act, March 1933: 91–2; and Centre Party, 153
'Explanations' of Nazi inhumanity: chapter 1 *passim*; from German history, 9–12, 26–7; from Hitler's

239

'Explanations' of Nazi inhumanity:
(*cont.*)
character, 94-5; inadequacy of
many of, 222-3; *see also* German
'characteristics'

Family: and traditional society,
32-3; and industrialization, 51-2;
and World War I, 59-60
Furtwängler, Wilhelm: 156

German 'characteristics': mili-
tarism, 13-18; arrogance, 18-21;
subservience, 21-2; crudity, 22-
24; cruelty, 24-6
Gestapo: *see* SS
Goebbels: 78, 112-14, 132
Göring: 69, 70, 74, 77, 90, 132
Grese, Irma: 173-5

Himmler: 74, 124-6; and apartheid of the mind, 166-73; *see
also* SS
Hindenburg: and January 30, 1933,
66-74; death of, 93; 129
Hitler: extraordinariness of, 27-8;
and January 30, 1933, 65-75;
gradual methods of, 76-9, and
chapter 3 *passim*; foreign policy
of, 76, 79; intelligence of, 94-7;
and fantasy, 97-101; oratory of,
114-5; pioneer of future, 206-12,
and chapter 5 *passim*

Ideology: and totalitarianism, 82-6;
Nazi, 102-12; and chapter 4
passim; *see also* racialism
Industrialization: general, 30-1,
38-9; and workers, 39-41; and
Mittelstand, 41-6; and aristocracy, 47-51; and culture, 49-51;
and family, 51-2

January 30, 1933: 65-75; and
Army, 69; and Cabinet, 69-70;
and Communists, 70-1; and
possible civil war, 71-3; and
possible Polish aggression, 73

Jews: anti-Semitism, 107-12; and
lack of resistance in camps, 200-
204; and chapter 4 *passim*
Junkers: 19-20, 47-8

Mass society: and Nazi régime,
28-9; and irrationalism, 55-6;
and January 30, 1933, 74; and
totalitarianism, 81-9; and chapter 5 *passim*
Mittelstand: and industrialization,
41; and politics, 44-6; and revolutionary conservatism, 45-6;
and Nazism, 63-4; and June 30,
1934 Purge, 146

Nationalist Party: and January 30,
1933, 65; and Cabinet, 1933,
69-70; liquidation of, 92
Nazi party: and totalitarianism,
81-2; growth of power of, 89-101
Nietzsche: 11, 54, 74-5

Pius XII: and Jews, 121-4
Police: *see* SS
Propaganda: and totalitarianism,
86; growth of control of, 112-24
Prüller, Wilhelm: 173, 175

Racialism: and totalitarian ideology, 83-6; and Nazism, 105-12;
and chapter 4 *passim*; and
Western World, 231-3; *see also*
Jews
Reason: and industrialization, 54-
56; and irrationalism, 54-5; and
mass society, 55-6
Religion: traditional, 34-6; and
workers, 40; and industrialization, 52-4; *see also* Centre party,
Churches
Resistance: associations necessary
for, 148-9; and *Kirchturmspolitik*,
149-52; and Social Democrats,
151-2; and Centre party, 152-3;
and Germans' low opinion of
politics, 153-4; civil servants
and, 154-8; ordinary German

and, 158–60; and Jews in camps, 200–4; *see also* Army, Churches and chapter 3 *passim*
Rohm: 98, 134–6

SA: 72, 74, 77, 89, 98, 134–6
Sex-and-sadism. in Western World, 217–20
Social Democrats: and industrialization, 39–40; liquidation of, 92; lack of resistance, 151–2; *see also* Workers
SS: 2, 3, 70, 77, 90–1; and totalitarianism, 86; growth of power of, 124–6; and Army, 143–4; and concentration camps, chapter 4 *passim*; volunteers in, 175–6, 179–80; sadism of, 176–7, number on concentration camp duty, 177; doctors, 184–5
Stalin: 3, 22, 81, 85, 94, 211; *see also* Communism

'Top' history: 4–5, 28–9, 93
Totalitarianism: chapters 3, 4, 5 *passim*; novelty of, 79–80; characteristics summarized, 80–9; comparisons and contrasts of Nazi Germany with England, 207, France, 207–8, others, 208, Communist Russia, 208–11, Italy, 211, Japan, 211; future of, 212–33; possibility in Western World, 213–25; in underdeveloped world, 226–33; *see also* Army, Churches, Economy, Hitler, Ideology, Nazi party, Propaganda, SS
Traditional society: characteristics of, 31; slowness of change, 31–2; agrarianism, 32–3; aristocratic, 33–4; Religion and Reason in, 34–6; breakdown of, 39–60, chapter 2 *passim*; in underdeveloped world, 206–12

Versailles: terms of, 60–1

Weimar: failure of, 61–5; *see also* January 30, 1933
Wiesel, Elie: 192–3
Workers: and industrialization, 39–41; and Nazism, 63–4; and illiberalism, 111; *see also* Social Democrats
World War I: welcomed, 56–8; effects of, 58–60

Youth movement, Nazi: 113–14